A Moderate Compromise

A Moderate Compromise

Economic Policy Choice in an Era of Globalization

Steven Suranovic

palgrave
macmillan

A MODERATE COMPROMISE

First published in 2010 by
PALGRAVE MACMILLAN®
in the United States—a division of St. Martin's Press LLC,
175 Fifth Avenue, New York, NY 10010.

Where this book is distributed in the UK, Europe and the rest of the world, this is by Palgrave Macmillan, a division of Macmillan Publishers Limited, registered in England, company number 785998, of Houndmills, Basingstoke, Hampshire RG21 6XS.

Palgrave Macmillan is the global academic imprint of the above companies and has companies and representatives throughout the world.

ISBN: 978–0–230–10517–1

Library of Congress Cataloging-in-Publication Data

Suranovic, Steven M. (Steven Michael), 1960–
A moderate compromise : economic policy choice in an era of globalization / Steven Suranovic.
p. cm.
ISBN 978–0–230–10517–1 (hardback)
1. Globalization—Economic aspects. 2. Globalization—Political aspects. 3. International trade. 4. International economic relations. 5. Social justice I. Title.

JZ1318.S873 2010
337—dc22 2010013064

A catalogue record of the book is available from the British Library.

Design by Newgen Imaging Systems (P) Ltd., Chennai, India.

First edition: November 2010

10 9 8 7 6 5 4 3 2 1

Printed in the United States of America.

CONTENTS

ILLUSTRATIONS

Tables

Figure

PREFACE

As the twenty-first century began, the world was in the midst of a dramatic new wave of globalization. More than ever before, products and information were moving swiftly around the globe at an unprecedented pace, fueled by an explosion of supercomputing capacity, a burst in worldwide telecommunications, discoveries of new energy resources, and a dramatic reduction in transportation costs. The pace of change, both economically and socially, was probably faster than any human society has experienced before.

One result of this rapid change has been the significant improvement in living standards, hundreds of millions of people being lifted out of poverty, and a rapid increase in the number of billionaires around the world. Another result has been significant dislocations of peoples, some who have migrated either into cities or across national boundaries, some who have lost jobs because of the fervent rise of international competition, others because multinational companies move factories and jobs to the countries where the costs are lowest. Along the way ideas have changed and institutions have been disrupted from one generation to the next. Cultures have adjusted and evolved, leaving people disconnected from the safety and security rooted in tradition.

It is easy to blame globalization as a root cause of these newfound insecurities. In a single word, globalization captures the complex interconnectedness and fast-paced changes that are affecting every country and every society worldwide. Globalization captures the dynamism and opportunities as well as the struggle and strife.

Using the term "globalization" to describe these complex changes is fitting because the term itself is nebulous. It is not restricted to economic changes but also encompasses political, social, cultural, and religious adjustments. Thus, to say that globalization is responsible for the perceived positive or negative effects on individuals, businesses, and countries, is much like saying no one is responsible. Furthermore, when no identifiable entity can be charged with inducing globalization, it becomes easy to resign oneself to the proposition that globalization is inevitable. Certainly this is one of the conclusions reached after reading Thomas Friedman's popular and detailed accounts of the globalization phenomenon in *The Lexus and the Olive Tree* and *The World Is Flat.*[1]

Nonetheless, even though globalization has a certain inevitability to it, individuals, businesses, and especially governments can influence the way in which globalization affects people. Consequently, one of the most provocative and engaging debates in recent years has been about what to do with globalization policy. In its simplest form, the debate about globalization policy refers directly to international trade and investment. For example, the question of whether governments should pursue free trade or should restrict trade and investment flows has been a debate raging in policy circles for hundreds of years. In a broader sense, globalization can relate to almost every public policy under consideration. Indeed, because of the world's interconnectedness, one country's labor policy, environmental policy, health care policy, or regulatory system can easily affect people far across the globe. Thus virtually all public policy concerns have become a part of the discussion over globalization policy.

At the end of the first decade in the twenty-first century the debate over globalization policy intensified. The bursting of the U.S. housing bubble and a subsequent financial crisis quickly spread around the globe. Real estate and stock market prices plummeted over 50 percent in some countries, and more than $15 trillion of wealth was wiped out within several months. With risk and uncertainty rising, household and business demand for autos, steel, chemicals, and many other products began to fall, resulting in massive worker layoffs, rising unemployment, and negative GDP growth rates worldwide. A global recession had begun, more severe than any in recent memory.

Whenever things go wrong, it is natural to place blame on whatever events immediately preceded it. Looking back several years or decades, one feature of the world that stands out prominently is rapid globalization. Consequently, policies that have clearly promoted globalization, such as free trade, deregulation, business outsourcing, and lenient enforcement of immigration policies, are now under intense scrutiny and reevaluation as policy makers decide how to cope with the crisis.

However, if one were to ask an average person what was the main cause of the world's 2008–2009 economic crisis, a more common response than "globalization" would most likely be "greed." Many people believe that excessive greed was the source of overlending in the housing market, the source of the complex derivatives that were poorly understood and difficult to value, the source of overconsumption and overborrowing, and even the source of expanded international trade and investment. Indeed, to many people greed is the root cause of globalization itself.

Concerns about greed and its effects are not new and have been a part of the debate about international economic policy for a long time. As early as the WTO ministerial meeting in Seattle in 1999, opponents of free trade and globalization voiced concerns about the allegedly greedy, profit-seeking, multinational corporations, who have supported and promoted institutions such as the World Bank, the IMF, and the WTO; institutions that in turn have facilitated the rapid movement toward globalization. Protesters at the annual meetings of the G8, at the World Economic Forum at Davos, or at the G20 meetings, decry the high salaries earned by the CEOs of large corporations and the growing inequality of income around the world. In their view the rich are getting richer and the poor are getting poorer. They contend that corporations, greedy for profit, exploit poor workers, threaten endangered species, despoil the environment, and endanger the sustainability of the planet. If these opponents of globalization were wary about the economic system before the crisis, they are even more wary after it.

Indeed, in the wake of any major economic recession, democratic popular sentiment allows for, and even demands, dramatic policy changes. In the 1930s, at the onset of the Great Depression, governments around the world reacted to rising unemployment rates by significantly raising import tariffs and increasing regulatory control over the economy. Similar interventions occurred in the midst of this recent crisis with government takeovers of financial and manufacturing firms, emergency government stimulus packages, and subsidies to keep important industries afloat. In contrast to the 1930s, only minor increases in protection occurred, largely because countries have mostly maintained their trade liberalization commitments under the WTO.

Because this crisis seems unlikely to resolve itself quickly, it is almost certain that significant policy reevaluations and adjustments are forthcoming in countries around the world. Indeed, a severe economic crisis virtually guarantees policy changes in democratic societies because citizens will demand that governments take action. Additionally, the greater the economic problems, the more accepting citizens will be for larger and more dramatic changes. However, although there is a danger of overreaction, the crisis affords opportunities as well. The key opportunity is that the crisis will fuel widespread interest in how to make the economic system work more effectively.

Because the crisis is severe, many more people than usual will listen to popular opinion around the world and reevaluate their own fundamental philosophy. Although there is great diversity of opinion, popular views tend to gravitate toward one of two poles: those who favor greater regulation and government interventions and those support free and open markets. On the one hand, those who had been wary of globalization before the crisis will argue that the lack of government regulation allowed greed to get out of hand in financial markets and will point to the inherent instability of a free market system. They will tend to support strong new regulatory control by governments. On the other hand, defenders of free markets will make the case that the current economic crisis is not caused by lack of government but rather by government intrusions into the market. Many have said that too much regulation is to blame; for example, that government incentives to expand home ownership and implicit government guarantees to Fannie Mae and Freddie Mac considerably increased the riskiness of the financial system.

Of course, there are extremists on both sides who express their views almost with religious fervor. These more extreme views often seem to dominate the discussion. More often than not, extreme-view holders tend to exaggerate both the positives of their own views and the negatives of their opponents' views. An important consequence is that it is very difficult for new observers in the debate to acquire objective information about how the economy works and the likely impacts of various policies.

That makes this a teachable moment. In the midst of an economic crisis, there is a window of opportunity to argue for policy reform to a larger-than-usual audience. Normally, it is only the academic researchers, policy wonks, and legislators that pay close attention to globalization policy issues. These individuals have studied the issues closely and have contributed to the current state of knowledge. However, the economic crisis will induce many more people to ask what happened, why did it happen, and more importantly, what should we do next?

What is needed most is a simple guide, accessible to a wide range of people, from experts to the average citizen; a compilation of the arguments on all sides of the globalization debate; an evaluation of the theoretical and research methods that are used to support the often conflicting claims; a dispassionate review of the strengths and weaknesses of the different positions; and a simple and comprehensive solution that can bridge the divide that so often seems to separate people.

This book offers a solution to these problems by proposing a simple but comprehensive set of principles to guide policy choice for the next century—a century of globalization. The task is accomplished by looking deeply into the core of the arguments on all sides of the globalization debate, stripping away the rhetorical chaff and academic complexity that obscures understanding, and discovering the kernels of truth that lie at the heart of every opinion.

This book argues that the kernels of truth—behind every policy position taken on any side—invariably involve three simple principles that are shown to be mostly fair using a broad definition of fairness and justice. In other words, adherence to these simple principles is mostly consistent with standard views of social justice. The book then identifies a moderate compromise solution consisting of a set of government policies that are fully consistent with the three principles. The mix of policies that arises are called moderate because they fall in an intermediate position between the extreme left and extreme right policy positions: to accept these principles and guidelines requires all sides to compromise. What makes this proposal different is that the compromise position is shown to adhere to the fundamental principles of justice that all sides are seeking. It is true that accepting this compromise requires everyone to give up or rethink some of their existing assumptions and policies, but it would not require them to give up their fundamental principles.

The book also offers a unique new method to guide to policy choice. Instead of using traditional cost-benefit analysis, which focuses on outcomes, this book proposes we focus on the process. Instead of policy makers responding to every new problem with a new set of policies, this book suggests we establish fixed rules that guide behavior in both good times and bad times. Instead of engineering a better future outcome, this book proposes we give people the freedom to take the economy and their lives wherever they choose.

This book advances these classical liberal traditions in a unique way. The first part of the book, chapters 2–5, looks carefully at traditional economic analysis and concludes that the results are much less certain and convincing as a guide to policy than is typically presented. It also examines in detail the common arguments for social justice and fairness. Here too the book argues that fairness considerations alone are an insufficient guide for policy choice. These weaknesses in the traditional methods are obscured in the popular rhetorical discussions largely because of the realities of the political process in a democratic society. The book also argues that simply relegating policy decisions to whatever comes out of the democratic political process is fraught with complications and is unlikely to result in outcomes that conform completely to basic principles of justice. Nonetheless, despite the weaknesses in these traditional methods, we have no choice but to continue along in the same old way, at least until there appears a simple, obvious, and convincing alternative rationale and mechanism for policy choice.

The second part of this book, chapters 6–11, suggests an alternative to our current policy choice process. The conclusions are most consistent with the views promoted by Adam Smith, Ludwig von Mises, Friedrich Hayek, and Milton Friedman. The book promotes the advantages of individual freedom and free markets, arguing for acceptance of an unencumbered spontaneous economic order, Hayek's term for Adam Smith's "invisible hand." The book argues that a principled moderate position is neither conservative nor liberal, at least as those positions are currently defined in the United States. Instead, the moderate compromise is best described as classical liberal, or libertarian.

Along the way the book explains the key economic lessons about international trade. It integrates economic theory, empirical analysis, political economy and ethical considerations. Most importantly, the presentation is simple. The most effective ideas are those that can be explained even to nonexperts. Among some of the issues discussed are:

- Why trade liberalization will redistribute income making some people better and others worse off
- Why we cannot know precisely who will gain and who will lose from free trade
- Why free trade may not improve the well-being of some countries
- Why a compensation policy (compensate the losers with gains from the winners) is both impractical and inoperable in a democracy
- Why empirical methods cannot determine which policies are best
- Why the democratic political process affects the objectivity of information in the globalization discussion
- Why fairness is multifaceted and contradictory in its application, despite its inherent reasonableness
- Why the competitive process is misunderstood
- Why business often seeks to prevent competition, not promote it

- Why free markets and competition do not generate good outcomes for all participants
- Why the relatively disadvantaged will suffer more in the competitive process
- Why the losses caused by competition should be tolerated nonetheless
- Why there are widely disparate opinions about the suitability/morality of profit seeking
- Why not all profit seeking by firms is good
- Why some profit seeking is imperative for a well-functioning economy
- Why altruism is not the answer to egoism
- Why a generalized social safety net is the best way to establish a compassionate free market economy
- Why nonprofit institutions can play a critical road providing for the social safety net, and
- Why the application of three simple principles can ensure that public policies generate outcomes that are both socially just and highly efficient.

ACKNOWLEDGMENTS

I would like to acknowledge the support of the Institute of International Economics and the Institute of Global and International Studies at the George Washington University's Elliott School of International Affairs. Special thanks to Susan Sell for organizing a book incubator resulting in many helpful suggestions from Susan Aaronson, Steve Charnovitz, Tamar Gutner, and Virginia Haufler. Conversations over the years with Bob Goldfarb, Mike Moore, Shahe Emran, Arun Malik, Stephen Smith, Bryan Boulier, Phil Levy, and Herman Steckler contributed to the style and substance. I am also grateful for the research assistance from Kyle Renner, Kara Heitz, Juan Srolis, Merium Haq, and Semehar Isaac. Finally, I remain continually grateful for the loving support of my family, my children, Ben and Katelyn, and M Victoria Farrales.

CHAPTER 1

Introduction

We study economics because we care about people. The global economic system produces and distributes goods and services to over six billion people around the world. These goods and services contribute to people's sustenance, shelter, warmth, security, entertainment, knowledge, and self-worth, which, in turn, affect their happiness.

If we can understand how the economic system generates positive effects on well-being, then we might also learn what can be done to make the system work most effectively. How well the system works depends on policy, which includes a country's legal system, the laws and regulations that are in place, and the practices and customs of a country's businesses and households. Thus, if we study economics because we care about people, then we must also care about policy. Every theory and empirical evaluation relates in some way to policy evaluations.

Which set of policies is best for a country is a subject of endless debate. Although the collection of knowledge about the economy and how it works is extensive, it has not produced anything close to a consensus identifying the best set of policies or practices. A lack of consensus exists in many areas, including health care provision, energy policy, industrial policy, tax policy, environmental policy, and monetary and fiscal policy. In each of these areas, debate about appropriate policy rages on.[1] The policy debate is especially contentious with regard to globalization.

Globalization can refer to many different things: the expansion of trade and investment across countries, the advancement of telecommunications and the widespread use of the Internet, the changing cultural and religious attitudes and beliefs in many regions, and the conflicts that arise between peoples. The debate about globalization involves discussions about trade and finance, the environment, global climate change, cultural identities, labor laws, natural resource usage, economic sustainability, agriculture, national security, and much more. Although the issues are extremely diverse, this discussion focuses primarily on economic globalization.

After the Great Depression, many nations embarked on a gradual systematic dismantling of trade barriers. The General Agreement on Tariffs and Trade (GATT) facilitated this movement by engaging countries in successive multilateral trade liberalization rounds committing member countries to reciprocal tariff reductions. The Uruguay round, the last completed GATT round, created the World Trade Organization (WTO); countries committed themselves to an expanded set of trade liberalization measures involving agriculture, services, intellectual property rights, and import quota systems. As barriers to trade were dismantled over the years, the volume of international trade and investment grew rapidly. This expansion of economic activity is clearly one of the more significant aspects of globalization. Nevertheless, as movement to freer trade became more widespread around the world, doubts about free trade as an appropriate policy choice also began to grow.

Although many developing countries joined the WTO in the 1980s and 1990s, some representatives from those countries now feel that the WTO agreements are tilted in favor of the large economies like the United States and the European Union. The latest WTO round of trade liberalization efforts (the Doha round) has been stalled for several years. Protests against the WTO and other international organizations have become commonplace.[2] In the United States, fast-track authority, the congressional green light enabling the U.S. president to negotiate free trade agreements, has expired and seems unlikely to be renewed anytime soon. Finally, the rapid expansion of two new economic giants, China and India, is arousing fear across the globe. In the United States, dozens of pieces of legislation have been proposed in the last few years (though none yet approved) targeting Chinese imports. Doubts about trade have extended to doubts about globalization in general.

In the popular press there are numerous suggestions that the traditional view about freer trade is overly optimistic and even that economists themselves are beginning to rethink the standard prescriptions. Some have argued that although the principle of comparative advantage may have been true decades ago, it is not longer valid because production factors (such as labor) are able to move between countries as never before. In addition, the advent of telecommunications has opened up opportunities for service sector trade that now affects high-wage jobs in developed countries. One notable economist, Alan Blinder, does not denounce free trade, but has suggested that the current wave of globalization may result in a loss of as many as 40 million service sector jobs in the United States.[3] The *Wall Street Journal* quoted Dani Rodrik, a noted Harvard economist, "... global trade negotiations should focus on erecting new barriers against globalization, not lowering them, to help poor nations build domestic industries and give rich nations more time to retrain workers."[4] Even Nobel laureate Paul Samuelson, the founder of modern economics, emphasized that free trade may not always lead to national gains.[5]

To outside observers these statements seem to announce a paradigm shift in the profession. It seems that economists are realizing that free trade may not be so good after all. However, to insiders these statements really do not reveal anything that has not been known to economists for at least the past half century. Although the patterns of trade are different and the pace of change is faster than before, the underlying principles and processes require few adjustments in our thinking. Modern economics really does tell a very consistent story; however, in many ways the presentation and dissemination of ideas has not been very effective.

Ineffective communication has resulted in a popular misunderstanding about what economic theory and empirical studies tell us about free trade and globalization. Rodrik (1997, 72) wrote that

> International economists in particular have been too Panglossian about the consequences of globalization.... They have been too quick to paint those who have taken a more concerned stance as ignorant of economics or as closet protectionists (and sometimes both). Largely as a consequence they have shut themselves out of the broader policy debate.

As a result, groups with different interests have become increasingly polarized, thereby contributing to a rising contentiousness over trade and globalization issues and a growing uncertainty about how best to step forward.

Globalization is complicated. Because it touches on so many separate issues, it also touches many people with a myriad of occupations, cultures, and nationalities. Each person looks at the globalization phenomenon from a different perspective, drawing upon a unique set of personal information shaped by one's education, cultural identity, and distinct view of morality. It follows that there are a multitude of views about what is right and wrong about globalization and what the most appropriate set of policies should be. As such, the globalization debate provides an ideal issue around which to discuss the more general problem of how to determine the most appropriate policies, especially policies that can appeal to a wide set of interests.

This book is largely about method. What is the most effective way to choose policies? The book approaches the issue by first outlining the traditional arguments supporting both free trade and free markets as well as the arguments supporting policy interventions in trade. The focus of this discussion is to assess how certain we can be of the conclusions reached via alternative investigative methods. In other words, we carefully reflect upon the results of models, both the theoretical and empirical evaluations, together with the ethical and political considerations, and ask if the answers researchers provide should convince an *objective observer* what are the best policy choices.[6]

Overview of the Book

The question of policy choice is clearly normative, seeking to identify what "should" be done, rather than merely asking positive questions about "how" things work. Nevertheless, to discuss what is best, one must also know something about how things work. The study of positive economics is needed to tackle the normative issues.

The book is laid out in two parts. The first part examines the intellectual arguments and political methods used to support and choose policies. This part examines the theoretical approach, the empirical approach, the fairness and social justice approach, and the political approach. It concludes that although we have extensive knowledge about many important interrelationships in the world economy, the extent of our knowledge does not rise to the task before us. An objective observer would have to conclude that our current state of knowledge about the effects of policies from a theoretical, empirical, ethical, or political perspective, does not point to a particular set of policies that can be generally accepted to be best.

The first part of the book also emphasizes that while current research suggesting best policy options should not be convincing to an objective observer, it is usually more than adequate to convince nonobjective observers. Nonobjective observers are those who recognize their position in society and the economy, and act to implement policies that serve their own particular interests. This group includes virtually everyone currently engaged in the political, social, and economic debate about policy. In short, nonobjective observers refer to what others call "special interest" groups, and everyone in society is a part of many special interest groups. These special interest advocates use theory and empirical research to infer how their interests will be affected by various policies. Once effects of policies are inferred, these groups enter into the political discussion to sway popular opinion to support their policies. In other words, there is considerable bias in the discussion surrounding policy choices: special interest groups are inclined to accept and promote the validity of research that tends to support their positions and to deny the research that opposes their positions. Their positions also motivate the political discourse and tend to push policy outcomes in the direction of greatest influence rather than in the direction of what might be deemed best in some more general sense.

It is natural that teachers, professors, and authors all transmit their knowledge and ideas to others through the filter of their own particular experiences and interests. Although the degree of objectivity surely varies from presenter to presenter, it is often difficult to know which presenters are more objective. This poses a challenge to anyone trying to understand our current state of knowledge and who wishes to use this information to identify appropriate policies. This book takes the problem associated with bias and nonobjectivity very seriously. Although evaluation bias might be impossible to overcome completely, perhaps, with a pointed awareness of the problem, we can present a mostly objective evaluation of our current state of knowledge relating to globalization policy issues.

Because the objective evaluation in the first part of the book concludes that current methods of policy evaluation are inadequate, there is a clear need for an alternative. The second part of the book suggests an alternative method in the form of a simple heuristic mechanism to guide policy choice. The choice mechanism is derived by focusing attention on the debate about profit seeking, with profit defined very broadly.

Free trade advocates, following the wisdom of Adam Smith, tend to believe that profit seeking by firms and individuals have positive social effects. Many believe profit seeking—greed even—is good. In contrast, supporters of social justice and fairness tend to believe that profit seeking on the part of firms and individuals contributes to many of the problems we witness in the world. For many other people, profit seeking and greed are not only bad, but also immoral.

This book suggests that it is not profit seeking, greed, egoism, or a lack of altruism that is the real problem. Rather, the problem is the way in which profit is achieved. The book distinguishes between three methods of acquiring profit: involuntary transfer, voluntary transfer, and voluntary exchange. Transfers occur whenever one person gains at another's direct expense. Theft is a simple example of involuntary transfer, whereas charity is an example of voluntary transfer. Voluntary exchange arises whenever a mutually voluntary trade between two parties occurs.

The suggested heuristic choice mechanism involves the implementation of laws, policies, and institutions that promote voluntary exchange and voluntary transfers while limiting or prohibiting involuntary transfers. It is shown that adherence to these principles are mostly fair with respect to an extensive set of fairness principles described in the first part of the book. The book also argues that the heuristic mechanism can account for many of the concerns of policy proposers from multiple sides of the policy debates. As such, the mechanism provides a moderate compromise solution.

With respect to globalization policy directly, the book unconditionally supports free trade and international factor mobility. The book shows that popular exceptions to free trade, such as trade remedy laws, agricultural export subsidies, and strict immigration laws directly conflict with the heuristic mechanism.

Following the mechanism also helps to delineate an appropriate role for government. The book proposes that government is needed to prevent involuntary transfers and to enable voluntary exchange and voluntary transfers. What is needed are property rights, enforcement of contracts, a national defense, police protections, and laws against theft and corruption. These government interventions protect citizens from the losses provoked by others. Similarly, laws to inhibit monopolization, provision of bankruptcy procedures, and avoidance of impediments to trade both domestically and internationally promote voluntary exchanges. Finally, the provision of public goods and social insurance such as unemployment compensation, welfare, and the provision of roads and parks, commensurate with the taxpayers' desires, enable voluntary transfers.

The book is laid out as follows: Chapter 2 discusses what economic theory can tell us about the effects of globalization and trade on the well-being of individuals. The chapter emphasizes several important results. First, any policy action, whether trade liberalization or trade protectionist policies, will cause a complex redistribution of income internationally; in other words, any policy change will generate both winners and losers. The economic solution to redistribution is to compensate the losers with gains from the winners. Effective compensation occurs whenever gains to the winning groups are sufficiently redistributed to the losing groups such that everyone can be left better off. However, to succeed, compensation requires that the policy change generate net benefits.

The chapter continues with a description of the trade policies that may be national-welfare-enhancing policies. Although many economic models conclude that free trade is welfare improving, this is only likely in very simple models. When more realistic market complications (a.k.a. imperfections) are included in models, it is common to see that well-designed policy interventions, rather than free trade, can raise national welfare.

The chapter concludes by highlighting two significant problems that are apparent from a review of the theoretical literature. First, there is no clear policy prescription for improving national welfare. In some instances free trade may be best; in other instances a different type of policy intervention may be best. There is no way to know unless we can measure the magnitudes of the positive and negative effects. Second, even if we could identify national-welfare-improving policies, there will still be winners and losers, requiring a compensation scheme to ensure that everyone benefits from the policy. Here too there is a measurement problem: for compensation to be effective, we would need the net total benefits to be positive and how much each person wins and loses. Although theory can teach us about the nature of the effects of various policies, because of the complexity, theory alone cannot tell us what the best policies are. We simply cannot be sure that free trade—or any other type of policy—is best.

Chapter 3 considers the effectiveness of empirical measurement in evaluating policy options. It evaluates the methods used to measure the costs and benefits of different policy options and whether these investigations can determine which policies are national welfare enhancing and who are the likely winners and losers. If we can measure the size and incidence of the effects, then we can also identify which policies are best.

The chapter concludes that despite the tremendous advances in data collection and computing capacity, an appropriate evaluation requires a level of detail that we simply do not possess. The studies that are done are either too partial (incorporating only narrow impacts) or too general (measuring aggregated averages that masks the redistributive effects). Thus, a truly objective observer should recognize the inconclusiveness of this research and determine that empirical analysis cannot tell us what to do about policy.

Chapter 4 considers the policy arguments made by proponents of social justice. Many who oppose policies promoting globalization argue that openness to trade and investment is fine and good as long as the policies are just and fair. Many of these arguments are very compelling. Nevertheless, the use of an ethical criterion to judge policy choices proves to be problematic as well.

The chapter identifies and describes multiple fairness and justice principles used in globalization policy debates. Each fairness principle, while individually reasonable, also tends to contradict other fairness principles. The larger implication is that every policy, whether interventionist or not, can be justified as being either fair or unfair, simultaneously. This conclusion should lead an objective observer to conclude that fairness and justice cannot tell us how to choose the best policies.

Chapter 5 considers the policy decision process in a democratic society, focusing on the question of whether democracy can provide a mechanism by which the best policies might be chosen. One possibility is that disparate individual interests are aggregated within a representative democratic framework, resulting in policy choices that reflect a kind of collective-average ideal.

The chapter explains why the economic ideal, in which overall benefits are maximized and losers are compensated with the gains of the winners, is unlikely to arise in a representative democracy. Instead, special interest groups are more likely to initiate policies that result in concentrated benefits for a few at the cost of dispersed losses to the many. The democratic process is also a contributing factor explaining why objective evaluations, especially those revealing significant uncertainties, tend to be ignored in the policy debates. In the end, an objective observer would conclude that because of the prominence of nonobjective influences (i.e., special interests), democratic processes are very unlikely to effectively choose the best policies.

Chapter 6 begins the second half of the book by introducing the alternative approach to choosing best policies. This approach involves the application of a heuristic choice mechanism applying three simple principles. The mechanism states that policies should be chosen that (a) support free and voluntary exchange between individuals, (b) oppose involuntary transfers between individuals, and (c) enable voluntary transfers between people.

The approach is practical because it eliminates the need to conduct complex empirical investigations to determine the welfare impacts of policies. Instead, attention is focused on the guidelines and whether they are supported or opposed by the policy. It is labeled a moderate compromise approach because it promotes the strengths and mitigates the weaknesses of the previous approaches. The chapter emphasizes with several examples how many objections to policy proposals on various sides of the debate are essentially violations of one or more of these fundamental principles. The succeeding three chapters examine each principle in turn.

Chapter 7 considers the many ways in which involuntary transfers arise. The most common example is simple theft or violence against another person. To protect individuals against these threats, countries have laws that inflict penalties to offenders that are found guilty of these infractions. These types of policies are shown to be consistent with the heuristic policy choice mechanism and as such begin to build a case for appropriate government policies.

The chapter extends the analysis to many other situations, including cases in which government interventions themselves enable involuntary transfers. In these cases, proponents of the policies are those whose special interest is satisfied, whereas those opposed tend to recognize the involuntary nature of the policy. Strict application of the no-involuntary-transfer rule would eliminate from consideration many policies that have been implemented, largely because special interests over time have exerted their influence in the democratic process.

Chapter 8 highlights the well-known result that all parties benefit from voluntary exchange. The chapter proceeds to explain the dynamic workings of a competitive system. Although such a system will generate mutual benefits to the trading parties, it will often not work to the benefit of other people who are external to that pairwise trade. In other words, although every individual trade is win-win, because new pairwise trades will often substitute for previous trading patterns, some firm's successes will cause other firms injury. This is akin to what Schumpeter called the process of "creative destruction."

The chapter also highlights the positive incentive effects that come from the fear and anxiety generated by the competitive process. In other words, the positive effects of competition are actually inspired by the negative aspects of competition. Without the destructive process, there are fewer incentives to produce goods and services that are more desirable to consumers; that is, without the pain, there will be less gain.

Recognizing and understanding these features of the competitive process are very important: first, because supporters of free markets often exaggerate the benefits of trade and globalization; and second, because opponents tend to use the negative effects that arise from competition to tilt policy choices in the direction of their special interests. Both reactions make it much more difficult for an outside observer to ascertain the objective truth about the effects of policy options.

Chapter 9 explores applications of voluntary transfers. The innate desires that people have to help others in distress motivate a substantial amount of charity and philanthropy throughout the world. Much of this occurs within households when income earners transfer benefits to others in both their immediate and extended families. Much also occurs as individuals contribute to support their churches, synagogues, and mosques. Voluntary charitable contributions fund many nongovernmental organizations (NGOs) such as the Red Cross, the United Way, and Doctors without Borders. Finally, the charitable giving of very wealthy individuals has resulted in the formation of many philanthropic organizations like the Gates and Ford foundations.

However, all charitable giving is not created equally; not all charity represents voluntary transfers. Instead, some charity involves a kind of payment for the provision of goods or services. For example, much of the giving to religious organizations finances the building of a church and supports the clergy who in turn provide religious teaching and other services to the contributors. As such, this is more like voluntary exchange than voluntary transfers. Similarly, contributions to NGOs like Greenpeace fund the lobbying and education services related to the promotion of a particular cause or special interest. To the extent these activities are successful, they may represent payment for the successful invocation of involuntary transfers toward the special interest group members.

In addition, some activities that may seem to be involuntary transfers, such as government taxation, can be interpreted as voluntary transfers instead. This is because the problem associated with free riding in the provision of public goods can motivate a desire on the part of a collective of people to relent to taxation, coupled with punishment for nonpayment, to support the provision of a social safety net.

In chapter 10 the heuristic mechanism, described in detail in the previous four chapters, is applied to a series of globalization and public policy issues. This chapter highlights the alternative approach that does not rely on aggregate cost-benefit analysis. There is no need to determine who wins or loses, and no need to discern whether a country is better or worse off. Indeed, we can throw much of that analysis away because it will never be any better than inconclusive. We can also ignore many of the common appeals to justice and fairness, as these often involve partial applications that are ultimately contradictory.

Evaluation of policies in light of the three heuristic principles is shown to be straightforward with respect to some policies, but much more difficult with respect to others. For example, on the one hand, the policy of free trade is easily shown to be consistent with the three principles. On the other hand, intellectual property rights provisions are more difficult to evaluate because they involve granting anticompetitive monopoly rights to motivate the incentives to innovate.

Chapter 11 concludes the book with a bold globalization policy suggestion for the United States: a graduated and unilateral movement to free trade and international factor mobility. Acceptance of the heuristic mechanism as a reasonable approach to policy choice makes this suggestion a logical next step. However, such a policy is fraught with obstacles; the first being a general lack of understanding of the way in which a truly free market system can work. This book will clear up some of the misunderstandings. The second obstacle is the political system, which acts more to promote concentrated special interests than those of a truly objective observer. However, suggestions for overcoming the political obstacles are beyond the scope of this book.

In the end, the book provides a critique and analysis of our current methods of globalization policy evaluation, draws the conclusion that an objective observer should find all of these methods to be inadequate, and provides a viable moderate compromise alternative that involves a simple heuristic mechanism derived from three simple principles. However, even though the simple principles should be noncontroversial, the policies derived from those principles will more than likely conflict in one way or another with many common ideological positions, save perhaps the classical liberal tradition. Thus, general acceptance of this approach requires a compromise, especially on the part of those who hold more extreme ideological positions.

CHAPTER 2

Why Economic Theory Cannot Tell Us What to Do about Policy

Much of what theory can teach us about the appropriate role for government policy can be gleaned by understanding what theory teaches about international trade. This is because international trade theory has largely used what are known as general equilibrium models to understand the effects of trade and domestic policies. General equilibrium models offer a comprehensive view of an economy because they account simultaneously for impacts in the output markets, labor markets, and capital markets. Any policy affecting one market is shown to affect every other market both domestically and internationally. Although the focus of trade theory is primarily on trade of course, the general conclusions that derive from studying these models have a much broader applicability.

For many reasons, what to do about trade policy and policies concerning globalization are highly contentious. Many economists support a free trade policy because economic theory suggests that free trade can raise economic efficiency, raise average incomes, and can generate greater economic growth. Economists often say that countries will benefit from free trade, thereby positing that an improvement in national benefits, or national welfare, is a criterion for policy choice. This criterion is an application of the traditional philosophical principles of utilitarianism outlined by Jeremy Bentham and John Stuart Mill almost two centuries ago.[1] Economic theory and models implicitly accept this principle whenever they address the welfare effects of policies.

We might ask, what do people mean when they say that a "country" benefits from trade? After all, countries cannot feel a thing! To economists it means something very precise; a country benefits when the total real income gains to some people exceed the income losses to others; it means there is a Pareto improvement; it means that the net benefits, however measured, are positive; it means that average standard of living rises.[2] It does not mean that every person in the country will benefit from free trade. This is an important point worth emphasizing because it is one of the reasons many people oppose free trade and globalization.

Rodrik (1997, 3) points out that, "economists' standard approach to globalization is to emphasize the benefits of the free flow of goods, capital, and ideas and to overlook the social tensions that may result." Indeed, although advocates of free trade will often acknowledge small, temporary adjustment costs, or even some social tensions, they will usually be quick to turn attention to the long-term benefits. The implications of these arguments seem to be that even if someone suffers a welfare loss, it will be temporary and will be made up with eventual gains in income to compensate. Thus, it is sometimes argued, if we allow enough time to pass, everyone will indeed benefit from trade. Unfortunately for free trade advocates, whereas benefits from free trade will certainly occur for some people, perhaps even many people, economic theory is also very clear that some individuals will suffer income losses from free trade even in the long term. In other words, there is no assurance from theory that free trade is good for everyone, even eventually.

Economists who support free trade recognize these income redistribution effects. The economic solution to the redistribution "problem" is a proposal to provide compensation. Compensation is a transfer of income from those who gain to those who lose. If done right, compensation can ensure that everyone in the country will realize benefits from free trade. However, for compensation to work, the sum of the gains in the overall economy must exceed the sum of the losses. In other words, compensation can only be completely effective if there is an overall increase in economic efficiency.

The next reasonable question to ask is whether economic models and theories demonstrate that free trade will lead to increased economic efficiency, or in other words, to net national economic welfare gains. Unfortunately, here the answer is no! Some models do suggest this, but many others do not. The ones that do show efficiency improvements tend to be the ones that are simpler in structure; those that do not show improvements are the ones that incorporate greater real-world complexities.

The notion that free trade may not be best for countries, may be surprising to some, but in fact is a standard result from international trade theory; one that has been known for a very long time. Indeed, Paul Samuelson, one of the founders of modern economics, described the notion that free trade is always good for countries as "a popular polemic untruth." He argued that, "it is dead wrong about the necessary surplus of winnings over losings (when countries move to free trade)."[3]

The real-world complexities that make free trade less likely to be beneficial overall are known as market imperfections and market distortions. These terms capture a wide variety of problems including pollution, unemployment, market externalities, information asymmetries, oligopoly markets, cultural influences, and many others things. In fact, it is these "problems" that many critics of trade liberalization claim economists do not take adequately into account.

The critics are both right and wrong. They are wrong because economics has incorporated many of these problems into their analyses and have derived some very general and somewhat unsettling results. The critics are right too, because it turns out that their criticisms highlighting the problems of free trade are often valid. In particular, it has become straightforward to show that free trade may not raise the nation's welfare in the presence of most types of market imperfections.[4]

The purpose of this chapter is to explain the effects of trade liberalization by describing the results from a range of economic models and theories. The conclusions drawn at the end of the review are only those that are virtually indisputable, meaning any objective observer should accept these results as valid. But widespread acceptance can only be achieved because the results are very weak; in other words, what can be said with near certainty is not very much. Nonetheless, the lessons that result, apply not only to the debate over trade policy, but also to the issue of policy choice more generally; the definitive statements that can be made about trade policy are the same statements that can be made about any policy decision.

Redistributive Effects of Trade Liberalization

Income redistribution effects arise in a variety of trade models. That redistribution occurs may not be too surprising, but the complexity of the redistribution is best understood by considering how and why it arises in different economic models.

In general, income redistribution occurs whenever prices change. Prices are the signals that other agents use to make their own decisions. When prices change, it affects consumer demand, producer supply, intermediate input demand, wages, rents, and many other things. It is the change in prices that causes some to win and some to lose.

In the simplest trade model we imagine there is only one product being exported from one country to another. For example, imagine that a trade liberalization agreement results in a reduction in the tariff on an imported product, say, shrimp. A tariff reduction reduces the price of shrimp in the importing country. Consumers of shrimp, including the food-processing companies who make shrimp-based products, restaurants who purchase shrimp, and final consumers who purchase raw shrimp for cooking in their own homes, all will pay less for shrimp and thus benefit from the lower prices. Domestic shrimp fisherman, facing a declining price of imported shrimp, will be forced by greater import competition to reduce their own prices or face a decrease in demand. Regardless of how they respond, domestic shrimp producers will suffer losses. The third effect of a tariff reduction is a decline in tariff revenue collected by the federal government.[5] Less revenue will either require an increase in taxes to offset the decline or a decrease in spending resulting in the loss of some government services. Of course, the government could borrow more to make up for the shortfall but this would just mean pushing the effects off until later. In any case, taxpayers or government-spending beneficiaries eventually will lose out.

When tariffs are reduced by large importers, it will also cause an increase in the world price of shrimp.[6] Foreign consumers of shrimp will pay more for shrimp at the market, in restaurants and for other shrimp products and will lose out somewhat. Foreign producers of shrimp will benefit expand production and see profits rise.

Thus, even the simplest model of trade presents a fairly complex redistribution in welfare around the world as a result of trade liberalization. Trade liberalization will cause income to be redistributed between at least five distinct groups in both the importing and exporting country. Consumers of the products whose tariffs are reduced will gain in real income in the importing country, but consumers of those same products in the exporting countries will lose income. Owners of firms producing the liberalized products will lose real income in the importing country but will gain real income in the exporting countries. Finally, since government tariff revenues will most likely fall, recipients of government program benefit, or taxpayers, will lose real income.

Redistribution in More Complex Trade Models

The Heckscher-Ohlin-Samuelson (or Factor Proportions) model assumes there are two countries (say, the United States and Mexico) producing two distinct goods (say, clothing and autos) using two factors of production (say, labor and capital). The model assumes workers can work in either industry and will seek the highest wage. Since the model presumes a capitalist economy, someone is assumed to own the capital equipment and machinery, which earns that person a rent. Workers and capital owners use their income to purchase the food and clothing the two industries produce on the basis of their own desires. Firms decide how much food and clothing to produce, the prices to charge, and the wage rates and rental rates so that total supply of each good and factor equals total demand.[7]

The key assumptions of the model are two real-world regularities; first, some industries use more capital per worker in production than other industries; and second, that some countries have more capital available for use in production per worker than other countries. For example, if autos production use more capital per worker than clothing production, then auto production is called capital intensive and clothing production labor intensive. Also, if the United States has more capital per worker overall than Mexico, the United States is called capital abundant and Mexico labor abundant. One key result of this model is that in free trade the capital-abundant country exports the capital-intensive good while the labor abundant country exports the labor-intensive good.

A very interesting result arises with respect to income distribution in this model. When two countries (such as the United States and Mexico) open up to free trade, first prices change, and as a result, the real income of the country's abundant factor increases while the income of its scarce factor falls. In other words, free trade generates an increase in the income of capital owners in the United States and a decrease in the income of workers. In Mexico the reverse occurs; workers' incomes rise while capital owners' incomes fall. Trade creates winners and losers, but this time the effect is based on the source of one's income. If someone earns wage income in the United States, no matter in which industry he works, he will lose from free trade. If someone earns wage income in Mexico, he will lose from free trade. The reverse is true for capital owners in each country.

In another variation of this model (known as the specific factors model), economists have considered what would happen if an input factor cannot move between industries. This assumption is relevant because in many instances workers develop skills that are specific to the industry in which they work. For example, clothing workers know how to sew but cannot operate robotic auto assemblers. If the clothing industry lays off workers and the auto industry is hiring, these workers might not be employable in the expanding auto industry. Similarly, capital equipment is typically designed for one specific purpose. The robotic assembly equipment in the auto industry cannot be used effectively in the clothing industry. Impediments to factor mobility are real concerns for workers and capital owners threatened by import competition.

These models demonstrate that when trade is liberalized and a factor is specific to an industry, those factors stuck in the export industries, benefit, while the factors stuck, or specific, to the import-competing industries lose. Once again, there are winners and losers, however, the reason why individuals gain or lose changes based on the structure of the model.

Finally, economists recognize that the ability of factors to move across industries improves as time passes. For example, given sufficient time, a worker can learn new skills and find a job in a completely different industry; the seamstress can learn auto assembly skills. Also given enough time, capital equipment eventually depreciates and new investment can be used to purchase newer types of equipment, possibly in a completely different industry. However, because the mobility of a factor changes over time, who gains and loses will also vary with time.

Economic models suggest then that in the short run, before labor and capital can adjust easily to other industries, trade liberalization will harm all income earners in the import industries, and benefit all income earners in the export industry. Eventually, after factors adjust to new sectors in the long run, the country's abundant factor will gain while its relatively scarce factor will lose. This result implies that some individuals will gain in the short run and lose in the long run. Other will lose in the short run and gain in the long run.

General Implications

Economists have developed even more complex models of international trade including some with multiple goods, multiple factors, and multiple countries. However, regardless of the complexity of the model and regardless of which features are included or excluded, there is one basic result that almost all[8] models of international trade display: trade liberalization causes income redistribution. This occurs because free trade causes the prices of many goods and services to change; some people benefit while others lose from free trade.

Because income redistribution occurs whenever prices change, this same conclusion applies whether trade is liberalized or protected. It does not matter what new set of policies is put into place, any policy change, whatsoever, will cause prices to change and will also result in winners and losers. Thus, if countries lower export subsidies, or implement a carbon tax, or set new health and safety standards, or reduce the income tax, prices of some goods or services will change and this will cause a redistribution of income with some people benefiting and others losing.

In fact, even if there are no policy changes at all, other natural changes like the depletion of resource stocks, technological changes, changes in consumer preferences, and changes in fiscal and monetary policies all cause prices to change. This means that even when a country does almost nothing, there will be continual redistributions of income.

The income redistribution result is shown in simple trade models and becomes even more prominent in more complex models. There should be little doubt that this same result carries over to the real world.

As mentioned earlier, the solution to redistribution is to provide compensation to the unlucky losers caused by the policy change, paid for out of the extra earnings accruing to the winners. However, to make redistribution completely effective so that no one loses, the net benefits from the policy change must be positive. Or in other words the policy must cause an increase in national welfare. We explore this issue with respect to globalization policy in the next section.

National Welfare Effects of Trade Liberalization

Despite the redistribution, most advocates of free trade and globalization believe that, overall, trade liberalization will be good for countries. That belief derives from a substantial literature showing that trade can raise economic efficiency. Economists use the term "efficiency" to describe an optimal allocation of resources in production and consumption. More specifically, "Pareto efficiency" refers to an economic outcome in which it is impossible to raise the well-being of one person without simultaneously reducing the welfare of someone else. If it were possible to make one or several people better off without harming anyone else, then that situation is not efficient.

Comparative Advantage and Efficiency Improvements with Free Trade

In general, economic efficiency improves with free trade when countries specialize, or produce more, of the goods and services in which they have a comparative advantage. A comparative advantage, when defined in its most general form, arises when a country enjoys a price advantage (i.e., a lower price) in a particular good or service compared to another country. Different economic models show that a price advantage can arise because of cross-country differences in technology, because countries have different proportions of capital and labor, or because of differences in product demands.

Comparative Advantage via Differences in Technology

In the Ricardian model, countries are assumed to differ only in their productive capacities. It was in this model that David Ricardo first formally demonstrated the principle of comparative advantage. An important conclusion from the Ricardian model is that advantages from trade do not disappear just because another country has lower wages or is more productive in all industries. Ricardo demonstrated that by specializing in producing the products in which one has a comparative advantage, the world can expand total world output with the same quantity of resources. The expansion of output is the realization of increased economic efficiency that economists always talk about. Finally, given the expanded output, international trade can ensure that all countries in the model gain from the surplus that is created. In other words, without raising the quantity of resources, the world economy would be able to produce greater output and generate higher living standards for everyone. Economic efficiency will rise both internationally and nationally. This is how all nations can benefit from free trade.

Comparative Advantage via Differences in Resources

The Heckscher-Ohlin-Samuelson, also known as the Factor Proportions model, assumes differences in resources between countries and comparative advantage is determined by differences in factor proportions.

The capital-abundant country has a comparative advantage in the capital-intensive good and the labor abundant country has it in the labor-intensive good.

In the model, world production is maximized when the capital-abundant country produces relatively more of the capital-intensive good and exports it, while the labor abundant country produces more of the labor-intensive good and exports that. Although as discussed earlier, a movement to free trade redistributes income from the countries' scarce factors to its abundant factors, the net national welfare effect is positive. In other words, the sum of the benefits to the abundant factor is larger than the sum of the losses to the scarce factor. Thus, the model displays an improvement in overall economic efficiency with free trade, and with appropriate compensation provided, all people in all countries could conceivably be made better off.

Advantages via Economies of Scale

More recent models of trade focus attention on economies of scale. Economies of scale, also called increasing returns to scale, occur when a larger production volume enables cheaper production. For example, in heavy industries, such as chemical or steel production, the cost of producing each unit of output falls substantially if large volumes are produced at one place and time. Clearly in these cases it makes sense to produce at a very large scale so as to reduce the production costs per unit.

At the international level, the presence of economies of scale in production has been identified as a potential source of benefits from free trade. In this case, we would not say that trade is based on comparative advantage because it does not rely on differences between countries.

As an example, suppose two countries produce two goods, steel and chemicals, which exhibit economies of scale. One possible production arrangement is for both countries to close themselves off from trade and produce the two goods for themselves. In contrast, if one country were to specialize in steel production and the other in chemical production, and if each industry supplied its product to the entire world, rather than just one country, then the scale of production would be higher in these industries and the cost of producing each good lower (due to economies of scale). Thus, once again, because of international trade economic efficiency can be improved and the overall welfare of both nations increased.

Efficiency and the Division of Labor

In all cases efficiency improvements derive from one fundamental principle: the division of labor. From the time of Plato people have recognized that when individuals concentrate their productive effort along one production task, it becomes possible to significantly increase output. Adam Smith began his famous treatise, The Wealth of Nations with a detailed explanation of the division of labor.[9] Using an example of a pin factory, he explained how specialization in particular tasks within a production process would enable each person to become more efficient in that task, and when combined with others performing other tasks, would result in a substantial increase in the output of pins.

It is worth recognizing that the economic efficiency improvements from international trade, as depicted in all models of trade, are demonstrating that additional gains can be realized by extending the division of labor internationally. If individuals can reap benefits domestically through specialization and trade, then countries can extend these gains to its fullest potential via international specialization in one's comparative advantage goods followed by trade. To deny that international trade can be beneficial is to deny that the division of labor extends internationally. This seems highly unlikely. However, what one could argue is that other complications in the world may cause additional inefficiencies that overwhelm the positive effects caused by extending the division of labor. For this reason we take up the issue of market imperfections next.

Market Imperfections and Distortions

In all of the basic trade models, certain real-world complications, known as market imperfections or market distortions, are assumed away. When these imperfections are incorporated into the models, the traditional result that countries will gain from trade due to improvements in economic efficiency is undermined.

The term market imperfection is used to describe these situations because each represents a deviation away from the standard assumptions of perfect competition, upon which many economic models are based. Perfectly competitive models include numerous assumptions. Some of them are made because it is believed they describe an important aspect of the world. However, many other assumptions are made to simplify the analysis. In many ways, the world described by the model of perfect competition is indeed perfect. It is a kind of "economic nirvana": an idealistic outcome that we should never expect to arise naturally in the world or should we ever expect to attain it—except perhaps in a future life![10]

When economists build models of the world that incorporate imperfect competition they often describe these cases as second-best. The state of economic nirvana that arises in perfect competition is often referred to as first-best.

Next I will describe several models with market imperfections and discuss the implications for free trade for each of these, then will consider the implications for a world that is awash in imperfections, as we may well expect to see in the real world. As economists often cryptically proclaim, we live in a second-best world.

International Trade by Large Countries

The first hint students of international economics get that free trade is not always best for a country happens when they learn about optimal tariffs in a large country case. Countries are classified as large or small on the basis of whether their trade policies can influence the price of a product in international markets. Thus, when a "large" country places a tariff on an imported good, the price of that product in the rest of the world is pushed downward because of lower international demand. In contrast, a small country's import tariff would have no effect upon the price in the world market. Largeness also applies on the export side. If a large country introduces an export subsidy on a product, the price of the product in the world market is pushed down, this time because of increased international supply. A small country's export subsidy, however, has no effect upon the world price.

What students learn in an international trade class is that a relatively small tariff implemented by a large importing country raises national welfare; in other words economic efficiency improves with protection. The same positive effect on welfare is possible on the export side when a large country implements an export tax. In contrast, if any tariff or export tax is implemented by a small country, national welfare falls.

To see that it is not just a theoretical curiosity, one need only look to the welfare benefits achieved by OPEC countries during the oil embargo era of the 1970s. When oil supplies to the world market were temporarily curtailed, the world price of oil rose threefold and revenues streamed into OPEC government coffers. This is the same effect as described in models of a large country implementing an export tax. An export tax, or an export quantity restraint, by a large country raises world prices and results in a flood of revenues to the government. The effect was even more profound for oil because oil demand is very inelastic in the short run[11] due to a lack of cheap substitutes. From this, it is not hard to imagine that welfare improving import tariffs are also a very real phenomenon.

The reason free trade is not optimal in the large country case is because there is an apparent market imperfection. An imperfection exists here because a nation's ability to influence the world price gives it the same kind of ability as monopoly firms in a domestic market who are able to affect the market price. These price-influencing capabilities are assumed away in perfect competition. To get a truly perfectly competitive setting in international trade requires each country in the world to be too small to be able to influence world prices. This is what we assume in the small country scenario. However, when a country is large, it can use its international market power to influence the price to its advantage.

Surely the United States, European Union, Japan, and many other countries with large economies are also large importers and exporters of many products in international markets. Thus, this is a real feature of the world economy, not just a theoretical curiosity. The implication is that when countries have the "largeness imperfection," trade liberalization can actually lower national welfare. Or, in other words, in this setting free trade is not best.

Externalities

One very important type of market imperfection is known as an externality. An externality exists whenever activity in one market has an external effect on firms or individuals in another market, in a way that is not captured by (i.e., is external to) the original market itself. Externalities arise in production processes as when chemical production causes air and water pollution, or when research and development activities spill over to create innovations in other industries. Externalities also arise in consumption as when driving a private auto causes local air pollution or when cigarette consumption has social health costs. Externalities can be either positive or negative in their effects. Pollution causes negative externality effects, whereas landscaping of a corporate headquarters has a positive externality effect.

Infant Industry

A classic argument in support of protection is the infant industry argument. This argument goes back to the time of Adam Smith and before. It is commonly invoked today by less developed countries to support their significantly higher trade barriers.[12] It is also another case in which market imperfections in the form of an externality plays a role.

The argument suggests that new industries (infants) in underdeveloped countries are unable to compete head-to-head with firms in more developed countries since they lack the experience and knowledge necessary to reduce production costs. However, if these infant industries are given temporary protection, say in the form of import tariffs, then this will provide time for these firms to learn the skills and knowledge to reduce costs. Eventually, after adequate nurturing while young, these same firms will grow up and be able to compete as equals with the mature firms in the international market.

The market imperfection in the infant industry case is a positive production externality. Through production of a product, the firms in the infant industry are expected to learn how to reduce production costs and become more efficient over time. Economists refer to this as "learning by doing," The external effects of learning are experienced only later in time, perhaps many years after the initial protection is first provided.

If capital markets worked perfectly, then infant industries could easily borrow money in the early years to overcome early production losses, which would then be recovered after the long-term efficiency effects are realized. However, since capital markets rarely work this effectively, the external effects are incompletely captured by the market mechanism.

The market may also not capture the learning effects if they spillover into other industries. For example, if part of the learning process involves new cost-reducing management techniques and if the managers who implement these measures eventually take jobs in other industries, then these other industries may also achieve similar cost savings. Since these efficiency effects occur external to the industries that first created them, they cannot be captured by the market mechanism.

For these reasons, nonintervention in the presence of infant industries is a second-best outcome. It also means if the long-term benefits of production outweigh the early costs of protection, which indeed they might, then protection can improve overall welfare for a country. In contrast, if a country with potential infant industries reduce, or eliminate, trade barriers, then free trade could reduce long-term economic efficiency of a country in this situation. In other words, trade liberalization, or free trade, may reduce the national welfare in the presence of this type of market imperfection.

Pollution

A classic example of a negative externality is pollution. Water, air, soil, and aquifer pollution is caused in numerous production processes whenever active intervention to control that pollution is not undertaken. Examples include air pollution caused by traditional smokestack industries like steel, chemicals, and power generation; water and soil pollution caused by fertilizer and pesticide use in agriculture; and water and aquifer pollution caused by extractive mining industries. Pollution is also caused in some consumption activities; most notably the air pollution caused by household use of automobiles and water pollution in locations without sewage treatment facilities.

Pollution can have serious detrimental effects upon others. Industrial plants have sometimes dumped chemical waste into the ocean causing serious declines in the production of the nearby fishing industry as well as health problems among consumers of seafood. Air pollution causes breathing problems especially for people with respiratory ailments. Water pollution can damage the recreation and fishing industries downstream. Finally, aquifer pollution can affect the safety of public water sources and lead to serious long-term health consequences among consumers.

Economic theory shows that in the presence of production externalities, firms tend to over- or underproduce relative to what is best for society overall. When consumption externalities are present, consumers over- or underconsume relative to what is best. Theory also shows that government intervention with appropriately chosen policies can correct the over- or underproduction and consumption and result in an improvement in the nation's welfare. International trade theory has shown, in turn, that when these externalities arise among traded goods and services, trade policies can often be applied to improve the nation's welfare.

For example, consider a country that imports crude oil. The oil is refined into gasoline and used by consumers to power their automobiles. In the process of both production and consumption, air pollution is created in the community. The pollution has negative health effects especially upon those individuals with respiratory ailments. Thus, the use of crude oil exhibits a negative production externality in the refining process and a negative consumption externality when gasoline is used in automobiles. If a free market prevails, refineries will overproduce gasoline, and households will overconsume gasoline relative to what is best for the nation overall.

Trade theory shows that government intervention in the form of an import tariff on crude oil would raise the domestic price of gasoline, reduce gasoline refinery activity and consumption, and reduce the amount of pollution. Lower pollution would generate positive health effects in the community. Thus, a protectionist trade policy, if set at the appropriate level, will raise national welfare if the positive health effects outweigh the standard economic efficiency losses of protection. The reverse implication is true too; free trade, or trade liberalization, may lower national welfare in the presence of this externality. Free trade may not be the best policy in the presence of a negative production and consumption externality.

Cultural Externality Effects

Concerns about free trade and global markets have more recently involved the issue of culture. Most of the time, economists portray issues like culture as falling outside the realm of economic analysis. However, culture can be easily introduced as an externality effect.

For example, many countries are especially fearful that American music, films, and TV programs will push out local offerings and lead to the Americanization of their culture. For this reason, many countries have laws that require certain minimum levels of domestic programming for radio and TV broadcasts. Many countries also restrict the percentage of screenings of foreign films. From an economic theory perspective, this is another example of a market imperfection in the form of an externality.

These restrictions can be beneficial for a country because the cultural effects of imported products can be viewed as a negative consumption externality. In this case maintenance of cultural traditions embodied in music, film, and TV programming, benefits everyone in the community through the promotion of certain cultural understandings. Since each person's individual consumption is too small to have a noticeable effect on the community welfare, there will be a tendency to underconsume relative to what is best for society from a cultural perspective.

For these reasons, domestic regulations can raise the level of consumption of cultural goods, correct for the underconsumption, and if the cultural benefits outweigh the standard economic efficiency losses due to lower imports, then the national welfare can be increased with protection. As before, the reverse is also true: if cultural restrictions are eliminated as might be agreed to in a trade liberalization measure, the effect may be a reduction in the nation's welfare. Trade liberalization can make a country worse off in the presence of a cultural externality. Thus, it is conceivable that Europe might reduce its national welfare if it eliminated domestic content requirements on television and movie screenings.

Public Goods

Perhaps the most common economic argument in support of government intervention is the need to provide public goods. Public goods, of which national defense is the most notable example, have two defining characteristics: nonexcludability and nonrivalry. Economists have long known that a free market is likely to undersupply public goods, mostly because some beneficiaries are likely to free ride on the contributions of others. To solve this undersupply problem, governments can collect taxes and use the money to supply an adequate national defense. In this way government intervention can raise the national welfare of a country.

With the insight of the effects of market imperfections, we can now recognize that if government intervention can raise national welfare in the presence of public goods then public goods must represent a type of market imperfection. Indeed, in a pure perfectly competitive market model, we assume away public goods, imagining they do not exist. When public goods do exist, the inefficiencies that arise when a free market tries to provide them can be reduced with appropriate government intervention.

Indeed, from an economics perspective, the primary rationale for most public policies, is simply the correction of market imperfections and distortions. Regulatory policy to reduce pollution, taxes on cigarette and alcohol purchases, antitrust enforcement, unemployment compensation, the provision of a national defense, and income redistribution policies can all be justified by noting that they can correct for market imperfections and result in an improvement of a nation's overall welfare. As discussed above, in many instances trade policies can be applied in a similar way. When goods cross borders, trade policies can effectively correct for these same imperfections and result in an improvement in national welfare.

With perfect competition there are none of these worries or concerns. There are no public goods, no unemployment, no externalities of any kind. As a result, the very best domestic government policy is no policy at all. Laissez-faire is the term used to describe the total avoidance of all government regulatory, tax, and subsidy policies. When laissez-faire is applied to international trade, it implies free trade.

Policy-Imposed Distortions

But what if an economy were perfectly competitive in all respects, but then some policy is added, like a tax on cigarettes, or a production subsidy, or an import tariff? Economic theory shows that for any such policy, national welfare will fall. Government policies in the form of regulations or taxes and subsidies change prices and thereby distorts the allocation of resources causing a loss in economic efficiency. Although previous examples have shown that sometimes efficiency is improved with government policy, that only occurs when it corrects for the negative effects caused by an imperfection. In the absence of an imperfection, trade policy is the imperfection... it is a distortion. Economists sometimes call government taxes, subsidies, and regulations policy-imposed distortions because the distortion is caused by government action.

Once we recognize that government policy is a distortion in its own right, we can also realize something else very important; that the correction, or improvement, of one imperfection is actually achieved by implementing another imperfection or distortion on top of it. For example, consider the earlier example where a government places an import tariff on crude oil that in turn reduces the use of gasoline and reduces air pollution in its cities. In this case the government is placing a policy-imposed distortion or imperfection (the import tariff) on top of another imperfection (a negative externality). The tariff has two impacts: it corrects the negative externality, but at the same time it reduces efficiency. If the economic efficiency cost of the import tariff, is less than the economic efficiency benefit that results from the reduction in pollution, then the policy improves the national welfare. That means, somewhat paradoxically, two distortions can be better than one.

Indeed, there are only two ways to make the economy more efficient and move it closer to economic nirvana. The first method is to eliminate the imperfection or distortion directly. For example, if a country really were a small perfectly competitive economy with protective tariffs in place and with no other market imperfections present, then efficiency is best improved by eliminating the tariffs; simply move to free trade. However, if the imperfections are there naturally, as is the case with most externalities, then one cannot simply eliminate them. Instead, the only way to improve economic efficiency is to impose an additional, appropriately chosen, policy-imposed distortion.

I say appropriately chosen because it is necessary that the corrective distortion be set at the right level. It is easy to show in the pollution case, for example, that if the tariff were set too high, then the efficiency losses caused by the tariff may overwhelm the benefits caused by reduced pollution. Thus, the tariff must be set at the proper level to generate the positive efficiency effects.

Other Externality Effects

There are many other examples of market imperfections or distortions that we could explore including the presence of monopolies or oligopolies, the problem of imperfect information, and the nonclearing of markets, which arises with unemployment. However, these examples are sufficient to demonstrate the main point: in the presence of a market imperfection it is possible for a government to intervene in a calculable way to improve national economic efficiency and raise the average well-being of its residents. The common method to correct for these problems is the use of government taxes, transfers, and domestic regulations.

Theory of the Second-Best

In studying the effects of various types of market imperfections economists derived an important complementary theory called the "theory of the second-best." Second-best theory was first formulated by Robert Lipsey and Kelvin Lancaster in the 1950s.[13] A key finding of this theory was to show that if a market imperfection were present, the addition of another distortion could actually improve the outcome for a country.

Second-best theory also demonstrates another critically important proposition: the presence of one imperfection or distortion in an otherwise perfectly competitive economy, immediately changes the optimal policy response everywhere else in the system. This is a very significant result.

For example, consider a small economy importing and exporting many different products with no imperfections present or distortions in place. In this case we know that the optimal policy is zero tariffs and zero export taxes or subsidies. In other words, free trade is optimal in every market. However, suppose the government, contrary to the policy advice of its economic advisors, imposes a tariff on imports of one good. One might conclude that this not so bad since the government is choosing free trade for every other import and export good and perhaps this is true. However, according to the theory of the second-best, the optimal policy for every other good and service is no longer free trade. Once a distortion is placed into the system, it will upset the optimality conditions for every other substitutable good or service in the economy. With one distortion present, the optimal trade policy for other goods and services may be a small tariff, export tax or an export subsidy; we can no longer assume that free trade everywhere else is best. This result has profound implications for our main question: whether free trade is beneficial for a country. It is also one reason why the theory of the second-best is one of the most important results in all of economics.

What Is the Imperfection?

All of the previous examples, and many more, in which government intervention raises economic efficiency and national or international welfare can always be interpreted as a correction of a market imperfection through the use of a policy-imposed distortion. This is one reason why there are very few interesting new welfare findings in international trade theory. For example in recent years press reports have begun to suggest that the case for free trade has been weakened by new trade theories. Back in the 1980s, theoretical work on strategic trade policies showed that government subsidy or taxes could be used to shift profits from foreign firms and raise a nation's welfare. It seemed, free trade was no longer the best policy. In 2004 when Paul Samuelson published an article suggesting that outsourcing could make a country worse off, once again the popular press declared that the foundations of free trade were weaker than previously believed.[14]

To trade economists, these results were not surprising or new. Once you recognize that trade policy can correct for innumerable market imperfections, any new model or theory that demonstrates that free trade is not best should inspire only one question: what is the imperfection in the model?

In the case of a large importing country, the imperfection is monopsony power in trade. Similarly, in the case of a tariff on crude oil that reduces pollution, the imperfection is a negative externality. In the case of an infant industry, the imperfection is a positive production externality. These are just a few examples of the many imperfections that exist. For each imperfection, it is highly likely that an appropriately chosen trade policy can raise national welfare.

Reducing Distortions

It is logically tempting to think that if a distortion causes a reduction in economic efficiency, then reducing that distortion will improve efficiency. This proposition is true only when there is just one distortion present. If there are multiple distortions or imperfections present simultaneously, then the theory of the second-best shows that the proposition is no longer generally valid. In a sense we have already seen this result in reverse. In the previous section we noted that one imperfection could be corrected to an extent by appropriately implementing another policy distortion. Since adding a distortion or imperfection can be better than just one, it must mean that subtracting one distortion or imperfection can be worse than having two. Moving from two distortions to just one can arise only by reducing or eliminating an existing one. There is a classic example of this phenomenon in the trade literature.

Free Trade Area Formation

Free trade areas are an excellent example in the trade literature that displays surprising results because of the presence of multiple distortions. It has been known for a long time that when a country enters a free trade area with another and lowers its tariffs to zero, it is possible for the country to make itself worse off.[15] In other words, despite moving toward free trade, a step that in many circumstances improves economic efficiency, instead it is possible, though not assured, that economic efficiency declines. To economists this is the classic case of trade diversion.

This result, that an FTA can reduce economic efficiency and make a country worse off, can be interpreted in the context of the theory of the second best. When a country establishes an FTA, it is indeed a step in the direction of the economic nirvana of free trade, however, it is only a partial step. Since the FTA partners continue to maintain tariffs against other countries, some market distortions remain in place. When a tariff is removed only against one country, the liberalization can have the surprising effect of making the remaining distortions more distorting.

Effects with Multiple Imperfections

Trade diversion is the most notable example in which reducing a distortion can lead to a reduction in a nation's welfare. However, what is true in this specific case, is also true more generally. Whenever there is more than one imperfection or distortion in an economic system, reduction or elimination of one distortion need not result in an improvement in economic efficiency and national welfare. It might, but it just as easily might not. The most important implication of this result is what it says about a movement to free trade.

Trade liberalization represents a reduction in some policy-imposed distortions, whereas free trade is the elimination of some policy-imposed distortions. If either of these actions occurs while other market imperfections or distortions are in place, then there is no guarantee, from theory, that economic efficiency and national welfare will improve. It may rise, but it just as easily may not. Below we will consider what we would need to know to determine if the effect of trade liberalization is positive or negative in a real-world setting. Before that we consider an alternative justification for free trade that does not depend on this knowledge.

Real World Implications

Almost all economic analysis of policy options in a model with market imperfections assumes that there is just one imperfection to be corrected. In those circumstances, it is fairly straightforward to determine the optimal policy and to compare the best trade policy with the best domestic policy. However, things become increasingly complicated if there are numerous imperfections and distortions at work simultaneously. Surely, this is the situation most reflective of the real world.

In the real world, some industries create positive externalities, others negative externalities. Some firms have market power and can affect their market price. Some products are differentiated within an industry. Some consumption activities cause positive externality effects; others cause negative effects; others still cause both positive and negative effects. Unemployment is more likely to develop in some labor markets and is less likely in other markets. Products display different degrees of public good characteristics. Participants in many markets must deal with imperfect and asymmetric information. Finally, some countries have monopoly and monopsony power in trade.

These imperfections not only exist, but they vary in strength and importance across industries and across countries. In some countries, labor markets are more flexible than in others. Some economies have greater problems with environmental externalities than other countries, partially because of the age of the capital stock and the choice of fuel. Information problems vary from country to country. Some counties have bona fide infant industries; others do not. The extent of monopolization varies widely and is always changing, especially as some countries privatize state-owned enterprises.

In addition, every country implements a complex mix of domestic tax and regulatory policies, all of which represent market distortions relative to the pure state of economic nirvana. Each one of these distortions affects supplies and demands and thereby affects the prices faced by producers and consumers of virtually every good sold in an economy. Any time that prices change, it affects the production and consumption decisions of economic agents, which in turn, interact with the market imperfections that are present, for better and worse. These price effects will also ripple through the economy affecting intermediate goods industries, labor, and capital markets and consumption markets for substitutable goods.

Simply imagine any country and think about all the policies that government has put into place. There are social security taxes, income and property taxes, profit and sales taxes. There are agricultural support programs, subsidy programs for low income households, and food stamp programs. There are programs for health insurance and medical treatment, unemployment compensation schemes. There are health and safety regulations, anticompetition policies, and environmental regulations. In addition, we should not forget about the operations of the country's legal system and its security systems, including police and fire protection, national guard operations, and the national military defense.

Of course, for each of these domestic policies there is a rationale; the policy was put into place for a reason. More than likely, the reason will involve the correction of a market problem; some type of market imperfection. If a country is lucky, the collection of policies in place will have moved that country closer to its optimum, its highest level of national welfare. But how would we know if this is the case?

The Theory of the Second-Best and Ethanol Subsidies

The theory of the second best teaches a very important lesson that is pertinent here; every policy-imposed distortion and every market imperfection affects the optimal policy choice everywhere else in the system. Consider an illustrative example; suppose a country implements a production subsidy on ethanol. The stated rationale for the subsidy may be to stimulate cleaner fuel sources, to mitigate concerns about global warming, and to reduce dependence on foreign oil. These rationales represent corrections of market imperfections, one correcting for a negative environmental externality, another promoting the public good provision of national security. However, we can speculate about the effects of this policy to see what ought to be taken into account to choose the correct subsidy level.

First, the subsidy to ethanol production will increase ethanol supply forcing the price down relative to gasoline and lead to substitution of ethanol for gasoline by consumers. This may lower overall carbon emissions and have a long-term positive influence on the global temperature. The subsidy will also reduce demand for gasoline and the imports of crude oil from the rest of the world. However, the ethanol subsidy may also increase the demand for corn, an important input in ethanol production. This will raise the price of corn and inspire an increase in corn production. Greater corn production may stimulate greater demand for fertilizer and, because of its use, cause greater water pollution in some areas. Higher corn prices may also raise the price of beef and pork thereby encouraging people to substitute more vegetables in their diet. This may have a positive health effect by lowering average cholesterol levels in the population. Reduced demand for beef might also lead to unemployment in the beef industry. For those workers with specialized skills, they may be unemployed for a long period of time leading to higher unemployment compensation expenditures. Despite causing mixed effects on food output, if the overall effect of the subsidies were to raise agricultural production, that could increase the security of the nation in the event of a major war. However, greater corn production might be undertaken largely by conglomerate agribusinesses forcing a more rapid decline of the family farms and a subsequent loss of a national cultural heritage.

These are just a small set of effects one policy might cause. Not only does a policy affect the activity it is directed toward, but it also affects every related activity. Changes in these related activities, in turn affect an even larger set of activities related to these related activities, ad infinitum. To the extent that the related activities and subactivities influence different sorts of market imperfections or distortions, it will also change the effectiveness of every other policy that was put into place to correct them. This means that to assess the appropriateness—that is, the optimality—of any one policy requires knowledge about the level and effect of every other policy and imperfection that might be influenced either directly or indirectly.

Stated in terms of policy choice: if one policy in a complex interconnected economy is changed, it will change the optimal level of every other policy in the system. The only way to identify the optimal policy mix is to accurately specify the entire economic system and solve for the best policies. Stated in terms of effects: if you change one policy in a complex interconnected economy, it will cause positive effects to occur due to some of the imperfections and distortions and negative effects to occur due to other imperfections and distortions. The only way to know if a particular policy will have net positive or negative effects is to accurately specify the entire economic system with all of its market imperfections and then calculate the effects of the policy change.

Economists generally know about this result, but it is very uncommon for anyone to emphasize the problem. In part that is because these results undermine just about every policy prescription ever made. To advertise these results loudly reduces the reliability of many of the policy claims by the economics profession. Further, without some viable alternative what would be the point of advertising this? Thus instead, recognition of these effects is more likely to be found only in footnotes or mentioned briefly in a conclusion of a policy paper. Lal (2006, 55) reveals the quiet admission of this problem by quoting Greenwald and Stiglitz (1986, 258):

> We have considered relatively simple models, in which there is usually a single distortion . . . Though the basic qualitative proposition, that markets are constrained Pareto efficient, would obviously remain in a more general formulation, the simplicity of the policy prescriptions would disappear. Does this make our analysis of little policy relevance? The same objection can, of course, be raised against standard optimal tax theory. (Some critics might say, so much the worse for both.)

The term "constrained Pareto efficient" is the same as saying there are market imperfections. The rest suggests why critics can argue that such simple analysis does not say very much about policy choice in the real world. Lal concludes with a pithy remark, "Quite!"

The real problem with an optimal policy choice that will correct for the vast array of market imperfections that are scattered uniquely through every economy, is that it is unsolvable from a theoretical perspective because of the enormous complexity. It is true that governments do engage in some degree of cost-benefit analysis to decide whether to introduce new policies. It is also true that additional issues of potential concern are being incorporated when conducting these evaluations. For example, in the United States many proposals for government projects are required to conduct an environmental impact assessment before the policy is implemented. In this way, the potentially negative externality effects can be incorporated into the decision process. While it is true that this is a step in the direction of completeness, at the same time, it masks the fact that numerous other market imperfection impacts are never even considered in these same studies. Also rarely, would a government decide to adjust the level of all other policies whenever a new policy is being implemented (as would be necessary if we were truly optimizing).

The Problem of Chaos

One way to mitigate this problem of optimal policy choice is to argue that even though every change in the economic system affects everything else in the economy, the magnitude of the effects will vary in a systematic way. For example, the effects of an ethanol subsidy will have its largest effect in the ethanol market itself. It will have a pretty big effect in the corn market since corn is an important input. The effect in the vegetable and beef markets, being one more industry removed, should be affected to a somewhat smaller degree. The effect on health because of changes in cholesterol consumption or the effect on pollution due to increased fertilizer usage will be even smaller because these effects will be separated to the third degree. In other words the effects beyond the initial market are likely to dampen with each degree of separation from the original policy. Thus, if the effects of all policies follow this systematic pattern of dampening the farther removed an industry is from the initial distortion, then although we might need to consider the implications of a policy change across several levels of effects, we do not really need to consider them across the entirety of the economy. While the problem may still be quite complicated, with the "dampening effects" assumption it is now much less complicated than originally suggested.

The counterargument to this dampening story is chaos theory. Chaos theory has been popularly represented by the following metaphor: one beat of a butterfly's wings in Texas may be sufficient to cause a tornado to form in Florida a week later. I suspect this example leaves many readers puzzled. Is that really possible, one may wonder? The answer is unknown; the story is merely an illustration of something that is seen in a mathematical system.

The mathematics of chaos is not really that difficult. Researchers have discovered that some seemingly simple mathematical relationships display chaotic behavior. Chaotic behavior occurs whenever a very small change in initial conditions (like the flap of a butterfly's wings) can have a dramatically different effect upon the outcome (the tornado). One example of chaos in a mathematical system shows up in the Mandelbrot set. The Mandelbrot set plots different colors depending on whether a simple series converges to a real number or whether the series diverges to infinity (which is a very different outcome). The discovery of chaos demonstrated that if you moved a parameter input in the series by a very small amount (say, from 5.00001 to 5.00002) the value of the summation, the outcome, can change enormously.

A globalization example of chaos might be something like ethanol subsidies. Suppose an ethanol subsidy, by encouraging a series of impacts that propagates through the global economy over time, saves the world from the disastrous effects of global warming. The oceans do not rise 50 meters, hurricanes do not grow to magnitude 15, and the summer temperature on the North Pole does not rise to 40°C. Suppose without the subsidy the world does experience these terrible effects. In this case, avoiding a small change in policy (the subsidy) pushes the human race to extinction (chaotic effect). Of course, this is a fanciful, make-believe example. I would not expect an ethanol subsidy to matter very much in the long run; but then, that is because I do not know whether a chaotic effect exists in this situation or not.

It is true that chaos theory does not prove anything about the way the world works. Instead, chaos theory should simply raise suspicions of seemingly reasonable assumptions, such as the expectation that the effects of policy changes in an economy will have a dampening effect as the degree of separation from the policy increases. If chaos is present in some real-world situations, it would mean that small changes in policy affecting one market could have very large impacts somewhere else. Once again we can never know what the effects of a policy change will be unless we can accurately specify the entire economic system with all of its market imperfections and calculate the effects of the policy change.

Conclusion

In a nutshell, the definitive lessons about trade policy that we learn from economic theory are:

- trade liberalization will cause a complex redistribution of income with some individuals realizing welfare improvements but others realizing welfare losses;
- due to the complexity of the real world, it will be difficult to identify all but the most immediate effects of trade liberalization;
- due to the presence of numerous market imperfections and distortions it is impossible to determine whether trade liberalization will induce net national benefits or net national losses; and
- after trade liberalization, because of the complexity of the redistributive effects and the inability to know if the net welfare benefits are positive, it is impossible to design a compensation scheme to ensure that everyone benefits from trade liberalization.

Thus, the only thing we can be absolutely sure of, on the basis of economic theory, is that trade liberalization will cause some to benefit economically and others to lose. This result is virtually indisputable; it is difficult to imagine anyone arguing convincingly otherwise. The inability to identify the winners and losers may not be obvious to some observers since every economic model does identify who gains and who loses. However, one must remember that the real world encompasses all of these individual model effects simultaneously. Although general equilibrium models display a wide array of effects as they propagate through labor, capital, and goods markets domestically and internationally, these models never come close to capturing the complexity of the real world. Each model gives us a glimpse of some of the effects, but they do not enable us to pinpoint the detailed outcomes with any reliability.

The argument that free trade may not raise overall national welfare should also be well known, at least in the economics profession, but here too the results comes mostly by imagining a real world that is much more complex than any single model. In a well-specified model it is usually possible to pinpoint precisely which policy option is best. However, some models show free trade is best, while others show that government policy interventions are best. Thus since the world is comprised of features displayed in all of these models, an objective observer should recognize that in reality the effects of a free trade policy are simply unknowable. Finally, the inability to compensate may also not be so obvious to many people since many economists do support compensation as a necessary component of trade liberalization actions. The standard example is the use of trade adjustment assistance to aid workers who lose their jobs because of a free trade agreement. However, it should be obvious even to supporters of compensation plans, that these actions probably do little more than quiet the most vocal adversaries of free trade agreements and have no chance of compensating the vast numbers who lose without knowing why.

Of course, because there will always be gains and losses from any policy change, those who want to believe that free trade is the best policy for a nation will have plenty of positive impacts to point to that can support that view, as long as they ignore the many negative effects, or discount their importance in some way. Thus if someone suggests that trade liberalization is beneficial for a country because it will generate efficiency improvements, or if someone says that protection is harmful for a country because it will reduce the incentive to innovate, he is right. At the same time, any individual who wants to believe that trade protection is best for a nation can show plenty of evidence to support that view, as long as they ignore or discount the many negative effects caused by these policies. Thus if someone suggests that protection may be beneficial for the country because it will save workers from losing their jobs, or if someone says that free trade is harmful to a country because it will spoil the natural environment, theory says that he too may be right.

Finally, what we learn from trade theory applies more generally to any government policy. The redistributive effects described here arise solely because trade policies change prices. Since every other tax, subsidy, or regulation will affect prices as well, every new government policy, or any removal of a policy, will cause a redistribution of income. The multitude of market imperfections and distortions are affected as much by domestic policies as they are by trade policies. This means that any government policies will cause some positive impacts, some negative, and because of the complexity of the international economy, it will be impossible to know whether national welfare is raised or lowered because of the policy. This also implies once again, that the use of compensation to ensure everyone benefits from any new government policy is well-nigh impossible. This is why economic theory cannot tell us reliably what are the best policies to choose.

There are two possible ways out of this quagmire. One method is empirical measurement. Data collection, computational methods, and computing capacity have all expanded enormously in the past century. When theory cannot give us a definitive result, one answer lies in measurement. Indeed, when theory gives us several possible outcomes, it is common for economists to proclaim: "it's an empirical question!" The empirical answer is offered in the next chapter. The other way out is to devise a method of choosing policies that recognizes that positive and negative effects are the norm. In this case we ask the question, under what circumstances is it generally acceptable to implement a policy that will redistribute income between people. This approach will be explored in the second part of the book, chapters 6–11.

CHAPTER 3

Why Empirical Data Cannot Tell Us What to Do about Policy

Economic theory strongly supports the following two conclusions: first, trade liberalization will result in a complex redistribution of income; and second, depending on the circumstances, trade liberalization can lead either to an improvement or to a reduction in a nation's total welfare. Although theory can identify some of the characteristics of those who might gain and lose, without careful empirical measurement, it is impossible to know precisely who will gain and lose how much from freer trade. Whether national welfare rises or falls is important too, since economists often assuage the income redistribution concerns by suggesting that compensation be given to the losers from trade, drawn from the extra benefits accruing to the winners. However, the only way to ensure that everyone gains from free trade after compensation is if there is a positive national welfare effect from trade liberalization.

Economic theory does not provide incontrovertible support for the proposition that free trade is national welfare enhancing, however. Although many theoretical models highlight the improvements in economic efficiency likely to arise when countries trade more freely, many other models provide arguments for why free trade may not be the best policy when there are market imperfections and distortions present. Because every country has a highly complex and unique mix of these imperfections, and because these will differ from country to country, theory can only reveal that the set of optimal policies will also differ from country to country. Only by analyzing the empirical data in particular countries would it be possible to determine what that set of policies might be, or to determine if trade liberalization will be beneficial for any particular country. All of which points to the need for empirical measurement.

Simple Empiricism

One way to apply data to the theory is with what might be called simple empiricism, which uses empirical observations to suggest tendencies or inclinations. For example, suppose the trade data indicates that a country currently exports agricultural goods and imports electronic goods. Suppose collected data also shows that this country has many more unskilled workers per unit of capital than most of its trading partners. Using this broad aggregate data we can match the factor proportions theory to the data and suggest that trade liberalization is likely to reduce real income for individuals in the import-competing electronics sector but will raise real income for individuals in the exporting agricultural sector, at least in the short run. In the longer run we could say that the country's relatively scarce unskilled workers would experience income improvements while the country's relatively scarce owners of capital may experience income reductions.

For analytical simplicity, economic theory usually considers the effects of one policy change (such as trade liberalization) while assuming all other variables in the economy remain fixed at their original values. This means that while trade liberalization may cause import-competing industries to lose income, this is only ensured in the model when no other income improving economic effects are also occurring. However, in a real-world situation many other changes are always taking place simultaneously. Changes such as technological improvements, changes in management, outsourcing, and advertising effectiveness can all positively influence the outcome in a particular import-competing industry. If some of these changes occur simultaneously with the movement to freer trade, incomes in import-competing industries might actually rise instead of falling.

For these reasons, theory and simple empiricism only suggest tendencies rather than predicting outcomes. We can reasonably say that trade liberalization will tend to cause—or that the probability is higher for—incomes to fall in import-competing industries. However, this is different, and less definitive than saying, trade liberalization will surely cause incomes to fall in import-competing industries. Unfortunately, theory combined with simple empiricism is never sufficient to predict actual outcomes.

Sophisticated Empiricism

The alternative approach is what we might call "sophisticated empiricism," by which I mean the use of econometric and statistical methods to search for correlations or cause and effect relationships or to develop empirical simulation models of the economy.

Using multiple regression analysis and other advanced techniques, it is possible to analyze whether, and to what extent, a whole collection of variables may have on a particular objective. For example, trade liberalization may be only one among many changes that could have influenced wages, growth rates, or productivity. Other pertinent variables might be labor force and capital stock growth, interest rates, and R&D spending. Using regression techniques it is possible to assess the influence of trade liberalization while simultaneously taking into account variations in other variables that may have also affected the same outcomes. If a positive effect is found, one can more convincingly argue that trade liberalization has indeed raised wages, growth rates, or productivity levels.

Another common empirical research approach involves the construction of what are called computable general equilibrium models (CGEs), also known as applied general equilibrium models (AGEs). These approaches begin with standard trade models, such as Heckscher-Ohlin-Samuelson (HOS), and introduce numerical estimates of their parameter values. Using a computer simulation it is possible to introduce a policy change, such as trade liberalization, and use the model to predict estimates for production, consumption, trade changes, employment changes, and wage and welfare impacts on various groups in different industries. The models can show, at least at a high level of aggregation, which industries will benefit from free trade, which will lose and whether the net national effects will be positive or negative.

These empirical studies complement economic theory by quantifying the cause and effect relationships and by providing some evidence regarding the validity of the theories. Although researchers know that empirical evidence cannot prove the validity of theories, there is certainly widespread belief that if a theory or relationship cannot be supported by at least one or several instances of empirical evidence attesting to it, then the theory becomes suspect. In other words, consistency of the data with the theory is a necessary, though not sufficient, condition to be believed.

Interestingly, in practice, failure of a theory to match empirical evidence does not necessarily lead to the refutation of that theory. An example of this was the discovery by Wassily Leontief in the 1950s that the United States, a capital-abundant country, did not export capital-intensive goods as predicted by the HOS model. The "Leontief paradox," as it became known, did not lead researchers to throw away the model. Instead they developed ways of explaining why either the model was incomplete, or the data was inadequate. Thus, theory refutation inspired creative activities to reconcile the data with the theory. In many instances this process generates a much richer understanding of the variables that influence outcomes and the problems associated with measuring those variables.

The Empirical Answer

Despite some well-known problems regarding the inability of models to convincingly verify theories, researchers and others do use empirical studies to support policy positions. Indeed, most of the arguments made by free trade advocates and opponents alike rely on numerous empirical studies that support the policy prescriptions being advanced. The list of studies lending direct or indirect support to trade liberalization is extensive. Here are just a few recent examples.

One recent example of direct support is a survey of a range of studies by Bradford, Grieco, and Hufbauer (2006) that suggests that trade opening since World War II has added at least $800 billion to the U.S. economy. They conclude that future trade liberalization can raise U.S. incomes and standards of living. Other studies look indirectly at specific results that seem likely to correspond to generally good outcomes. Thus, Trefler (2006) provides empirical support that tariff reductions between the United States and Canada resulted in sizeable increases in labor productivity. Since higher labor productivity should tend to raise wages and incomes and inspire GDP growth, the study supports the view that trade liberalization is good. Edmonds and Pavcnik (2005) provide a third example by suggesting that trade liberalization can result in less child labor usage in developing countries. Although they do not say that it will lead to less child labor, their evidence that a higher incidence of child labor is not an automatic outcome of trade liberalization softens concern on that point.

Nevertheless, many other empirical studies lend support to free trade opponents. For example, Traca (2004) shows that trade liberalization causes a decline in real wages and welfare of unskilled workers. Parikh

(2006) suggests that liberalization may lead to an unsustainable balance of payments position. Finally Grieben (2005) suggests that Southern-originated trade liberalization can result in an increase in Northern wage inequality.

Many of the books about globalization today involve lengthy arguments about why the "evidence" supports the author's point of view and why any counterarguments are notably weaker. The purpose of this chapter is not to undertake a comprehensive evaluation of the empirical literature or its ability to verify theories. Instead, I will make several simple observations about the reliability of empirical studies with regards to the policy debate of trade liberalization.

The relevant multipart question with respect to trade liberalization policies is: can empirical studies, with a reasonably high degree of reliability, either individually or in combination, identify who benefits and who loses from trade liberalization over time and show whether the net national effects are positive? A more general policy question is, can the optimal set of economic policies for an economy be identified with a high degree of reliability using empirical methods? Finally, rather than requiring a strong result that the policy be optimal, we can ask a weaker question: Can we use empirical methods to determine which policies will make things better for a country?

Computable General Equilibrium Models

In the last chapter we discussed how to identify the optimal economic policies in the presence of multiple imperfections and distortions. This question is an extremely difficult one to answer because of the complex market interactions both within a country and internationally. Because of market interconnectedness and the widespread distribution of market imperfections, theory suggests that every policy that is implemented or changed by a government will generate a complex ripple effect of both positive and negative changes across the economy both immediately and over time. The overall impact of any policy change can only be identified if we can effectively measure these effects now and in the future.

An even more difficult question to answer is what the set of policies would be to optimize the well-being of people within an economy or around the world. In other words, what are the set of policies that will maximize a country's well-being? Economic theory shows that the answer to this question needs to account for the fact that every policy change affects the optimal policy level of every other policy within the economy. For example, if you reduce tariffs, then the optimal environmental policy, the optimal labor policy, the optimal competition policy, and all other policies will change as well. In principle then, one cannot evaluate the best trade policy in isolation from all of the other domestic policies that are already in place.

Probably the best and most direct way to account for these cross-market interactions is to construct a model that mimics these complexities as closely as possible. The closest economists have come to developing such a model is the computable general equilibrium (CGE) model. A general equilibrium (GE) model incorporates the simultaneous interaction between goods markets and factor markets across at least several industries. GE models capture the connections of households, firms, governments, and the foreign sector operating through different markets. Thus, in a general equilibrium model, a change affecting one market will have ripple effects throughout the rest of the economy. A CGE model quantifies the interindustry relationships using actual data collected from real economies.

The starting point for a CGE model is an input-output (I-O) table for an economy. An I-O table separates production into multiple sectors or industries, such as agriculture, forestry, minerals, manufacturing, and services. The number of sectors specified can range from a handful to over one hundred depending on what data are available. An I-O table presents measured values for the amount of production from each industry that is used as an intermediate input into every other industry. In addition the table provides final good production from each sector. An I-O table is appended with information on labor and capital inputs in industries, demand patterns between consumption, investment, government, and the foreign sector, among other information to create a social accounting matrix, or SAM.

Variations of CGE models may expand the number of labor inputs using data about the number of workers with different skills employed in different industries. On the consumer side, a CGE model can specify households with different income levels and consider variations in consumer preferences and income distribution. Typically the models assume perfect competition but adjustments can be made to allow for economies of scale in certain industries. Numerous such adjustments and extensions have been made as CGE models have been further developed and improved over the years.

The values in a national input-output table for a particular economy are based on the measured values in one year. Because it is difficult to compile all of these numbers, I-O tables are typically constructed only once every five years. Also, since the purpose of a CGE model is to consider how an economy will adjust after policy changes are made, additional information about the supply and demand elasticities is needed. Elasticities measure how demand and supplies change in response to variations in prices. Estimates of these elasticities are typically drawn from other studies in the literature.

Once constructed and quantified, the models are used to simulate the effects of changes in some of the key parameters. For example, tariffs on imported goods can be lowered, or eliminated, to simulate the effects of free trade area formation. With a detailed CGE model, the ripple effects on production, consumption, and government spending levels throughout the economy are numerically specified. Thus the models will indicate the magnitude of the effects in different segments of the economy. They can also be used to assess the overall national welfare effects of policy changes.

CGE models have become very popular in assessing the effects of trade liberalization for several reasons. First, these models are the best available for predicting changes in industry production levels and the number of jobs in a sector. Since much of the political discussion about trade liberalization often focuses on job effects, these models contribute to that debate. Second, CGE models provide the most complete evaluation of effects arising from economic policy changes. Thus, it is easy to sell these models to users in policy circles on the basis of sophistication. However, this sophistication can act as a drawback since it is sometimes difficult to explain their precision. There is also skepticism that because of the complexity of the models, researchers could plausibly vary parameter values to produce virtually any result a policy maker might desire.[1]

Nevertheless, despite the complexity of these models and the hard work and expertise that goes into creating them, it is reasonable to ask how close they come to answering the questions we would like to answer. In other words, can CGE models be used to convince us that trade liberalization is a good thing in some general aggregate sense? Can CGE models be used to identify the winners and losers from trade liberalization so that an appropriate compensation can be made? Unfortunately the answer to these questions is no; not now, not in the near future, and probably not even in the distant future will these models provide convincing answers to these critical questions. What follows are a few reasons why.

Aggregation

First, CGE models can identify winners and losers, but only at a high level of aggregation. CGEs are currently unable to identify income changes at finer levels of detail. The industry classifications consider industries like "manufacturing." For the manufacturing industry the data reveals how much intermediate and primary inputs come from various sources. For example, the data might show that for $1 of manufactured goods output, $0.02 came from the agricultural industry, while $0.31 came from the service industry, etc. The data would also indicate the value of capital and how many workers were employed in the industry, which in turn is used to identify productivity values.

In reality, the manufacturing industry consists of production processes as diverse as semiconductors, clothing, food and beverages, machine tools, automobiles, and airplanes. At the micro level, the intermediate input proportions and capital and labor productivity will also vary greatly within the industry. Thus, when trade liberalization occurs, it can be expected to affect different manufacturing industries differently. Perhaps one manufacturing business using more capital will expand, while another using more services will contract. This would in turn change the input proportions and productivity values that, in the empirical model, are assumed to be fixed at the level of all manufacturing. When policy changes are made, a CGE model assumes that these aggregate industry relationships are maintained. In other words, manufacturing output will always require the same proportion of agricultural and service industry inputs and will maintain the same productivity of capital and labor.

Despite these problems, aggregation is necessary for two reasons. First, despite the advances in computing capabilities, CGE models take considerable time to solve. Computing requirements rise exponentially as production and consumption agents are separated into finer details; thus, the more aggregated the data, the less computation time and the easier it is to compute a solution. Second, aggregation is necessary because disaggregated data is simply not available across an entire economy. Although more data are beginning to be collected for some industries, it is expensive to collect detailed data describing the production and consumption processes. At best surveys can be done for some businesses and households and inferences drawn about the rest of the population. But this requires strong presumptions about regularities across a diverse economy.

Parameter Estimates

A second shortcoming of CGEs is that they assume that economic adjustments in the future will mimic patterns displayed in the past. This assumption is implicit because all parameter values are based on past data. The I-O coefficients are usually updated only once every five years, if that. For some countries, I-O tables may not exist or there may have been only one such table constructed in recent years. In some cases, creative methods, such as cross-entropy techniques, have been developed to use more recent economic data to update the social accounting matrices to better reflect the values that prevail nearer the time of interest.[2] Of course, past data is the only data available. Nevertheless, to carry this data forward to the future in simulations means that a very important assumption is being made: the parameter values are unchanging.

Unfortunately, parameter values are quite likely to change over time because trade liberalization will change the composition of production within each aggregate industry. Thus within each aggregated sector some businesses will expand while other will contract in response to freer trade. These changes should affect the input proportions from other industries measured in the I-O tables. In addition, some parameter values may be drawn from studies that are five, ten or even 15 years old. And yet CGE models presume the future will mostly conform to the patterns of the past.

Incomplete Coverage

Perhaps the biggest problem with CGEs is the failure to include many of the market imperfections and distortions that surely are present in real economies. CGEs generally assume that markets are perfectly competitive, that full employment of all resources, which includes workers, always obtains, and that there are few market imperfections present. The models will incorporate some of the policy-imposed distortions by simulating government tax and tariff collections and expenditures. Also, sometimes the model will focus on a particular issue, such as environmental problems or economies of scale, and incorporate at least that one imperfection into the model. However, despite modest attempts to add realistic feature into the models, there will always remain numerous other imperfections and distortions that cannot be included due to the sheer complexity.

Ken Arrow recognized the exclusion of one important imperfection when he wrote,

> The most important novel development in microeconomics in recent years has been the recognition (by economic agents and by economists) of asymmetric information as a basic element in economic interaction.... I think it fair to say that none of these developments have been reflected in CGE models. The reason is clear. Economists have not developed any successful way of going from the individual decisions and outcomes of small-group interactions to the economy as an interacting whole.[3]

Information asymmetries are an important feature of the world that affects economic decision making at the micro level. Since it affects all micro-level agents, it will also affect macro-economic outcomes like those being predicted in CGE models.

However, the problem is much more serious; not only information asymmetries are missing. Most models are missing a complete and accurate representation of labor and capital market rigidities, environmental effects, strategic behavior in oligopolistic markets, social and cultural effects, positive and negative externalities, and public goods, among many others.

The theory of the second best teaches that the only accurate way to assess policy impacts is to recognize all of the market imperfections and distortions simultaneously. To exclude one or more means that policy evaluations will certainly be incomplete and thus more likely to be incorrect. Thus, to assess whether free trade is good or bad from a national perspective, while using an incomplete model of the economy, should by no means be convincing to any policy maker or any objective observer.

Jagdish Bhagwati, a prominent economist who has contributed substantially to the trade literature, summed up a common professional impression of CGE models when he wrote, "in fact I consider many of the estimates of trade expansion and of gains from trade—produced at great expense by number-crunching at institutions such as the World Bank with the aid of huge computable models, and then fed into the public policy domain with the aid of earnest journalists—as little more than flights of fancy in contrived flying machines" (Bhagwati 2004, 230). Unfortunately, for policy prescriptions, a review of the problems inherent in computable CGEs suggests he is exactly right.

The Value of CGEs

If CGEs are viewed with such apprehension, we might ask whether they are of any usefulness whatsoever. The answer is a restrained yes.

Many times when policy discussions occur, participants in the debate often talk as if the policies will have a narrow effect only in the industry of interest. For example, if the steel industry argues for a protective tariff, they will emphasize the protection of jobs for workers, often as if that is the only relevant effect. A careful economic analysis of the issue, however, will point out the effects on consumers of steel products, the effects on other industries who use steel as an input, the effect on government revenues, the effects on income to different production factors, the effects on the environment and much more. Indeed, one of the important lessons of economic theory is recognition of the interconnectedness of markets. These relationships are nicely described using general equilibrium models.

CGEs put numbers into the theory to demonstrate the kinds of pattern changes that may occur from various policy changes. As such, they are helpful in highlighting the complexity of the potential effects. In other words, the simulations can depict how policy changes will ripple through the economy even affecting industries that appear quite remote from the steel sector.

Sometimes the results of CGEs show outcomes that the researcher cannot easily explain because the process is hidden deeply in the complex mathematics. For some this becomes a source of criticism for these models, however I think these unexplainable outcomes are one of the main reasons CGEs are informative. Even though these models are nowhere near the complexity needed to mimic the real world, they still are complicated enough to be incomprehensible sometimes. If models much simpler than the real world can display policies with incomprehensible impacts, then what does that imply about our ability to understand the effects of real policy actions in real-world economies? Surely it should strongly diminish any hope that we can confidently predict the specific effects of policy actions in the real world.

The results of CGE analysis will always display complex interactions, the general patterns of which will surely occur. However, the predictions of any CGE model will also surely be "flights of fancy." They should not be used to inform policy choices because they cannot answer the questions: (1) who will gain income and who will lose from the policy change, and (2) will the nation be better off after the policy change? Without answers to these questions we cannot be sure that the policies will be good for the nation, nor could we implement a compensation scheme to ensure that everyone benefits.

Indeed, Kehoe (2005) conducted an evaluation of three of the most prominent CGE models from the early 1990s used to project the effects of the NAFTA. He found that all of the models drastically underestimated the effects on trade between the countries. Thus, the results of these models, though extremely sophisticated, should simply not be trusted.

Piecemeal Empirical Investigations

The popular perception in the economics field today is that economic theory requires empirical support to be believed. For this reason trade theories that suggest positive economic effects as a result of trade liberalization have been taken to the data, as it were, to see if the results can be verified. Numerous empirical studies exist in the literature that suggest positive outcomes from trade liberalization. Although all researchers acknowledge their limitations, they are also likely to believe that each study moves us closer to the truth. There is power in numbers. Most would agree that if only one study showed support for free trade then the proposition that free trade is good would be accepted only with great reservations. However, if two or three or a hundred studies using different data sets and different estimation techniques also show support for free trade, then the case for free trade strengthens substantially. Although studies opposing free trade may weaken the case for free trade, these can be countered with more analyses showing support. The impression is that continuing empirical research steps us closer and closer to the truth.

Based on the philosophy of science literature, especially that of Karl Popper and Imre Lakatos, most researchers accept that empirical data cannot be used to verify theories.[4] Just because the data is consistent with a theory does not prove it would be so in all instances. Instead it can only be said that in the instances tested, the data is consistent with the theory. An example of the potential problem is illustrated in Taleb (2007). Consider a simple theoretical statement or proposition: "all swans are white." If this proposition were tested empirically in Europe and the Northern hemisphere by looking extensively at bird species and noting the color of all swans, the theory would have been supported over and over again. However, once Europeans discovered Australia, the theory would fail upon the first sighting of the Australian black swan. One of Taleb's central propositions is that scientific knowledge is much less certain than it often appears and that empirical observation is not sufficient to prove very much.

The purpose of this section is not to review the literature in the philosophy of science, but rather to suggest a few reasons why the empirical literature tending to support trade liberalization makes a weaker case for trade liberalization than is commonly suggested. The main reasons highlighted are, (a) partial analysis does not identify the total effects, (b) many effects from trade liberalization are immeasurable, (c) researcher confirmation bias can tarnish objectivity, and (d) the Bayesian method is not applicable.

Some researchers may argue that empirical tests are not designed to inform policy debates, instead they simply represent tests of theories versus alternatives. In this view, theories and tests of theories are designed to be positive economic analysis that simply try to explain "what is" rather than normative analysis attempting to support what "should be." Although this bifurcation makes some sense, it is unrealistic to think that public policy advocates are not using empirical results to build support for their preferred policies. Simply listen to any policy debate and take note of how many times "numbers" are used to support a position. Since even purely positive studies can be used in normative discussions, it still makes sense to consider them in terms of their policy implications.

Partial Analysis

Because the question, will free trade promote an increase in the overall national welfare, is very broad and difficult to answer, researchers simplify the questions to make them more manageable. This is both reasonable and necessary. For example, a researcher may inquire whether trade liberalization in a group of countries has affected GDP growth or poverty, or wage inequality. Each of these is only a partial question however.

For example, while it is certainly true that GDP contributes to the well-being of a nation, it is also well accepted that many things people care about are not captured in this measure. For example, GDP is a measure of a country's annual production of all goods and services. It does not account for income inequalities, does not include negative effects like pollution caused by some productive activities, does not capture benefits caused this year by previously produced products such as used cars and houses, and only imperfectly accounts for inflationary effects. Furthermore, GDP measures production not consumption. When a nation runs a trade deficit, its national consumption expenditures exceed its productive output and this contributes to a higher standard of living than represented by its GDP.

Nonetheless, because evaluating all of these impacts is very difficult, it makes sense to answer the simpler partial question. Thus, many studies have indicated that trade liberalization has indeed been associated with faster real GDP growth for many countries in the past. This result is used by advocates of free trade to suggest that trade liberalization is a good thing. And it may well be a good thing. However, several studies using partial and incomplete indicators of well-being are insufficient to prove that trade liberalization raises national welfare. Skeptics can reasonably argue that GDP growth is not everything people care about, and just because GDP grows does not mean we should choose free trade. This counterclaim is just as plausible because we simply cannot know very much about overall effects from a partial analysis alone.

Immeasurability

One reason partial analysis of the effects of policy changes is necessary is because many of the effects from policy changes are simply immeasurable. Consider, as an example, the effects of trade and globalization on culture. Some argue that globalization leads to the decline of traditional industries. An early example of this effect was the decline of the Indian textile industry in the 1800s after the introduction of new weaving technologies and trade with Britain. The cheap textiles imported from Britain devastated the industry. In modern times one will notice the resistance that prevails in developed countries to liberalization of agriculture. In the United States they talk of the destruction of the family farms. In Europe they fear the loss of the pastoral countryside and the rural reminders of a simpler time. In Japan they maintain agricultural traditions with rice paddies in the middle of urban areas.

Although one can argue that references to cultural traditions by supporters of agricultural restrictions are merely a rhetorical cover for their real concern (i.e., fear of losing income), it seems reasonable to imagine that cultural considerations can affect people's well-being. Indeed these utility effects can be modeled as a negative externality, a kind of market imperfection, which can then justify the use of trade restrictions to preserve culture. However, to implement such a policy appropriately would require the measurement of the effects of trade on culture and the subsequent influence on individuals utility or well-being. As far as I know this has never been attempted, largely because the idea of culture itself is rather fuzzy and because enumeration of its effects, even if possible, would certainly be based on a considerable number of arguable assumptions.

If culture is accepted as a relevant factor in assessing the effects of globalization, and if it cannot be measured convincingly, then one can never assure people that freer trade is indeed a good thing. Negative effects on people from cultural changes could overwhelm other positive effects such as GDP growth. Indeed, perhaps the inability to measure cultural effects is a reason economists seem reluctant to accept it as a possible motivation for trade restrictions. Cowen (2002) is one economist who clearly accepts that culture matters. His book provides an extensive overview of the effects of globalization on culture around the world. Although he makes no attempt to measure the effects, he does argue that cultural changes are not all bad and that the positive effects of cultural change caused by globalization may overwhelm the negative effects. Of course we can never know if his argument is valid unless we could somehow measure culture convincingly.

A similar issue arises with the recent issue of global climate change. If energy usage rises because of increased economic activity inspired by globalization, then the increased carbon emissions into earth's atmosphere may be causing a dramatic shift in the earth's climate. Average temperatures are expected to rise across the planet, possibly causing changes in rainfall, increases in the number and strength of hurricanes and typhoons, and the melting of large land ice masses, thereby causing a rise in the ocean level. Economic damage may be catastrophic, especially if a rising ocean buries coastal cities under meters of water, if superstorms become commonplace, and if changes in ocean temperatures influence regional climates. For example, there is some concern that rising ocean temperatures could stop the Gulf Stream that carries warm water toward Europe. If the Gulf Stream stopped, Europe would become much colder, greatly affecting agricultural production and many other economic activities.

Indeed significant global climate change would surely have important and perhaps catastrophic effects on the world's economy. But how much of an effect is an open question. In fact, the issue is so complex that the extent of the damage is impossible to assess. Perhaps this is one reason some people are unwilling to accept climate change as a real phenomenon, believing instead that it represents a left-wing conspiracy to wrest control of people's lives.[5]

Of course, difficulty with measurement will not prevent researchers from making assessments. Nevertheless, consumers of this information need to be aware that all assessments of such far-reaching and global phenomenon will be based on an enormous number of assumptions, some of which will certainly turn out to be invalid. In the same way as CGE analysis, assessments of global climate change can be helpful in providing a "sense" of the kinds of outcomes that are in the range of possibilities. However, also like CGE studies, they are quite likely to be wrong in their details ex post.

Confirmation Bias

One well-known problem in empirical research is known as confirmation bias. This occurs when a researcher begins with an expectation that a particular result is true and then searches selectively for evidence to support the expectation. Some evidence of this problem seems apparent in econometric testing.

For example, most trade economists generally believe that free trade is a good thing for a country. A search of the empirical literature on the effects of trade liberalization finds many more studies tending to support free trade and few tending to oppose it. One possibility to explain this pattern is that the actual evidence more strongly supports the positive effects of trade liberalization. In this case no confirmation bias exists. However, it may also be true that results tending to support trade liberalization are more likely to be published in trade publications since the reviewers of these papers will also be economists who tend to believe in the net benefits of free trade. If empirical researchers recognize that the bias exists, they may be inclined to only submit papers that have the expected results.

Observation of the standard operating practice in economics may support this claim. For example suppose a researcher decides to study the empirical effects of trade liberalization on poverty rates. Initially, a model will be used to identify all of the variables that may influence poverty in a country and the way in which these variables may interact. The model will be used to inform the specification for an econometric test, and data will be collected for the test.

Quite frequently, when the test is run the first time, the results are mixed. The initial hypothesis, that trade liberalization reduces poverty, may be only weakly supported or perhaps even rejected. At this point the researcher has a choice. Either she can attempt to publish these "weak" results, or she could check to see if a stronger result might be obtainable.

Suppose however that this researcher "believes" that that trade liberalization should reduce poverty. In this case, she will be inclined to also believe that something was wrong either with the model specification or with the data. In all but the simplest empirical studies there are always a variety of "problems" with the data. For example, rarely is the available data for a study precisely the data a researcher would wish to have. Thus, proxy data is used as a substitute.[6] The proxy data may or may not mimic the behavior of the ideal data that was unobtainable. Standard operating procedure in the profession is to rerun the study, sometimes hundreds of times, with different data and different model assumptions. Indeed, most of the development of econometrics involves improvements in techniques to compensate for the myriad of data problems that can arise. If alternative specifications with alternative data provide greater support for the hypothesis, then it is generally believed that this new specification and data is "correct." This process is sometimes called data mining, or massaging the data to secure a better fit with expectations.

Unfortunately, it is impossible to know whether the final model specification and data proxies are closer or further from the truth. This would be especially true when the researcher has a preference about the final result. If the researcher approached the problem completely objectively, he might conduct his research study very differently. For example, first he would fully investigate ex ante precisely the "best" data available and the "best" possible test of the hypothesis. Then, he would run the model once and publish whatever results were obtained. In this way, confirmation bias might be reduced.

Problems with confirmation bias are not unknown to empirical researchers in economics. For example, Leamer (1983) provides suggestions on how to improve the empirical procedures with an appropriate use of sensitivity analysis that considers a range of studies that vary with different assumptions about the prior beliefs of the researcher. The example he offers considers the deterrent effects of the death penalty. He shows how a researcher using one set of assumptions can reach a conclusion that the death penalty reduces homicides. However, by altering the model, either including or excluding variables deemed important or not, he is able to show that some equally plausible models shows the death penalty actually raises the homicide rate.

Procedures involving alternative tests such as these have become common practice in economics. In order to have a paper published today in the best economics journals, most research must show that a particular result is supportable under a variety of model specifications and with alternative data assumptions. These procedures surely act to reduce confirmation bias, but it is unlikely to eliminate it entirely.

Bayesian Inference

Most researchers would agree that one or two empirical studies supporting the argument for freer trade would not be too convincing. Nonetheless, most may also accept that if numerous studies, conducted by many different researchers, using many different data sets, over many different periods of time, all show support for trade liberalization, then the case is much more solid. Even with substantial evidence such as this, one should never claim that the point has been "proven." However, one can claim that the probability that trade liberalization is overall good for a country is certainly higher. Strong believers in free trade may even believe that the probability free trade is good for a nation is very close to 100 percent.

The idea that the probability of a hypothesis being true rises as more supporting evidence is accumulated is know as Bayesian inference or Bayesian updating. For example, suppose, perhaps based on economic theory alone, someone believes that free trade is good for a country with probability 40 percent. Afterwards, every empirical result the person reads that supports the original hypothesis increases his belief in free trade a little bit. Similarly, every empirical result that casts doubt on the proposition reduces the probability. If studies supporting free trade are greater in number and also more believable (perhaps because of the care and rigor of the analysis), then his impression that free trade is a good thing will grow.

While Bayesian inference is a perfectly valid principle, there are several problems in applying this process to the issue of trade liberalization and globalization. First, remember that trade theory teaches that trade liberalization will always cause benefits to some individuals and losses to others. Thus, a finding that some overall good will result from trade liberalization is not surprising. Furthermore, the good outcomes are likely to arise in the form of improvements in economic efficiency, which will translate into higher incomes and national GDP. The negative effects are more likely to arise because of market imperfections, which may involve effects like pollution, global climate change, cultural changes, and national security concerns. These latter effects are much less easily measured than the efficiency effects.

Thus, if researchers do empirical studies using the most readily available data, and if that data is more likely to display the positive effects of trade liberalization, then they are more likely to produce empirical studies tending to favor trade liberalization. Furthermore, if economists also harbor some bias in support of freer trade, then the studies they decide to pursue are also more likely to show support for trade liberalization. While Bayesian updating may lead people to believe more strongly in free trade, that perception could be because of a bias in the type of studies conducted and the type of data available.

A second problem with the Bayesian approach is that no one really knows how to precisely determine the probability values. Although it makes sense that the greater the number of studies favorable to free trade, the greater the probability that free trade is a good thing, it makes a big difference to policy makers if the increase is from a 40 percent to a 90 percent probability or from a 40 percent to a 43 percent probability. In the former case, if most people accepted the probability values, then the hypothesis that free trade is good would be accepted by a near consensus. In other words, empirical testing would be sufficient to convince most people what is most probably true. However, if the probability rises only from 40 percent to 43 percent, then empirical tests are not likely to change popular opinion. Also, since there are so many impacts from freer trade and globalization that are almost impossible to measure effectively, it seems unlikely that we could be anywhere near 90 percent (or even 80% or 70%) certainty that free trade is an overall good thing.

Finally, even if empirical testing were sufficient to convince most people that free trade was good for a country overall, that still is not sufficient to guarantee that everyone will enjoy the benefits of freer trade. Only after an appropriate redistribution will the gains be adequately reallocated so that all people may benefit form the net welfare improvement. But, redistribution requires identification of winners and losers in highly complex economies. Unfortunately, empirical analysis has not come anywhere close to accomplishing this objective.

Conclusion

Is free trade ultimately the best policy for countries to pursue? The theoretical literature says that trade liberalization will surely generate a complicated mix of winners and losers over time and that the sum total effects are uncertain. The only way to determine the answers, presumably, is to go out and measure the effects. The fundamental questions that need answers are:

- which individuals will gain and lose from freer trade, how much will they gain and lose, and when will they gain and lose?
- will the sum of the benefits over time to those who benefit from trade liberalization exceed the sum of the losses to others?

If both questions can be answered affirmatively then the choice of policy is clear. Free trade coupled with an appropriate compensation scheme can raise everyone's well-being in the future. However if we cannot answer these questions then the standard cost-benefit approach to policy choice is hopeless.

Unfortunately, the conclusion of this chapter is that empirical analysis does not provide an effective method to decide what kind of policy actions to take regarding trade and globalization. Advanced empirical methods cannot tell us whether free trade is good for a country overall and they cannot tell us precisely who will win and lose from policy actions. Empirical methods also cannot tell us precisely what set of policies would be optimal for a country from a national perspective. This means empirical methods cannot tell us what to do about policy. Free trade might be best for a country, but we cannot know for sure. Some combination of domestic and trade policies might be best for a country, but we cannot know with sufficient certainty what that set of policies would look like.

These conclusions follow despite the fact that empirical methods have improved significantly over the past century. Data collection and computing capacity continue to grow. The care and rigor applied in the best research in the discipline is impressive. However, despite these advances, the questions that can be asked and the phenomenon that can be measured effectively remain much too simplistic in comparison to the complexities that prevail in the real world. Thus, while a good study will provide the very best answer possible to the question being asked, that question by necessity will be extremely narrow in its scope. Indeed, even the full range of empirical studies from the beginning of the statistical era, are extremely narrow in scope. There are simply too many relationships that cannot be specified and too many effects that cannot be measured. It also seems unlikely, given how distant our current analytical state is from the complexities of the world, to expect that empirical analysis will provide an answer to these questions anytime soon.

Another perspective on this conclusion is possible with a simple analogy. We might ask whether the empirical investigations into the question of free trade and globalization are more like showing that the earth and planets revolve around the sun or showing whether the one sports team is better than another.

In the first case, Galileo's observations (empirical tests) that Venus displayed different phases, precisely like the earth's moon, was sufficient to convince most scientists that the heliocentric theory offered by Copernicus and others was valid. I do not know of anyone today who seriously doubts that the earth revolves around the sun. Thus, empirical observation and measurement was sufficient to answer this question definitively.

However, the question about which sports team is better is more difficult to assess. The first issue is how one should define the term "better." If the teams meet and Team A defeats Team B, some might find that sufficient evidence that Team A is better. But what if the teams meet several times and each team wins at least once? Or what if they never play each other? Sports enthusiasts typically can rattle off reams of statistics attesting to the superiority of their favored team. However, in most instances, for teams at similar competitive levels, different observers can reasonably reach different conclusions. It will be impossible to reach agreement by most observers on which facets of the teams are most important and what it really means to be "better." Thus, for this relatively simple question, empirical observations are not likely to lead most observers to a definitive conclusion.

The conclusion of this chapter is that the question—is trade liberalization good for countries?—is more like deciding which sports team is best than it is like deciding whether the earth revolves around the sun. The question itself is unanswerable, no matter how many numbers we collect or how much computing capacity we employ. If this is indeed true, then the debate over trade liberalization may be endless. Indeed if we look back over the past several hundred years, many of the arguments both in favor and against free trade have not changed very much. While it is true that more sophisticated mathematical analysis is often used to make the points today, it is not clear that this information is helping to move people or countries toward a consensus on the issue.

Indeed mathematical analysis may be more of a problem than a solution. One of the major advances in economics in the twentieth century was to apply the scientific method to economic issues. Economics began to mimic the physical sciences. Economic relationships were increasingly described using mathematical models with the necessary assumptions carefully specified. Results in theory required confirmation via empirical testing. In this way, tests of economic relationships tended to mimic tests of physical relationships.

A similar scientific approach is now applied to policy evaluation. To decide whether a policy is appropriate, the researcher collects data for countries with variations in the policy and using an empirical test, determines if the policy had positive or negative effects. However, an implicit assumption is being made here that may not be valid. Physical systems display regularities that may not arise in social systems. For example, water boils at 100°C at sea level. Given physical regularities, we expect water will boil at the same temperature today, tomorrow and 10,000 years from now. It will boil at 100°C in the United States, in China, and even on Mars (assuming the same atmospheric pressure is maintained). Social systems may not display this same regularity. Thus, if free trade is shown to improve GDP in a sample of 50 countries today, it may not follow that free trade will improve GDP in another sample of countries one hundred years from now. Changes in the behavioral patterns of participants in the system may prevent a replication.

The implication is that empirical methods in economics suggest a belief that economic and social relationships follow immutable patterns. With that belief, one may begin to see the economy like a large machine, whose parts interact with each other in discoverable ways and with the regularity of a physical system. Once we understand how the economic machine works, and once all of its effects have been measured, it becomes possible to use policy levers to produce more favorable economic outcomes. After all, policy changes are like changing the settings on the machine. Adjust the settings appropriately and one can make the machine work more effectively.

However, this scientific procedure is not very different from the socialist/central planning ideas of the past. Hayek (1988) deemed these intentions the Fatal Conceit, the idea that we could fine-tune a large macro economy using policy levers so as to produce an outcome that would be better in some overall sense. In a similar vein empirical tests used to support freer trade presume that by measurement we will determine that free trade is best and then implement the policy choice together with an appropriate redistribution to ensure that all will benefit. Hayek argued that central planning could never work and instead we should succumb to the workings of the private market. In a similar vein I argue that current empirical methods used in policy evaluation are not effective or convincing, therefore it is imperative to find an alternative choice mechanism.

CHAPTER 4

Why Fairness Cannot Tell Us What to Do about Policy

If we cannot identify who wins and loses, and we cannot measure outcomes very precisely, and we cannot compensate effectively, then how are we supposed to decide what to do? How are trade policies, or other public policies, to be chosen? One possible answer is provided by groups that have risen up in opposition to free trade and globalization. Many of them look upon economic theories and models with suspicion. They do not believe that economic efficiency is of utmost importance and remain unconvinced by empirical studies suggesting trade liberalization is a good thing. Instead, these groups unite around a call for social justice and fairness.

Fairness has become a rallying cry for a diverse and somewhat eclectic set of people. Although many of these groups accept there are some advantages to open markets and freer trade, they also contend that in many cases (perhaps most) free trade allows stronger and more powerful groups (such as multinational corporations) to take advantage of weaker, disadvantaged groups (like poor unskilled workers). In other words, they will often proclaim that free trade is unfair or unjust.

Justice is an effective rallying cry because everyone is surely in favor of justice and fairness. Probably this is why politicians often proclaim that they are in favor of free trade as long as it is fair. Indeed, Dani Rodrik (1997, 6) argues, "…one cannot produce a principled defense of free trade without confronting the question of the fairness and legitimacy of the practices that generate the consequences."

That fairness has many supporters is not surprising. But what exactly does fairness mean? The concept of fairness is a fuzzy one. Ask people what they understand fairness to be and you are likely to receive dozens of different responses.[1] This suggests that fairness does not have one concise and unchanging definition.

However, although fairness may be difficult to describe accurately and completely, the notion that something is unfair can sometimes rise up within a person with sudden conviction; simply remember an obviously bad call made against your favorite sports team, or the time someone cut in front of you in traffic.

In a previous article, Suranovic (2000) described the different ways in which fairness is used in trade policy and other public policy discussions. That paper presented seven distinct fairness principles. In this section I will reexamine those principles and apply them to a specific trade issue; antidumping. The chapter argues that each of these seven fairness principles is likely to be viewed as individually reasonable by most people. Nonetheless, the principles consistently conflict with each other when applied to particular situations. The chapter concludes that because of that conflict, any policy option can be viewed as fair with respect to some principles and unfair with respect to others. Consequently, fairness, broadly defined and applied, is inconsistent and therefore an inadequate policy choice mechanism.

General Principles of Fairness

People generally consider outcomes and processes to be fair if they conform to a common, or shared, set of standards. Parents instill these standards upon their children, which may vary across cultures, countries, and even families. As such, they form a set of individual expectations. Individuals consider outcomes or processes that conform to their expectations as fair, whereas those that do not are often described as unfair.

For example, a modern Western standard is the belief that all people are equal. This belief generates an expectation that two individuals should be treated the same way in certain situations. In the United States today, most people believe that all individuals should be allowed to use a public bus or drink from a public water fountain. However, just over 50 years ago it was legal to segregate blacks and whites on buses and to designate water fountains as "For Whites Only." Over time a general belief in equality has grown stronger. However, similar beliefs are not shared by all peoples and all cultures around the world. For example, in India the caste system has a long history of segregating individuals into particular professions on the basis of one's hereditary class or caste. Although Indian law has outlawed discrimination on the basis of caste, the system continues to hold sway over a vast population in the Hindu culture.

Many terms besides fairness are used to describe issues of right and wrong; terms like justice, equity, and morality. Although there are surely distinctions between these, delineating these differences is not absolutely necessary. Instead I will focus on popular conceptions of fairness, especially from the Western perspective, which has tended to focus on the standard of equality. From the French revolutionary slogan, "Liberty, Equality, Fraternity," to the U.S. declaration that "All men are created equal," to the U.S. Supreme Court's promise of "Equal Justice under the Law," to modern calls for equal treatment and equal opportunity, a standard of equality is regularly aspired to, but not always achieved.

Below, I will highlight seven ways in which fairness is applied in public policy discussions. Each principle, although often acceptable to diverse groups, may nevertheless be measured and applied differently. Thus, to evaluate a fairness argument, one should first identify which principle is being used and second how that principle is being measured and applied.

Each fairness concept has a long and voluminous literature associated with it in the philosophy, legal, and social science disciplines. The key innovation here is to present these concepts connected to one public policy issue, trade liberalization, and to suggest that these notions help form the basis for both support and opposition to globalization. If we wish to engage all sides in the public policy debate, then we need to understand the rationales for the positions that people take. As in Suranovic (2000), the intention here is not to argue that these fairness concepts should be used and applied, but rather that these conceptions are being used and applied. The readers are welcome to form their own judgments as to which is more or less important.

Equality Fairness

In many societies there is a strong belief in the equality of people. The standard of equality as applied to public policy discussions generally takes one of two forms: either applied to expectations about outcomes or expectations about treatment or behavior. In the first case, observers desire outcomes, such as wages or income, to be more equally distributed and is therefore labeled distributional fairness. The second case involves concerns about equal treatment in certain situations and is labeled nondiscrimination fairness.

Distributional Fairness

One of the major stated concerns about globalization is that the rich are getting richer and the poor poorer, resulting in an increase in inequality both within countries and around the world. Whether that statement is true or not, it is clear that concern about inequality is prominent in public policy discussions. While the issue occupies a voluminous literature, we need to emphasize only a few key points.

First, the concern about inequality is based on a presumption that all people are equal in some sense. In what sense, is a question that is difficult to answer. Nevertheless, because many people have the sense of the rightfulness of equality, they also tend to believe that important life outcomes should be equal, or at the least, more equal. Which life outcomes are important, brings us to the second issue: what is the equalisadum, that is, the outcome to be equalized?

The answers are many, often determined as much by what is possible to measure, as by what is most appropriate. Thus although it is well accepted that income is not the only source of well-being, it is certainly an important source, and it is widely measured and reported. Individual wealth may be a better measure but is somewhat more difficult to measure and is reported less widely. Amartya Sen developed the notion that what is most important to equalize is "capabilities" or "functionings," which is somewhat akin to the idea of equal opportunity.[2] However, this concept is clearly much more difficult to measure effectively and convincingly.

In the economics literature a prominent thread of discussion in normative welfare discussions is the tradeoff between efficiency and equity, where equity refers to the widespread preference or concern for equality in economic outcomes. Notably, a free market economic system, which may generate the most efficient economic outcome and the best use of scarce resources, may not generate a relatively equal distribution of income or wealth. How a society might deal with that issue has been very important over the past few centuries.

Surely one reason for the advent of socialist and communist ideologies was to offer solutions to the problems of a free market capitalist society, one of which concerned the expected inequality that would result. Today, in the aftermath of the breakup of the Soviet Union and the transition of China to a market economy, the socialist and communist systems have been largely discredited. Nonetheless, there remains in most societies around the world a continued concern about the issue of inequality. Although many would no longer demand that income, or wealth or some other measure, be equalized completely, there remains a strong desire for economic outcomes to become more equal than they currently are. As such, policies are often judged to be fair or unfair on the basis of whether the policies will cause more or less inequality, of income, wealth, opportunities, capabilities, or whatever else.

Nondiscrimination Fairness

The second way equality is applied is with respect to equal treatment, that is, nondiscrimination between people in particular situations. For example, the decision of hiring an employee is often expected to be conducted without regard to race, religion, gender, or age, because these characteristics are usually considered not germane. Nonetheless, it is acceptable for individuals to be discriminated on the basis of ability. The worker with more experience may rightfully be hired over a person with less experience because past experience contributes to the person's ability to do the job. Thus, nondiscrimination is considered fair whenever different characteristics, judged irrelevant to the decision, do not influence the decision.

Nondiscrimination fairness is precisely the basis for John Rawls' (1971) first principle of justice that says, "Each person has an equal right to a fully adequate scheme of equal basic liberties which is compatible with a similar scheme of liberties for all." It is also sometimes referred to as the principle of impartiality.[3]

In an international trade context, nondiscrimination is the basis for several principles of the WTO agreement. WTO countries have agreed to provide most favored nation (MFN) treatment and national treatment to all other WTO countries. MFN means that the best trade policy a country offers, such as a maximum or bound tariff rate, will be offered equally to all other WTO countries. The WTO agreement generally restricts a country from charging a higher tariff against one member relative to another. A commitment to national treatment requires that a country treat foreign goods, after clearing customs, equally to domestically produced goods.

Because judgments must be made as to when two groups should be treated equally and when not, this fairness principle, while widely accepted in principle, is also highly contested. Just as with distributional fairness, where people can dispute what is to be equalized, so too can people argue over when discrimination is acceptable and when not. In the WTO agreement, although MFN is generally applied for all trade issues, there are also a number of allowable exceptions to the rule. For example, MFN can be withdrawn because of free trade areas or when trade remedy actions, such as antidumping, are taken. In a domestic setting, although it would generally not be considered fair to charge a higher price for gasoline to whites rather than blacks, nevertheless it is generally acceptable for theaters to charge a different price to senior citizens for a movie ticket. This means that although policy observers may accept that nondiscrimination is an important principle, there continue to be divergent views about how or when it should be applied.

Golden Rule Fairness

The golden rule is often prescribed as a method to determine acceptable actions. In the biblical context it is often expressed as, "Do unto others as you would have them do unto you." If one accepts this rule of thumb, it is easy to understand why doing harm to others (e.g., stealing), and most other social admonishments are considered wrong or immoral.[4] If you do not want another person to injure you, then do not take the same actions that would injure him.

Although the golden rule is typically considered a moral or religious code, it is found in the philosophical literature as Immanuel Kant's categorical imperative and due to its widespread acceptability applies in public policy discussions as well.[5] A noteworthy application arises in the common expectation that people will abide by the "rules of the game." In a simple context, as when people play a board game or card game, cheating to gain an advantage for oneself both violates the golden rule and consequently, is quickly objected to as being unfair.

Across social settings different rules typically apply: national laws differ from state laws, which differ from the codes of conduct expected in a business environment. Sometimes the rules are explicit; the income tax laws are written down and published for all to see. Other times the rules are implicit, as with expectations about behavior in church. Regardless of the social setting and despite the fact that the "rules of the game" are sometimes hard to pin down, violations of explicit or implicit rules are generally considered unjust or unfair.

In international trade a notable rule is the WTO agreement itself, which consists of a series of promises or commitments that countries have made to each other. The promises by each member country induce a set of expectations for the other members. For the 153 WTO member countries, unfair trade is often proclaimed when another member has failed to live up to one of its previous promises; or when expectations are unfulfilled. Similarly, any time a country is judged to be violating any rule, law, or promise, whether explicit or implicit, the charge of unfairness is often applied.

In some instances, following rules or laws is often regarded as sacrosanct. For example, when other countries charge the United States with being protectionist because it applied higher tariffs against other countries in antidumping actions, the U.S. response is always that it lies within the rules of the game since antidumping actions are allowed by the WTO agreement. On this basis, these protectionist actions are perfectly fair. Note that when determining fairness in this situation, the observer generally does not inquire whether the antidumping procedure itself is "fair" in some other sense, only whether the procedure is allowable by law.

Reciprocity Fairness

Another important principle of fairness is based on the idea of reciprocity, a kind of quid pro quo. There are three different variations of reciprocity, depending on the value of the quid and the quo. Thus, when someone does something that has a positive effect on another person, that person is sometimes expected to reciprocate in kind with an equally positive response. This type of interaction will be called positive reciprocity fairness. In contrast, if someone does something that has a negative effect upon someone else, it is often deemed acceptable for the second person to also reciprocate in kind with an equally negative response. These types of interactions will be called negative reciprocity fairness. Finally, if someone does something that has no effect upon another, it is generally expected that the other person will not respond with a negative effect upon the first. This type of noninteraction will be called privacy fairness. Privacy fairness represents an expectation for autonomy or noninterference—to be left alone.

The "in kind" reciprocal action is also expected to be approximately equal in value to the value of the original action. Since the quid and the quo should be almost equal in perceived value, reciprocity fairness also represents an application of a concern for equality, but applied not to outcomes or opportunities but to bilateral transactions. Even with privacy fairness the expectation is that a zero-effect action will be reciprocated with an equal zero-effect response.

Adam Smith described positive and negative reciprocity in the Theory of Moral Sentiments: "To reward, is to recompense, to remunerate, to return good for good received. To punish, too, is to recompense, to remunerate, though in a different manner; it is to return evil for evil that has been done."[6]

Positive Reciprocity Fairness

Positive reciprocity fairness is a common feature of exchange between people. Whenever an economic transaction is made between two individuals, or two businesses, or an individual and a business, the two parties to the exchange believe that the value of what is given up is approximately equal to the value of what is received. If not, it is unlikely that both would agree to exchange voluntarily. Indeed, for trade to be viable, what both parties should believe is that the value of the item received is more valuable to themselves than the value of the item given up. This is the reason economic exchange is a positive sum game and both parties gain from the transaction.

Positive reciprocity is relevant in many other situations as well. International trade agreements, like the GATT and the subsequent WTO, involve negotiations between countries in which each side offers trade-liberalizing concessions in exchange for approximately equal concessions by its trading partners. When both sides believe the quid pro quo is substantial enough and approximately equal, trade rounds come to a conclusion. The Doha round of trade liberalization talks have followed a very slow progression largely because the developing countries felt the United States and European Union were not making sufficiently large concessions in the area agricultural liberalization. At the same time the United States and European Union felt the developing countries were not reciprocating enough by offering to reduce the bound values of their import tariffs. Since no party to a possible agreement felt the exchanges were sufficiently balanced, the current offers are viewed as unfair by both sides.

Another embodiment of positive reciprocity fairness is in the definition of the fair price in antidumping actions. AD actions, sanctioned in the WTO agreement, allow a country to raise trade barriers on imported products that are shown to be sold at less than fair value. One definition of fair value is a price that is approximately equal to the cost of producing the good after allowing for a reasonable profit. In this case, fairness is related to approximate equality of reciprocal values (the cost and sales price).

Negative Reciprocity Fairness

Negative reciprocity fairness arises in cases of revenge, retribution, or a redress of grievances. Revenge is one of the motivations behind punishment for those found guilty of crimes. Since criminals have killed, injured, robbed, or inflicted other damages upon others, it seems reasonable to require the criminal to suffer similar negative effects. For this reason, the perpetrators of serious crimes are either fined or incarcerated. The more serious the crime, the larger is the penalty; demonstrating an intention that the reciprocal effects be approximately equal in value.

In international trade, an application of negative reciprocity fairness is the allowance for suspension of concessions as a part of the WTO dispute settlement process. If a country is found to have violated one of its commitments under the WTO agreement, and if it refuses to come into compliance, the dispute settlement body (DSB) can allow the aggrieved country to suspend its previous concessions. A suspension means taking away some of the trade-liberalizing benefits that were previously granted. In this way some pain is caused to the violating country, and in keeping with the spirit of equality, the value of the suspended concessions, in terms of how much trade is affected, is meant to be approximately equal in value to the original harm caused by the violating country.

Privacy Fairness

Privacy fairness relates to situations in which the reciprocal effects are null or zero. It is often applied in situations in which a person may do something that has an effect upon oneself but not upon anyone else. Cohen (1986) defined a self-ownership postulate claiming that that a person has a moral right to use one's powers to benefit oneself as long as no harm is caused to others. Other people, viewing these actions from afar, will sometimes form opinions about what should or should not be done; what is right or wrong, even if those actions do not directly affect them. For example, a person may believe that smoking is wrong and object to another person smoking, even when that person's smoking is done in their own home with no external effect upon anyone else. Privacy unfairness may be charged especially if the person who objects seeks to restrict the private actions of another person.

One could argue that privacy fairness is just the null application of the golden rule. In other words, if you would not like others to interfere in your affairs or decisions then you should not interfere in the lives of others. To do so is unfair.

The most notable application of privacy fairness in international trade discussions is the issue of national sovereignty. Quite often some countries pressure other countries to change their trade or domestic policies. Sometimes this is done because the changes would have some positive effect on businesses in the advice-giving country. At other times it is suggested because it is perceived to be in the best self-interests of the other country. Even if the advice is appropriate, the country asked to change policies is often offended that the first country would presume to offer unsolicited advice. Privacy fairness issues arise whenever one person or country insists that another person or country mind their own business.

Maximum Benefit Fairness

Maximum benefit fairness arises out of a concern that decisions should be made that are "best" or "most appropriate" in some sense. While it is true that in many contexts this concern does not coincide with the use of the term fairness, occasionally it does. One simple example, is the decision to hire a worker for employment. If a firm considers several candidates, the usual standard is for the firm to hire the best-qualified worker; the worker that would best achieve the objectives the company needs from a worker in that position. If a candidate were hired that was clearly less qualified than another, many would judge the outcome as unfair. The expectation is that hiring decisions will be made on the basis of skill and abilities and not on other irrelevant criteria, such as whether the candidate is male or female.

In another context one might consider what is a fair method to allocate scarce donor organs to those in need of a transplant? The method that has been developed by the medical establishment considers the extent of the benefit accruing to recipients along several important dimensions. Thus, a younger person takes precedence over an older person. Similarly, a person who is weaker and may die sooner ranks higher than a person who could wait several months. In this situation, outcomes are judged to be more fair if the person who stands to benefit the most is the one who receives the transplant, hence it is an application of maximum benefit fairness.

In an international economic context maximum benefit fairness is a prime concern among economists since economic analysis typically focuses on the efficiency effects of various economic arrangements or policy options. Free trade is often promoted, largely, because it is expected to raise overall economic efficiency implying a greater overall benefit for the country. While surely some would contend efficiency is separate and distinct from fairness considerations, it remains true that efficiency (i.e., maximum overall benefit) is a valid concern for policy makers.

Thus, by including maximum benefit fairness as a distinct fairness conception we also can expand the set of criteria that are typically used to make judgments about policy options. Indeed, we might even claim that the set of concerns embodied in the seven fairness principles cover most, if not all, of the standard principles used to assess the appropriateness of different policy options or economic arrangements. Including maximum benefit fairness, then, allows us to consider the long-standing equity-efficiency debate within the parameters of what are defined as fairness principles.

The Application of Fairness to the Globalization Debate

The presentation of these seven principles of fairness is intended to show the distinct ways in which people make policy evaluations, not to argue for or against any particular principle or to suggest what weight should be given to each principle. Prima facie, it seems that each principle is commonly accepted and applied by most individuals in at least some situations. However, the fact that there are seven different principles means that individuals can, and do, pick and choose which principle to apply in every situation, often in a way that tends to serve their own interest. Also, as we will see with a few examples, the principles themselves can contradict each other when applied to a particular situation. The presence of these contradictions means the principles do not provide a basis for defining an unambiguous conception of fairness.

Another problem with the application of the fairness principles involves the scope of the application. For most policy choices, the policy effects are likely to be widespread and diverse. For example, the removal of a tariff will affect consumers of the imported product, firms in the import-competing industries, workers in those industries, as well as foreign consumers, firms, and workers. Fairness principles can be applied in light of the effects on domestic workers only, or the overall domestic effects, or on foreign firms only, or the effects worldwide. By changing the scope of the fairness application one can usually change the evaluation of a policy from fair to unfair or vice versa.

Finally, application of fairness principles often requires measurement of key variables, and these measures are frequently disputed. For example, some critics of freer international trade argue that globalization is leading to environmental degradation as polluting firms move facilities to countries that have more lenient environmental standards. Proponents of freer trade have countered by showing that the environmental costs savings are dominated by other cost concerns when firms make relocation decisions. In this case, while both sides may accept the same fairness principle, they may come to different conclusions because they measure and interpret the data differently.

These issues imply that for any policy under consideration it is usually possible to build one fairness argument that supports the policy and to build a differently configured fairness argument that opposes the policy. One need only to vary which principle is applied, the scope of the application, and the data used to measure the variables of interest. Below we consider the different ways a fairness argument can be built to support, in the one case, or oppose, in the second case, the WTO-sanctioned antidumping procedures, one of our so-called unfair trade laws. This policy serves as a useful example since most of the fairness principles arise in this case.

Fairness and Antidumping Procedures

Antidumping is a legal procedure that allows a country to raise tariffs on specific items if several criteria are satisfied. The procedures are allowed to all countries that are members of the WTO. Thus, most, if not all, WTO countries have antidumping legislation. When the criteria are satisfied, a country is allowed to raise a tariff against a particular foreign firm above the bound tariff rate negotiated in the WTO agreement.

In general, the AD procedures work as follows. First, a firm or industry must request its government to conduct an antidumping investigation. The government will seek to determine several things. First, they must assess whether the product is being sold in the country at a price that is less than reasonable value. One definition of "less than reasonable" is if the price in the import country market is less than the foreign firm's cost of producing the good. A second allowable definition is a price in the import country market that is less than the price charged in the foreign firm's home market. In economics, while pricing less than cost is known as dumping, pricing differently in different markets is commonly known as price discrimination. In either case, both have come to be known as dumping because of the legislation. The degree of under-pricing, in percentage terms, is referred to as the dumping margin.

If the investigation discovers dumping, the government must subsequently determine if the dumping caused injury to the domestic import-competing firms. Injury may involve falling revenues, recent accounting losses, worker layoffs, and other indications of harm caused to the domestic firms. If the injury can be attributed to the dumping then a green light is given to assess an antidumping duty. The duty is a tariff on imports of the product set at a level equal to the dumping margin. It is worth noting that governments often identify different dumping margins for different firms. This means that when the antidumping duty is assessed, it is set at a different rate for every investigated foreign firm.

Dumping Is Unfair; Antidumping Is Fair

Antidumping is known as an unfair trade law purportedly because it protects a country against unfair pricing practices by foreign firms. When foreign firms undercut domestic producers, especially by selling below the cost of production, it makes it more difficult for the domestic firms to effectively compete. To stay in the market, import-competing firms may be forced to lower their own prices, perhaps to a level below their production costs. The losses incurred by these firms would cause harm to the firm owners and employees by reducing profits and lowering wages. If losses persist for very long, the domestic firms may be forced to lay off workers causing the further damage of unemployment.

Additionally, the foreign firm is sometimes accused of predatory behavior. Predation occurs if, after a period of low pricing, the domestic firms are forced into bankruptcy, thereafter enabling the foreign firms to raise prices to near monopoly levels and recover their previous losses. Foreign firms may be able to withstand economic losses for longer than domestic firms if either the foreign firms have a near monopoly in their home market or if the foreign government subsidizes exports in some direct or indirect way. In the case of a foreign monopoly market, extra-normal profit at home can allow for a kind of cross subsidization within a firm. Given high profit in the home market, the firm could sell its exports below cost for a long enough period of time to drive its foreign competitors, who do not enjoy the same monopoly position, out of business. Foreign government subsidization works in a similar manner. Government subsidies either increase revenue over that achieved from sales of its product or reduce the cost of production. This can enable a firm to sell its product indefinitely at a price below cost in the foreign market and help force its competitors out of business.[7]

Several distinct fairness principles can be applied to argue that antidumping actions protect against unfair trade. Applying golden rule fairness one can argue that firms in different countries should play by the same set of rules, that there should be a level-playing field. Monopoly profit in a home market or foreign government subsidies, are usually viewed as a one-sided advantage for the foreign firms that enables them to more easily compete, take over market share and potentially force competitors out of business. If foreign firms did not have those "unfair" advantages, then all firms would face the same circumstances, i.e., the same rules. For many this argument is sufficiently convincing. However one can build an even stronger case.

Another common argument supporting antidumping procedures is that the procedures are themselves encoded in law and agreed to by the WTO countries. As such foreign firms are violating the rules when they engage in predatory or discriminatory pricing. Actions taken against these firms are allowable and thus are fully consistent with golden rule fairness.

The antidumping procedures themselves incorporate other fairness conceptions such as reciprocity. Recall that when AD duties are applied they are set equal to the assessed dumping margin. As such, the AD duties raise the domestic price of the foreign product to the level deemed "reasonable." The unfairly low price is equally reciprocated with the AD duty. Of course, some argue that the response in insufficient because it does not return the losses incurred by the domestic import-competing firms during the time the unreasonably low prices were being charged and before the AD duty could be assessed. On this basis, which involves measuring the reciprocal effects differently, one could claim that the AD duties should be set even higher.

Finally, antidumping measures are allowed for all WTO member countries. All WTO countries have agreed to the basic set of principles and procedures described above and each country can apply antidumping actions against any others within the dictates of the agreement. Thus, the nondiscrimination fairness principle applies to this situation.

Dumping Is Fair; Antidumping Is Unfair

An alternative perspective on these same actions is possible by broadening the scope of the analysis. The charge that unreasonable pricing is unfair is based on the narrow perspective of the domestic import-competing firms. Thus, it is not accurate to say that dumping is unfair overall, or unfair to the importing country, only that it is unfair from the perspective of the import-competing firms. However, the effects of dumping and antidumping have many other impacts on individuals in both the exporting and importing countries. If we include these wider effects, it is possible to reverse the perception of what is fair.

The effects ignored in the above fairness analysis are the impacts on the consumers of the affected products in the importing country. When foreign firms sell their products below cost, consumers are enabled to purchase the products at a lower price. An antidumping duty, however, will raise the price back up and eliminate these benefits.

According to privacy fairness one could ask what right the government has to restrict the mutually voluntary exchanges between the foreign firms and the domestic consumers. The antidumping duty interferes with the private actions of the domestic consumer and the foreign firm. Thus, from the narrow perspective of domestic consumers one can argue that dumping is fair while antidumping is unfair.

If we evaluate the national effects from "unreasonably low" foreign prices, it is conceivable that overall national welfare rises due to dumping. This means that the benefits of dumped products to consumers may outweigh the losses that accrue to the domestic import-competing firms. The same result follows when foreign governments subsidize their exporting firms; for importing countries the overall welfare effect of the foreign action is likely to be positive. If we imagine that a government's obligation is to do what is best for the nation overall, then allowing foreign dumping to occur maximizes national benefits, whereas antidumping actions reverse the positive effects and reduce national benefits. Accordingly, applying maximum benefit fairness, dumping is fair and antidumping is unfair.

Alternative arguments against antidumping procedures challenge the assumptions made by those who consider dumping to be unfair. For example, one of the most compelling arguments for why pricing less than cost is unfair is the presumption that the foreign firm intends to set low prices to force its competitors from business. However, evidence that foreign firms have ever been able to do this effectively is very rare. In the United States, the first antidumping code, dating to 1916, required a demonstration that the foreign firms intended to prey on the domestic firms. However, this law has almost never been applied, largely because it is very difficult to impossible to demonstrate. The current version of the U.S. antidumping code, which dates to 1922, relaxed the requirements to show predation intentions, and the current law now only requires price discrimination with injury. Thus, arguments alleging predation as a reason dumping is unfair is unsubstantiated empirically and thus weakens the fairness argument in support of antidumping.

A recent charge of unfairness with respect to antidumping procedures recently made its way to the WTO dispute settlement board. Foreign countries charged the United States with using unfair procedures in the way in which it calculates dumping margins. The procedures are known as zeroing. When calculating the dumping margin the United States looks at many different sales of the product made by a firm in the domestic country, sometimes spanning several months. In most instances the prices charged to different buyers at different times will vary. Because of the variation it is also common to find some instances where the price charged was "less than reasonable" and other instances where the price charged was reasonable. The dumping margin is calculated as the average dumping margin across these different sales. However, when the United States calculates the average, it eliminates, or zeroes, the margin for all sales that were reasonably priced.

Foreign countries have charged that the zeroing procedure results in a larger than reasonable, or unfair, dumping margin and that the procedures violate the commitments made by the United States in the WTO. In addition, if the dumping margin is being set too high, then the application violates the principle of reciprocity. A WTO dispute panel reviewing the case has already ruled against the United States and has requested that it eliminate the practice. At this time, the United States is reviewing the situation and has not yet made changes to its antidumping procedures. The lack of action is often construed as a failure to abide by the agreed rules of the game and is considered unfair by most foreign observers.

Conclusion

Evaluation of the fairness of antidumping procedures provides a specific example that demonstrates how fairness principles can be used to construct an argument that a trade policy is simultaneously fair and unfair. Opposing conclusions are possible by picking different fairness principles, by altering the scope of the application of those principles, and by picking data favorable to the case one is making. This inconsistency in applying fairness principles to evaluate policy choices can easily be shown in virtually all public policy discussions. In other words, every policy option under discussion can be reasonably argued to be both fair and unfair.

For example, free trade is considered unfair to domestic workers when foreign firms face less stringent, and hence unequal, health and safety requirements and lower minimum wages (nondiscrimination fairness). Free trade is considered unfair because low wages paid to foreign workers contributes to poverty and inequality (distributional fairness). Free trade is also considered unfair when firm owners make greater profit by laying off workers in the domestic economy and moving factories abroad (golden rule fairness). However, free trade is considered fair trade because it reduces economic inefficiencies and contributes to an increase in average living standards (maximum benefit fairness). Free trade is considered fair because it consists of millions of mutually voluntary and reciprocal exchanges (reciprocity fairness). Finally free trade is considered fair because to restrict trade interferes in the exchanges of private parties (privacy fairness).

Politicians are astute to this inconsistency. This is why virtually every politician in the United States claims to support free trade as long as it is "fair trade." After all, how can anyone be against fair trade? At the same time, without providing any details about specific policy choices, the phrase is virtually meaningless since any future policy choice can always be justified on the basis of several fairness principles. Meanwhile, a voter may be fooled into believing that the conception of trade fairness held by the candidate must be the same as his own, especially if the voter does not recognize that fairness arguments can be manipulated to serve whatever purpose one desires.

The broader implication is that fairness, as commonly applied, is simply not effective as a policy choice mechanism. Its conceptions are too broad, and it appears impossible to identify a set of policies that a near consensus of people would judge to be fair.

The even broader implication is that still another policy choice mechanism has been shown to have serious deficiencies, on top of the deficiencies already described for pure economic theory in chapter 2 and empirical cost-benefit analysis in chapter 3. Indeed, if we accept these problems, then objectively we may well conclude that the popular arguments used to support policy choices, either free trade or something else, have little hope of obtaining a near consensus.

Nevertheless, all of these mechanisms for policy choice have popular appeal. Supporters of free trade gather evidence from economic theory, empirical studies, and sometimes justice principles to argue the case for trade liberalization. At the same time a diverse group with alternative views build up their own set of arguments by appealing to theory, empirics, and fairness and justice considerations. For any objective observer on the sideline trying to make sense of it all, it is difficult to decide which group, if any, is right.

Part of the problem is the underlying assumption that one side must be right, and the other wrong. Either a free trade policy is the best or one of the suggested alternatives must be best. One might think that the objective is to determine who has the story right. But what if nobody has it right? What if there is no way to identify the most efficient or the very best set of policies for a country? What if it is impossible to design policies that everyone agrees are "optimal," or "best," or "fair"?

The last three chapters have argued that uncertainty is the appropriate, albeit unfortunate, conclusion to draw. Current knowledge, while admittedly providing good insights into the workings of the global economy, is simply not able to provide a near consensus answer to the most critical globalization policy questions. The questions that need answering are: (1) what is the best mix of policies to optimize overall national and international welfare; and (2) because a movement to that best mix would undoubtedly result in a complex pattern of gains and losses, can we identify the winners and losers adequately enough to implement an effective compensation scheme? We cannot answer these questions effectively using economic theory or empirical analysis, and we cannot answer them using principles of fairness either. None of these methods can answer the questions with the kind of scientific precision that we show for physical relationships; for example, like showing the earth revolves around the sun or that water boils at 100°C at sea level. The truth is, we come nowhere close. Social "science" is not like the physical sciences. The changing nature of human responses means there is an insurmountable obstacle in the way. Curiously, although we should be able to see the obstacle; logic should convince us it is there, and still, no one seems willing to acknowledge it. Why is that?

One answer is provided in the next chapter; the answer is politics. Actual policy choices are made via the political process. Most countries today have some variation of democracy, wherein the will of the people is translated into policies. However, this process requires a collection and transmittal of information, which in turn greatly affects the way in which information is disseminated.

The political process also offers one more possible solution to the policy choice dilemma. Since policies are chosen via a political process, perhaps democracy itself is an adequate method to search for and choose the best possible policy options for a country. Democratic choice represents a way to balance the interests of different constituents. The next chapter explores how well the political process works to choose appropriate, or "best," policies.

CHAPTER 5

Why Democracies Will Not Choose the Best Policies

Economic theory supports the contention that many people will suffer losses because of globalization, but it also clearly shows that many other people will benefit. Because globalization will not affect everyone equally, and because there are many winners and losers, globalization is naturally contentious. The contentiousness inspires a continual discussion of appropriate policy.

What should producers and consumers, governments, and international organizations do about globalization? Should present policies be maintained or should they be adjusted? Perhaps free trade is best and we should continue the slow progression of trade liberalization. However, maybe freer trade is not such a good idea. Perhaps interventionist polices should be implemented to compensate those whose lives are most disrupted. Are current policies contributing to increases in poverty and economic inequalities? Are we doing enough to protect the environment? Are natural resources sufficiently abundant to sustain the world's growth and economic development? More importantly, can we ever know what the best set of policies is to deal effectively with all of these issues?

Economics proposes that we choose those policies that raise economic efficiency. When changes in policy cause some to lose, then implement an appropriate compensation scheme that transfers money from winners to losers so that all will gain. In contrast, social justice advocates argue that policies that are fair and just should be implemented. Although, in principle, both approaches are reasonable, for reasons discussed in the previous chapters, neither approach can convincingly identify a set of policies we ought to choose; instead, regardless of the policy suggested there are always sound counterarguments.

In addition, policy proposers sometimes seem to ignore the fact that decisions are not made by someone who can simply declare what policies will be enacted. Instead, policies are chosen in a political process. In the world today, that means mostly in a democratic setting with a representative government.

The political process is important to the discussion about globalization policy choice for several reasons. First, democracy provides a mechanism by which choices are actually made. The process is not theoretical; the process is real. Perhaps a democratic political process can translate the diverse interests and opinions of a country's citizens into policies representing reasonable compromise solutions. If so, then the political process offers a possible answer for how best to make policy choices. Secondly, policy choices are made by representatives of the people. Policies are made on behalf of the citizens who are in turn affected, both positively and negatively, by these choices. For the choice process to work effectively, information transmission is important. Information about what the people want or need flows from the citizens to the representatives. In between there are researchers, interest groups, and journalists, who are also citizens. The researchers, interest groups, and journalists convey additional information to both representatives and citizens to help them evaluate the options and make better policy decisions.

To be an effective policy choice mechanism, it is important that the information transmitted between parties be as reliable as possible. Unfortunately, because the collectors and transmitters of information typically have a stake in the policy outcome, information is not completely reliable. This poses a problem for achieving good policies and also makes it difficult for students of globalization to learn about the phenomenon objectively.

Because of politics in a democratic society, information presented by opposing sides in the globalization debate (or any policy debate) is purposefully biased. The process encourages the display of abundant confidence in the supporting information used to bolster one's case. The implication for outside observers is: do not believe everything you hear or read. Perhaps more importantly, do not think that one side has it right and the other wrong. The truth of the matter is more likely to be found in a convex combination of the extremes.

The fact that information is imperfectly known has important implications both for how a direct democracy would work and how its more practical variation, representative democracy, functions. In either case, imperfect information opens up a market for influence. The influence market is the topic of discussion in this chapter.

One of the best early accounts of decision making in a democracy was provided by Anthony Downs (1957). His paper provides an excellent description of the political choice process in a democracy by incorporating two important features. Downsian theory, as it is sometimes called, first incorporates the standard economic assumption that agents seek to maximize their own well-being. In the case of politicians, they seek the income, power, and prestige that come with running the political apparatus. The second critical assumption Downs makes is that information is imperfect. Indeed he states that, "lack of complete information on which to base decisions is a condition so basic to human life that it influences the structure of almost every social institution. In politics especially, its effects are profound."[1]

In this chapter we will use a series of simple games to illustrate some of the information problems associated with policy choice in a democracy. The policy choice we will consider is whether or not to implement free trade. I will begin by assessing the economic proposal to provide compensation under an assumption of perfect information. This outcome is untenable, though, both because of insufficient information and because policies are chosen democratically. Next we will consider situations with perfect information when transfers (sometimes also called bribery) can be used. These cases suggest one reason that secrecy or a lack of transparency may arise in political contexts. Finally we will consider the most realistic cases in which decisions are made democratically and with imperfect information about the outcomes. In these cases it is shown why information is twisted to suit political objectives, why lobbying arises, and how lobbying creates a drag on the productive capacity of the economy. Although policy choices are made in the process, it also appears that democratic choice in the presence of uncertainty may produce some extremely unsatisfactory results.

Choosing Policy—The Game Setup

Imagine a society with three agents, A, B, and C. We can think of these agents as three individuals, but it is probably better to think of them as three distinct groups whose members share similar interests. Suppose that no single group has a majority share, but that a coalition of A-B or B-C do make up a majority. For simplicity suppose the coalition A-C is not a majority. Thus, if Agents A and C each make up 20 percent of the voters and Agent B was the remaining 60 percent, then these conditions are satisfied. It seems reasonable to imagine that the groups immediately affected by trade liberalization (TL) may be small compared to the whole economy. This may well be true in a country like the United States since trade amounts to just 30 percent of the GDP. Also, trade liberalization is just one of many public policy issues under consideration at any one time. Thus, many people may have other higher priority issues and may be relatively indifferent to this one issue.

Choosing Free Trade: The Benevolent Dictator Case

Suppose a government must choose whether to implement a TL agreement. The alternative to implementing TL is to maintain the status quo. Suppose the returns, or payoffs, to each agent for each policy are as shown in table 5.1.[2] Initially, imagine that information about the returns is perfectly known to the three agents; however, we will relax this assumption in various ways later. The payoffs are set up to mimic possible outcomes shown in standard trade theory: one group gains, another group loses, while a third group, which may have no connection to that market, is left unaffected.

Given these payoffs, Agent A clearly favors trade liberalization (10 > 0) while Agent C favors the status quo (0 > –7). Agent B is indifferent, as the policy has no effect. The economic analysis of this situation would suggest what a benevolent dictator might do. A benevolent dictator would notice that trade liberalization offers a net positive overall effect of +3 (10 + 0 – 7 = 3). In addition, because there is a surplus, the money could conceivably be redistributed after the fact to ensure that everyone shares in the benefits.

For example, if after trade liberalization, Agent A transfers 8 units to Agent C and 1 unit to Agent B, as shown in table 5.2, then each agent will end up with one extra unit in free trade and everyone will

Table 5.1 Welfare Effects of Two Policy Options

	Agent A	*Agent B*	*Agent C*
Trade Liberalization	10	0	–7
Status Quo	0	0	0

Table 5.2 Implementing Compensation

	Agent A	*Agent B*	*Agent C*
Trade Liberalization	10 (1)	0 (1)	–7 (1)
Status Quo	0	0	0

(Arrows in table: 8 from Agent A to Agent C; 1 from Agent A to Agent B.)

be better off than in the status quo. In general, whenever efficiency improves in the aggregate, there will always be a redistribution that can ensure that everyone benefits.

It is for this reason, economists sometimes argue that societies should always (a) set policies to achieve the most efficient outcome and (b) worry about and implement an appropriate compensation scheme later.

Ah, if only life were so easy! Unfortunately, compensation, especially the total compensation described above, although easy to imagine, is extremely difficult to implement because of inherent uncertainties. The main problem in a more complex situation is to identify precisely who wins, who loses, how much they win and lose and when they will win and lose it. The answers to these questions can be guessed at, but they really cannot be known with a high degree of confidence. If one cannot know who should give what and who should receive what, then compensation becomes virtually impossible to implement successfully.

However, there is an even more obvious reason why compensation is an unlikely response: decisions are never made by a benevolent dictator with the knowledge and ability to move income around after the fact. Instead, in much of the world, decisions are made in a participatory democratic or semidemocratic process. In these kinds of systems there is no incentive to provide compensation, except when it can tilt votes or support in some direction. In summary, this ideal outcome is unlikely to arise. So, what might happen instead?

Direct Democracy with Transfers/Bribery

If the policy above (TL or status quo) is chosen democratically (e.g., by direct vote) and assuming information is perfect and everyone votes, the result in the above example would depend essentially on a coin toss by Agent B. Agent A will vote for TL, Agent C will vote against, and with 50 percent probability Agent B will choose TL.

Of course, it is in Agent A's interest for Agent B to vote for trade liberalization while it is in Agent C's interest for Agent B to vote for the status quo. Thus, both Agents A and C have an incentive to try to sway, or capture, Agent B's vote. Let us first consider how transfers can be used.

Start by assuming Agent A decides to act. Agent A needs to find a way to make it in Agent B's interest to support TL. One obvious possibility is a transfer of money or benefits. Agent A's transfer is also known as a side-payment or a bribe. But how much should Agent A offer to Agent B? The answer depends on several other factors.

Agent A will prefer to transfer as little as possible to win Agent B's vote because the greater the transfer the worse off Agent A becomes. In this example, 1 unit transferred from Agent A to Agent B is the minimum needed to induce Agent B to support free trade. However, Agent B might consider 1 unit to be insufficient, especially if there is risk. For example, if vote buying is illegal and if there is a penalty if caught, then the transfer might need to be larger to compensate for this risk. The transfer might also need to be higher if Agent B is aware of how much Agent A stands to gain with its vote. For example, if Agent B knows that Agent A will win 10 units and it is only getting, say, 3 units for its vote, Agent B may consider that an insufficient sum and demand a higher payoff from Agent A. For this reason, Agent A has a strong incentive to hide information about its total benefits from Agent B. Also, Agent A might wish to pay Agent B extra in order to purchase something more than its vote—its silence. Agent A does not want Agent C to learn about the transfer since that may induce competing bribes for Agent B's vote. Thus for both legal and strategic reasons, secrecy becomes extremely important in this scenario.

The amount of the transfer is indeterminate in general and will depend on the factors listed and the bargaining powers of the two agents. What we know is that the minimum transfer from Agent A is slightly more than zero, while the maximum amount is 10 units. Anything more than 10 would make Agent A worse off with TL than with the status quo.

Competition in Transfers

Next, consider what is likely to happen if there is competition for Agent B's vote; that is, what if Agents A and C both try to bribe Agent

Table 5.3 Competitive Transfers

	Agent A	*Agent B*	*Agent C*
Trade Liberalization	10 – 8 = 2	0 + 8 = 8	–7
Status Quo	0	0	0

B to win its vote. Suppose Agent A acts first and offers to transfer 2 units to Agent B in return for Agent B's vote for free trade. Since 2 > 0, Agent B should accept this offer. However, Agent C, upon learning that Agent A might step in and up the ante,[3] might offer 3 units to Agent B in return for a status quo vote. But then Agent A would come back and up the ante again.

In the end, the maximum bribe that Agent C is willing to offer is 7 units. However, Agent A's maximum bribe is 10 units. Since Agent A can afford to spend more on transfers than Agent C, Agent A will win this perfect information sequential transfer game. The final outcome might look something like that in table 5.3 with an 8-unit transfer occurring from Agent A to Agent B. In this case both Agents A and B will vote for free trade and that policy will be chosen.

Some interesting effects are worth noting here. First, compare this outcome with that implemented by a benevolent dictator. In this case, Agent C is a much bigger loser. After competitive transfers Agent C will quite likely look longingly at more egalitarian outcomes. Notice also that with competitive transfers, Agent A still wins, but not by as much as in the egalitarian case. Instead the big winner with transfers is Agent B.

Interestingly, even though Agent B had no stake in the original policy choice, it stands to gain the most in a world with competitive transfers. That may not seem fair. It seems especially unfair when we note that Agent A will only get 2 units of benefits rather than the 10 units that would accrue with free trade and without transfers. Remember also that Agent A's benefit arises because free trade allows the group to expand efficient production that in turn generates the monetary profit. Nonetheless, transfers erode these efficiency benefits for the winner; to come out just a little ahead may cost Agent A a great deal.

Finally, we can see the importance of secrecy to Agent A and why there is an incentive to keep these actions under cover. For strategic reasons, secrecy would be desired even if transfers were perfectly legal or recognized as a common practice. The incentive for secrecy described here also helps explain the desire for transparency by groups who seek more egalitarian outcomes. In this story Agent C would certainly look upon a secret meeting between Agents A and B with suspicion. Demands for transparency are motivated, in part, by a desire to prevent these kinds of secret dealings.

The second important point worth noting is that with transfers—and perfect information—the outcome chosen will be the one that maximizes national welfare; that is, it is the most efficient. Had we tilted the original payoffs to make the gain to Agent A only 6 units rather than 10, then the net national welfare effect from TL would have been negative at –1. However, in this case, Agent C would have won the transfers game and the status quo—which is the most efficient outcome now—would have been chosen.

To see that competitive transfers can lead to more efficient overall outcomes, consider the alternative set of payoffs shown in table 5.4. In this case, with no transfers, perfect information and direct voting, the status quo would be chosen since both Agents B and C would support it. However, the status quo is not the most efficient policy outcome. Trade liberalization provides a net welfare benefit of 2 units (10 – 1 – 7 = 2).

However, if Agent A were allowed to bribe, or transfer money, it could offer several units to Agent B to switch its vote. As before, competition would mean Agent C would get into the bidding war and up the stakes. In the end, Agent A would have to offer Agent B at least 8 units to win out over Agent C. The final outcome is displayed in parentheses. Agent A transfers 8 units to Agent B, leaving it with just 2 units. Agent B ends up with 7 units since it loses one from the natural effects of free trade, but gains 8 units from the bribe.

Again Agent B gains tremendously and Agent C loses again. But interestingly, as before, the policy chosen with competitive transfers remains the one that is most efficient. However, the one chosen in the absence of transfers is less efficient. This suggests that despite some obvious inequities, transfers nonetheless can have some positive effects. Indeed, as we will see next, public policy choice in a transfers game is better in some ways that the outcome in a lobbying game.

Table 5.4 Welfare Effects of Two Policy Options

	Agent A	*Agent B*	*Agent C*
Trade Liberalization	10 (2)	–1 (7)	–7
Status Quo	0	0	0

Notice that efficiency rises in both cases with "competitive" transfers and full information. If information remains secret or hidden however, then inefficient outcomes are more likely.

Consider the game presented in table 5.1 again. However, now imagine that transfers are not allowed so that if it is attempted it must be done secretly. Earlier we considered what would happen if Agent A tried to bribe Agent B to support free trade. Instead, suppose Agent C surreptitiously bribes Agent B to support the status quo. A transfer of, say 2 units would make Agent B better off and may be sufficient to induce Agent B to support the status quo. As long as Agent A does not compete in transfers, the less efficient status quo outcome may obtain. Hence, this demonstrates the significance of full information and competition to ensure that the most efficient outcome does indeed arise.

Perhaps because of the negative effects felt by the loser in transfer situations and because there is never perfect information about outcomes, bribery, is generally illegal in most settings. Thus, next we will consider the implications for policy choice in a scenario with no transfers and a lack of perfect information.

The Lobbying Game

Consider the same three-agent story from above with the same payoffs to the agents as listed in table 5.1. Now imagine that transfers are either not allowed or are impractical. Perhaps bribery is illegal and the cost of being caught is sufficiently large to deter the practice. Alternatively, transfers may be impractical, especially if Agent B is not an individual but rather a large group of voters. In that case there could be significant costs associated with identifying and transferring benefits to members of a large group. The larger the group, the higher will be the transactions costs and the more impractical transfers become.

Suppose that Agent B remains indifferent between the two outcomes, but now assume this is largely because it does not have adequate information about the effects of the different policies to know which is better. Agent A would still like Agent B to prefer free trade, and Agent C wants Agent B to prefer the status quo. But Agents A or C cannot use transfers, or bribery, to sway Agent B's vote. So what can be done?

The alternative is to play a lobbying game instead of a transfer game. The objective remains the same; convince Agent B to vote for a policy preferred by Agents A or C. However, now this is accomplished not with a direct transfer to Agent B, but by convincing it with ideas and information that one or the other policy is really in Agent B's interest. In other words, Agent A wants to convince Agent B that free trade is better in some sense than the status quo. Agent C wants to convince Agent B that the status quo is better.

However, in order for persuasion to work there must be imperfect information. The effects of the policies must be uncertain, at least to Agent B, if Agent B is to be swayed merely by ideas. But persuasion requires resources and effort. To convince Agent B will require communication; it is not without cost. If Agent B is a group rather than an individual, communication can occur through various media: newspapers, magazines, television, and the Internet. These methods require money or resources be spent. The information must be substantiated too. The more valid or true the information appears, the more likely Agent B will accept it. Thus, research into the policy effects by experts and other professionals can be funded to provide evidence that can be used to convince Agent B. These studies are costly too.

The maximum amount of money that Agents A and C would be willing to spend to gather and disseminate information to convince Agent B will be equal to the amount they would be willing to spend on transfers. If we imagine a sequential decision process, it might proceed something like this.

First suppose Agent C spends 2 units on research studies and lobbying supporting the status quo and broadcasts this information to Agent B. Given that Agent B was indifferent to the policies initially we might imagine that upon hearing only from Agent C, Agent B will be convinced to support the status quo. However, Agent A cannot sit back and watch. Agent A might now spend 4 units to conduct research and disseminate information confirming the benefits of free trade and broadcast this information to Agent B. With a larger amount of money spent and more effort by Agent A, it might be sufficient to sway Agent B to vote for free trade instead. However, Agent C cannot sit idly by and watch this, so it ups the ante and raises its lobbying budget to 6 units to support research and dissemination, and so on.

In the end Agent A can spend up to 10 units on lobbying while Agent C can spend up to 7 units. These are the maximums each agent can spend, although the limits may not be reached if some sort of détente agreement is achieved. Much will also depend on the marginal productivity of lobbying and its ability to sway Agent B to support one's position. If 1 unit spent on lobbying is equally effective for Agents A and C, then whoever spends the most money will win Agent B's vote; because Agent A can spend more, Agent A would win.

However, lobbying effectiveness per dollar spent will likely be highly variable. Thus, just because Agent A spends more than Agent B, it will not guarantee that Agent A wins Agent B's vote. So the lobbying game will be highly uncertain for Agents A and C especially since in reality there are many different strategies and approaches that can be tried beyond simply spending money to advertise the benefits of one's position.

Also, the amount spent will depend on the initial likelihood of winning without lobbying. If the contest is very close then each dollar spent on lobbying has a high chance of tipping the balance in one's favor. However, if there is only a 20 percent chance of winning without lobbying, then one may need to spend an enormous amount just to get it back to an even contest. If you believe that one's opponent has a large amount of resources, then it may not make sense to spend anything at all.

Resource Use in Lobbying

There are several important differences in the way the resources are used in the lobbying game compared to the bribery game. First, the resources spent in lobbying finance information gathering and dissemination. Resources—workers and capital—must be used to gather this information and disseminate it. With transfers, money is merely transferred from one individual, or group, to another. Transfers change who consumes the final goods and services, it does not represent a newly created resource-using service.[4]

The labor and capital used in the lobbying effort, however, do not produce anything directly used by consumers. Lobbying is a service, but it is not a service that enters into a consumer's utility function. To see this note that the lobbying information presented to Agent B is unlikely to be sold to it. Instead, in most cases it will be given away freely as will occur with campaign ads that appear in newspapers, magazines, and television. Lobbying is an activity entered into in order to shift benefits from some agents toward others. It is engaged in to win a contest. The true cost of lobbying is the opportunity cost, the value of the goods and services that could have been produced had the lobbying resources been employed in a directly productive activity. For these reasons lobbying is referred to by economists as a "directly unproductive profit-seeking activity" (DUP).[5] Another term commonly used as a synonym for lobbying is "rent seeking," which refers to the motivation for the process while DUP refers to the impact or effect of the process.

Once we recognize that lobbying is a DUP activity, we should also see a problem with the way in which we measure economic activity. Since lobbying is a service to the companies that hire people to engage in this activity, it is counted in the measurement of a country's national income. If workers are shifted from producing goods and services to lobbying activity instead, the GDP does not change, however the quantity of goods and services that sustains the national standard of living falls. In contrast, transfers simply rearranges who consumes what. There is no loss in valuable output, just a transfer from one agent to another.

The second difference between lobbying and transfers is that almost twice as many resources can potentially be spent on lobbying. In the transfers game depicted in Table 5.3, Agent A wins the game by transferring 8 units to Agent B. With that transfer, Agent C will not need to transfer anything, hence the total transfer will be 8 units. However, in the lobbying game, expenditures by one side are likely to be countered with expenditures by the other side, lest the other gain an advantage influencing Agent B. Competition for support doubles the expenditures. In the extreme, Agent A can spend up to 10 units while Agent C can spend up to 7 units. If the expenditures and the effectiveness of persuasion are about equal for both sides, then up to 17 units may be spent on lobbying.

As mentioned above, these 17 total units of expenditures to win the game are directly unproductive. Furthermore, the more competition there is in lobbying and the greater the potential gains and losses for the two sides, the greater the unproductive activity will be. In this example, 17 units might be diverted from useful production in order to win a contest in which the net benefit to society is only 3 units.

Thus, if free trade is chosen in the absence of lobbying, 3 additional units of useful goods and services will be available to society. However, when the potential winners and losers compete against each other in a lobbying game, the net effect for society will be a 14-unit loss in useful goods and services (3–17 = –14), assuming they choose free trade. If instead, the lower lobbying expenditures by Agent C were more effective in convincing Agent B, then the status quo would be chosen and the net effect on society will be (0–17 = –17), an even bigger loss. Thus although measured GDP would rise after free trade is chosen, the average standard of living in the economy will fall because fewer useful goods and services will be produced. This is a very important, but often unnoticed, aspect of lobbying in a democratic society.

One last feature of the lobbying game is similar to the transfers game: the big winner in the contest, curiously, is not one of the two agents trying to win. Recall that with transfers, it was Agent B, the swing voter, who gained the most. With lobbying, it is the lobbying agents themselves that gain the most. The lobbying agents are the people Agents A and C hire to engage in the lobbying activities. These information providers, who we can think of as a fourth agent in the game—Agent D—or, if the agents represent groups, as a set of individual's drawn from a subset of these groups, are the big winners.

One final inequity: because the benefits in the lobbying industry are likely to be larger than the benefits in the productive industries trying to win the contests, it is likely that this profession will attract the best and brightest individuals; which indeed it does. Lobbying firms hire individuals trained in some of the best universities and law schools, and these individuals are earning high incomes. Although it may be more accurate to say that these individuals are "capturing" large incomes, since their incomes come as a result of a transfer from the groups trying to win the contest, rather than from directly productive activity.

Incentives to Refrain from Lobbying

Because of the problems associated with lobbying, one might ask if there are incentives for either agent to refrain from the lobbying game. After all, if the possibility of large-scale success is low and the cost high, why do it?

Consider the outcomes under various scenarios—again from table 5.1. First, suppose almost-maximum lobbying occurs and Agent A wins Agent B's vote. In this case, Agent A will gain 10 units from free trade but will pay, say, 9 units for lobbying activity for a net gain of 1 unit. Agent C will lose 7 units from free trade but will spend, say, 6 units for lobbying activity for a net loss of 13 units. It seems senseless, especially for Agent C, to bother to engage in lobbying in this instance. If Agent C recognizes that it will lose 13 units with lobbying, it may choose to refrain so that its loss would be only 7 units. However, if Agent C does refrain from lobbying, then Agent A will recognize that it needs to do much less to convince Agent B to support free trade. That could inspire Agent A to lower its lobbying expenditures. Suppose Agent A reduces all the way to 1 unit. This represents just a little lobbying to guarantee support. However, by spending only 1 unit, Agent C now would have an incentive to reenter the competition. By spending only 2 units it may have a chance to win. However, as before, Agent A cannot allow this and would be inspired to increase its expenditures to 3 or 4 units, and so on.

What this implies is that while the no-lobbying outcome with Agent A winning the vote is actually better for Agent A, Agent C, and in general, neither Agent A nor Agent C has an individual incentive to refrain from lobbying. Instead each can raise its own chances of winning the contest through lobbying expenditures and will be inspired to do so to maximize its chances of success. This outcome is a classic prisoner's dilemma outcome. Individual self-interested behavior leads both parties to an overall inferior outcome.

The likelihood that agents will engage in lobbying is also higher when there is more uncertainty about the outcomes. On the one hand, if the payoffs are not perfectly known or if the effectiveness of lobbying to sway Agent B's vote is highly uncertain—which is most assuredly a real-world feature—then agents will be even more likely to try their luck in the lobbying competition. On the other hand, if all information about payoffs were perfectly known and if lobbying effectiveness were perfectly correlated with expenditures, then Agent A might be inclined to cut a deal with Agent C. The deal could consist of compensation if Agent C agrees to refrain from lobbying. For example, if Agent C recognizes it will lose any lobbying game, it can either refrain from lobbying completely, or threaten to inflict injury on Agent A by competing in lobbying. Agent A could conceivably buy off Agent C by agreeing to transfer, say, 2 units to Agent C if it promises to refrain from lobbying. In this outcome, Agent A might spend 2 units to bribe Agent C and, say, 1 unit on lobbying to sway Agent B's vote. In the end, when free trade is chosen, Agent A receives 7 units (10 – 2 – 1 = 7), Agent C only loses 5 units (–7 + 2 = 5), and there is just one unproductive unit wasted on lobbying. However, unfortunately this outcome may be unlikely in reality since it assumes near perfect knowledge about both the payoffs and the effectiveness of lobbying.

Lobbying and Rhetoric

In the previous section we discussed the nature of lobbying and its effects under the simple assumption that the more resources devoted to persuasion, the greater the chances of winning the contest. In this section we will look more carefully at the way in which persuasion is most likely to be effective. It matters not just how much money is spent, but also the way in which information is used to convince people. This is especially important because lobbying efforts can greatly affect our knowledge and understanding of what is true about the world. Unfortunately, to learn what is true, it is insufficient merely to listen to what is presented by the experts. Instead one needs to consider the motives and incentives of the groups presenting information, because these motives can bias the presentation.

Persuasion is only possible, or necessary, if some agents do not know something; that is, if information is imperfect. If all agents knew everything perfectly about the effects of different policies, then nothing one agent could say would affect what the other "knows" to be true. However, information is imperfect in several ways; ways which are not mutually exclusive.

One possibility is that some agents know the truth about the effects of policies, but other agents are uninformed. The informed agents are the "experts." Experts conduct scientific studies and careful analysis to identify the effects of various policy options. The uninformed agents are those people who simply have not taken time to learn what the experts already know. In this context, lobbying involves transferring information from the informed agents to the uninformed; a process of teaching and learning.[6]

A second type of imperfect information arises if no one can be certain what is true. Experts on the subject conduct analysis and do research studies but each study has a margin of error that makes it impossible to know with a high degree of confidence what the true effects of policy options will be. In this case lobbying involves persuading people that the likelihood they will benefit is higher if they support a particular policy.

The true nature of imperfect information is a mixture of these two cases. When considering the effects of various policy options, a small group of agents are likely to know with a high degree of confidence what the effect of a policy will be, or at least the effects for themselves. For example, import-competing industries know with high confidence that trade liberalization will harm their industry, at least in the short run. Similarly, export industries will know with high confidence that trade liberalization will benefit them in the short run. However, for most other people in the economy, the effects will be highly uncertain. Indeed it may even be highly uncertain for those who believe they will almost surely gain or lose in the short term. In the end, decisions are

Table 5.5 Welfare Effects of Two Policy Options

	Agent A	*Agent B*	*Agent C*
Trade Liberalization	(9, 11)	(–4, 4)	(–8, –10)
Status Quo	0	0	0

made not on the basis of what is "known" to be true, but rather what is "believed" to be true. Beliefs matter more than truth. The objective of lobbying is to sway beliefs about outcomes.

For example, consider the same game as before with two policy options; trade liberalization and the status quo, and three Agents A, B, and C. Consider the payoffs to the agents listed in table 5.5. In this game, instead of definite payoffs to each agent, the payoffs are given as a range. The range gives the high and low values that will arise for that agent with each policy choice.

For simplicity we can imagine a uniform distribution of values. This means the probability is equal, or uniform, for any particular triple-value (one value for each agent). Thus, the outcome (9, –4, –10) for Agents A, B, and C is equally likely to (11, 4, –8), which is equally likely to every other possible triple, where each number drawn is from each agent's range. The expected value for the three agents is calculated by finding the mean value for each agent. This computes to (10, 0, –9), respectively, implying that there is an expected net gain to the world economy because (10 + 0 – 9 = +1).[7]

This example is constructed to highlight several features. First, since any number in each range is equally probable, another equally probable outcome is, say, (9, –4, –8), in which case trade liberalization would cause a net national welfare loss. This implies that because of imperfect information, no one knows with certainty what the final impact of the policy choices will be for themselves or for others. Nonetheless, Agent A is certain trade liberalization will benefit it and Agent C knows trade liberalization will harm it. What Agents A and C do not know is the final realization of their gains and losses and the direction and magnitude of the effects upon Agent B. They also do not know whether the net effects from TL will be positive or negative.

This simple account of the lobbying game is a fair representation of the situation we face in democracies in the real world. As was discussed in chapters 2 and 3, trade liberalization, or globalization more broadly, will certainly generate winners and losers. A few of the big potential winners will have a high degree of confidence that they will gain, like

Agent A. In trade theories, Agent A corresponds to export industries or a country's abundant factor. A few of the big potential losers will also be highly confident that they will lose, like Agent C. In trade theories, Agent C corresponds to import-competing industries and a country's scarce production factors. Most people, probably the vast majority, will be like Agent B. This corresponds to workers and capital owners in the nontradable sectors. They will not have a clue whether they will gain or lose.

The nature of imperfect information in this example makes it a situation ripe for lobbying. Agent A clearly prefers trade liberalization, while Agent C clearly prefers the status quo. However, each agent needs the support of Agent B in order to adopt its policy. In the example, not only is Agent B uncertain whether it will gain or lose from trade liberalization, but the magnitude of its uncertainty is also greater. (Here the degree of uncertainty is easily measured as the range of values. Thus the degree of uncertainty for Agents A and C is 2 units, while for Agent B it is 8 units.) Thus, Agent B is a prime lobbying target.

Next, consider effective lobbying strategies in this context. What are the best ways for Agents A and C to convince Agent B to support their favored policy, and what are the implications and outcomes from this kind of lobbying competition?

Lobbying Effectiveness

To implement any policy in a democracy requires political support. Political support is obtained by convincing people that a policy is in their interest. The art of persuasion is called rhetoric and its techniques have been discussed since the time of Socrates, Plato, and Aristotle.

The issues discussed in ancient Greek times have changed little two and a half millennia later. As discussed in Nichols (1987), Plato and Aristophanes both expressed serious concerns about the use of rhetoric in political contexts. In Aristophanes' play, *The Clouds,* the protagonist seeks the assistance of rhetoricians who will help formulate an argument to convince a judge to forgive his debts to others. Rhetoric is imagined to be like the clouds that can take whatever shape is necessary for the circumstances at hand. Similarly, in Plato's *Gorgias,* Socrates argues that rhetoric is mere cookery; something that is designed to please the listener but which may have no regard for what is true and what the listener truly needs. In both cases, rhetoric is used to achieve private interests regardless of what is true.

In rebuttal, Aristotle argues that the rhetorician cannot be deceitful and hide behind his arguments. As Nichols states, "if a rhetorician is to be persuasive, he must show that his advice is advantageous to his audience, that what he is praising is noble, or that he has justice on his side. In such cases, his premises, his conclusions and his examples all reveal his character" (1987, 657). Aristotle acknowledged that concepts such as justice and the common good can never be as precise as the sciences, but through rhetoric they can become knowledge whose truth holds for the most part.

In the context of the simple lobbying game presented in table 5.5, the objective of Agent A is to persuade Agent B to support free trade, while the objective of Agent C is persuade Agent B to support the status quo. Agent B's support will depend on what it is most concerned about; thus, there are several possible approaches each agent can take. One possibility is that it is self-interested, caring only about the effect of the policy on itself. Alternatively, it might be socially conscious, in which case it might care more about the overall aggregate effects of the two policy options. Finally, Agent B might have a special interest that it is most concerned about. Perhaps it cares most about the environment, or sustainable development, or income distribution.

From Agent A's perspective, if Agent B's concerns are mostly self-interest, then Agent A needs to persuade Agent B that its payoffs will be in the range (0, 4). If Agent B is concerned mostly about the overall social effects, Agent A must persuade Agent B that the sum of the payoffs to all agents is positive. If Agent B has other concerns, Agent A will need to focus attention on those issues and convince Agent B that trade liberalization will have a positive outcome vis-à-vis those concerns. In like fashion, Agent C will wish to convince Agent B that the payoffs to trade liberalization lie in the range (–4, 0), that the sum total value of all effects are negative, that the environmental quality will decline, income distribution will widen with trade liberalization, etc.

More realistically, we can think of Agent B, not as one individual, but rather as a large group of individuals; some percentage of which care mostly for their own interests, another percentage that is socially conscious about a variety of issues. Effective lobbying will involve identification of the most significant of these concerns among the group so that resources can be directed toward appropriate campaigns. Gaining Agent B's support will mean convincing a significant proportion of this middle group to support one's favored policy.

But What Is an Appropriate Campaign?

If Agents A and C both determine that Agent B is mostly self-interested, then Agent A's task is to convince Agent B that TL will benefit him, while Agent C must convince Agent B of the opposite. If Agent B is mostly socially interested, then Agent A will argue the overall benefits will be positive, or that TL will be fair and just in some sense. Agent C will do the opposite. In any case, both Agents A and C will conduct research studies that tend to support the conclusions that will help make their preferred case. Since there is great uncertainty about the overall effects, it will be relatively easy for different researchers to come to completely different conclusions. Also, as was argued in chapter 3, it is impossible for any research study to incorporate and measure all of the impacts the policies may have. Thus, Agent A researchers can simply overemphasize the components that seem to make Agent B better off, or to make trade liberalization welfare improving. For example, they can point out that lower prices will be good for all consumers, or, they can focus on overall efficiency effects arising in standard economic models. At the same time Agent C researchers may argue that the threat to jobs may affect many industries and will emphasize adjustment costs that accrue to the import-competing industries.

Notice that the truth is not really important for effective lobbying. If the "true" effect of trade liberalization on Agent B were (+1), Agent C would have no incentive to reveal that truth if indeed Agent C knew it to be the truth. Of course, Agent A would be perfectly happy to reveal the truth in this case if it knew it, but would be equally unconcerned about the truth if the effect on Agent B were (–1) instead.

It is also worth noting that neither agent has any incentive to point out that the truth is really unknowable. If either agent were to take that position, it would immediately destroy its credibility and any hope that it could convince Agent B to support its policy. Thus, each side is induced, by the nature of the game, to argue that the effects of policies are more certain than they truly are.

Because uncertainty decreases the effectiveness of lobbying, the more credible or believable these studies are to Agent B, the more likely the information will persuade Agent B to vote in that direction. Thus Agents A and C will do whatever they can to enhance credibility. Research studies that are more sophisticated and complex will seem more credible than simple studies. This can work even if Agent B does not understand what the study is showing.

If the research was done by someone at a prominent university or research center, all the better. If one can enlist the support of "Nobel-Prize-winning" economists, that too can help garnish support. If one's policy is supported by someone famous, even though fame has little to do with knowledge or understanding of the policy effect, that is also beneficial. Thus, Hollywood movie stars can influence voters even though they are rarely experts on the subject.

More insidiously, if enhancing credibility can win more support, then reducing credibility can reduce support. This then becomes a strategy for the opposition. Each study released by Agent A, identifying positive effects of trade liberalization, will be criticized by Agent C. Weaknesses in the study are emphasized. Aspects that have been overlooked or ignored in the study are highlighted. This is easy to do, of course, because as discussed in chapter 3, every study is incomplete in its coverage; every study makes a series of assumptions each of which may not be true.

Even the very best empirical research study can be picked apart by someone who is an expert in econometric methods. This is true even when the study employs all of the latest empirical tools and techniques. The reason is that despite using the very best research "technology," every study must make an enormous number of assumptions. Challenge the validity of any of these assumptions, and one challenges the entire set of conclusions.

To be fair, the best empirical research studies are conducted with the utmost scrutiny and completeness. Thus, of course, the very best studies are less easily criticized. Nevertheless, even though the results of these studies are the very best the profession can muster, they remain the best possible in the face of extremely incomplete, inexact, or overly aggregated data. Although the results of these studies are "suggestive" of patterns or relationships, they remain quite distant from providing definitive "proof" of anything. This is one reason why virtually every research study concludes with the words, "and thus there is a need for further research."

Ad Hominem

Since the reputation of an individual making the argument can raise the credibility of a study, so then, impugning the reputation of the individuals associated with a study can reduce credibility. This often leads to the ad hominem arguments that are, unfortunately, all too common. As an example, consider Sen. Byron Dorgan's remarks about economists prior to arguing about the invalidity of the principle of comparative advantage in today's world: "These economists, puffing on their pipes, doubtless sitting in their sunrooms wearing their sweaters with leather-patched sleeves are meditating on the theory developed by David Ricardo in 1815."[8]

So, economists are pipe-puffing, sunroom-sitting, leather-patch-sweater-wearing, meditaters! Even though his ad hominem remarks are relatively tame, they nevertheless build upon a popular stereotype suggesting that academics are holed up in an "ivory tower" and completely divorced from the realities of the world.

Although these types of arguments are not germane to the issues at hand, they are used because they are often very effective. The intention is to portray the person making the opposing argument in such a way as to make him or her undesirable. In this way, a person whose opinion is not yet fixed will feel, even if only subtly, that he does not wish to be associated with that "type" of person. And if he does not wish to share company with the person, perhaps he will not wish to share opinions either. Psychologically these can be very effective statements even though logically they ought to be considered immaterial and even mean-spirited, especially since they develop or build upon stereotypes.

Exaggeration

For both agents, persuasion is more likely to be successful with an overemphasis of the strengths of your preferred policy and an underestimate (or by ignoring) the weaknesses. When two competing policies are being considered, successful persuasion is also enhanced by overemphasis of the weaknesses of the opposition policy and of course an underestimate of its strengths.

The reality of effective lobbying is that neither side has any incentive to present an unbiased account of the strengths and weaknesses of the policy proposals along with an accurate revelation about the degree of uncertainty. In political discourse it seems any leaning in the direction of objectivity (meaning recognition that the opposition may be making some valid points) becomes fodder for the opposition to attack and almost assuredly reduces support for your policy. Because the general public is smart enough to recognize that most policy choices will have some negative effects, each side will pay minor lip service to the negatives aspects of their own policy. Mostly, though, these references will suggest that the negative effects will be very small and temporary.

Hence, objectivity is locked in a kind of prisoner's dilemma because of the nature of political debate. Outside observers of the debate should be cautious. The truth may lie in some convex combination of the statements made by all parties to the debate, but it is unlikely to be found in the statements of any one party.

Can we expect more objectivity from the academic community? More so, perhaps, but probably not completely. Academics who study policy and advise policy makers will realize that taking a policy position and supporting it rhetorically (preferably using as much scientific empirical support as possible) is the best path toward success in the profession. Publishing opportunities and consulting jobs are all driven by demand for one's output, and if the output conforms to the political rhetorical needs, then it is more likely to be used and cited.

Conclusion

Policies are chosen via a political process. That means that ultimately, any discussion of appropriate policy choices must consider the interface with politics. This chapter has highlighted several important features of the democratic political process as it impinges upon the discussion over globalization policy.

First, the standard economic prescription to maximize economic efficiency and compensate any losers seems unlikely to be chosen in a democracy. If agents are self-interested and well-informed, those who stand to gain from a policy change merely need to convince a majority of decision makers to choose that policy. Winners stand to gain much more when compensation is not made and when only 51 percent is needed to secure a policy change, compensation need not be implemented. Indeed, it may be that compensation can be adequately implemented only if there is a benevolent dictator who is egalitarian minded and who has perfect information about the total effects of the policy. These conditions are never, even nearly, satisfied. An alternative is for most citizens to give up their self-interest motive and vote for egalitarian outcomes such as compensation. This too would seem to be quite unlikely.

Second, democracy may inspire the use of transfers, either money or some other benefits, to induce support for one's favored policies. But transfers, or more nefariously, bribes, are more likely to be effective if they can be done secretly. With secrecy it is possible to avoid the more costly outcome if there were competition in bribes. Secrecy also puts the nonbribing party at a distinct disadvantage and is one reason bribery is illegal in many contexts; but not all.

In some societies bribery is almost an accepted way of life, even if only grudgingly accepted. In these cases, competition in bribes may be the norm, which could ensure that the most efficient outcomes are chosen. However, even with an efficient outcome, all parties will not share in the benefits. Indeed, differing practices regarding the use of bribery to secure outcomes in both private and public venues creates difficulties for firms engaging in international trade and investment. If some agents use bribery freely when others are restricted because they are forced to follow their own country's laws, then those firms may be at a competitive disadvantage. Lastly, to ensure efficiency, the parties must have good information about the effects of the policies.

Because generally convincing information is not available for reasons outlined in the previous chapters, the democratic political process opens the way for lobbying. Indeed, lobbying, which involves transmitting information to persuade others to support your policy, cannot arise unless information is imperfectly known. The key concern with lobbying is that it is a directly unproductive activity; that is, lobbying diverts resources. The more lobbying, the fewer resources available to produce goods and services that contributes to standard of livings. Furthermore, when there is competition in lobbying, as there most assuredly will be, directly unproductive activity can multiply. The prime beneficiaries of the lobbying process may be the lobbying groups themselves since the groups who advocate alternative policies all transfer income to the lobbyists to help them win the political contest.

The second important aspect of lobbying in the democratic choice process is its effect on the way information is disseminated. Policy choices in democracies are made with majority support. Those groups who recognize they will gain or lose from a policy will disseminate information—lobby—to garner that majority support. The majority needed may be amongst members of the legislature or among the voting public, depending on the circumstances.

Lobbying involves the use of rhetorical methods to convince people to support a group's favored policy. Effective rhetoric often involves some bending of the truth. For example, supporters of a policy have incentives to overemphasize the positive effects of that policy and the negative effects of the alternative policies. This is why, for example, there is a popular impression that economists and other supporters of free trade believe that free trade is good for everyone; when in fact theory does not support that view. Also, the previous chapters argue that our knowledge about the global economy and the effects of policies is much more uncertain than commonly described. Rhetorical necessities can explain why there is an under emphasis on the weaknesses of research results. However, as a counterbalance, opponents of a policy do tend to emphasize the negative aspects of the opposing studies. Finally, rhetorical needs in the democratic political process may inspire bias in the investigation process itself. Research is more likely to be done in areas of current interest. Research papers are more likely to be read and cited when they offer clear support for a particular policy. In addition, groups who stand to gain from certain policies under discussion, will commission studies that tend to support those policies. The result is a clustering of studies supporting particular policy options, rather than an unbiased and objective assessment divorced from the objectives of special interests.

The entire lobbying process and its misrepresentation of information is also a potential source of disillusion for the electorate and may explain a drop in political participation. People regularly complain that they cannot believe politicians—and to a degree, this is correct. Politicians purposely frame arguments to support their proposed policies. While they do not necessarily lie, they do adjust the emphasis on the positives and negatives considerably. This is a natural consequence of the political system.

Most individuals are not specialists in international economics and have only a modest amount of knowledge about the global marketplace. As a result they must base decisions, such as who to vote for, or which legislation to support, on the experts who study, interpret, and communicate the workings of the world. However, these experts are engaged in a kind of ideological tug of war, using all techniques possible to sway a few more individuals to join their side. Because the true nature of the world is extremely complicated and messy, it becomes impractical to express a nuanced argument supporting your favored position. Nuance is not describable in a 30-second sound bite. Nuance also breeds confusion and that means there is less chance the average person will understand it. In addition, to express the true nature of the world, with all its ups and downs and all its uncertainty, will very likely lead people to switch to the rosier (and clearer) scenario provided by one's opponent.

For some people there is no predicament because they eventually join one camp or the other, grab hold of the ideological rope along with their fellow believers and begin pulling! Many of these individuals begin to believe all the "truths" that their side is presenting.

However, for the moderates, or the confused, or the seekers of truth, or those who just cannot make up their mind, there remains an uneasy feeling about the whole process. I suspect this is a prime source of political apathy. Many people believe that no one is telling them the truth, and with the increase in distrust comes a quiet disillusionment with the entire system.

Although democracy does provide a mechanism to choose policies, the tendency for the process to distort information makes the process problematic. Perhaps, Aristotle's notion is valid: that political discourse can arrive at a compromise solution between groups with heterogeneous interests.[9] Alternatively, it is possible the political system is not leading toward any particular outcome. Perhaps it is leading us in circles. For example, lobbyists will support maintenance of the political system, because, as long as there is contentiousness in public policy circles, money will keep being transferred in their direction. Next, since there really is no way to be certain of the overall effects of policies—at least not definitively or convincingly to all—and since there will always be expected winners and losers from every policy change, contentiousness is self-propagating. Third, governments, that implement policy changes, always need to be doing something to justify their existence. Hence "new" policies are always being proposed. Finally, policy researchers have little to no incentive to upset the process. No side can admit the degree of uncertainty in their own studies lest the opposing side gain an advantage. No side can waver from the position that its own analysis is asking the right questions, building the right model, collecting the right data, using the most appropriate empirical technique and discovering the most appropriate policies. Thus, while democracy may have the potential to solve the policy choice problem, it is not clear it does so effectively in its current configuration.

The remaining part of the book will suggest a new method for choosing policies. That method involves description of set of compromise principles that can guide policy choices. These principles will provide a justification for policy choices that are likely to generate outcomes that are pretty good from both a cost-benefit perspective and from a fairness perspective as well.

CHAPTER 6

The Pursuit of Profit

Economists and others, who support globalization, tend to look favorably upon profit seeking by firms. Neoclassical economic models are built on the assumptions that firms maximize profit and consumers maximize utility. Adam Smith's famous passage about the butcher, brewer, and baker is often used to suggest that self-centered, even egoistic, profit-seeking behavior can have positive effects for the economy:

> It is not from the benevolence of the butcher, the brewer, or the baker, that we expect our dinner, but from their regard to their own interest. We address ourselves, not to their humanity but to their self-love, and never talk to them of our own necessities but of their advantages. (Smith, 1937, para I.2.2)

Smith is arguing that the economic system provides for our wants and needs because, first and foremost, people are trying to help themselves, and they do so by producing and selling meat, beer, and bread to others. These market outcomes are not achieved because of altruistic behavior. We do not appeal to other peoples' humanity when we seek our sustenance, but rather to their self-interest.

Many who view profit seeking, and egoistic behavior, almost as an evil in society, do not share Smith's notion that social benefits arise from self-interest. These groups argue, for example, that large multinational firms use their size and power to take advantage of others. Firms manipulate consumers' demands with advertising,[1] they influence government policies to favor their interests, and exploit the lower skilled workers in their companies by pushing wages down to unlivable levels. Indeed, firms may avoid environmental protections, shift jobs to low wage countries, tolerate unsafe working environments, prevent workers from forming unions and may even hire child labor in countries where worker protections are lenient or nonexistent—all in the name of profit!

This chapter will argue that there are really two different types of profit-seeking behavior. The first type, described by Adam Smith, will be referred to as voluntary exchange. From the idea of voluntary exchange comes the notion that free market activity can generate benefits for everyone—that trade is a positive sum game. The second type of profit, emanating from the concerns of many social justice groups, will be labeled transfer profit. From the idea of transfer profit comes the notion that benefits to some groups arise from the detriment caused to others—that interactions are a zero-sum game. However, there are two variations of transfer profit; the first, analogous to theft, is labeled involuntary transfers and the second, analogous to gift giving, is labeled voluntary transfers.[2]

In subsequent chapters, I will elaborate upon these concepts of profit seeking and discuss their prevalence in today's global society and also examine the fairness characteristics of each type of profit seeking and note that voluntary exchange and voluntary transfers are largely fair under most interpretations while involuntary transfers are largely unfair. Finally, understanding and using the distinction between these two variants of profit seeking provides a heuristic mechanism, a stepping stone, to guide policy choices in this complex globalizing world.

What Do We Mean by Profit?

In business accounting, profit is defined as the difference between a firm's total revenue and the total cost of its inputs. It is the money left over after all the normal expenses of the company have been paid. Accounting profit represents the return to the owners of the firm since they have the right to retain any surplus for themselves. In a private firm, the owners may also be employees, in which case profit will be a surplus above what they pay themselves in wages. If the firm is a corporation with shares of stock issued, then profit will often be distributed in the form of dividends to the shareholders.

Economic profit is defined slightly differently as total revenue minus full economic cost, which, in addition to the cost of productive inputs, includes normal profit to the owners of firms for the risks they incur in running the business. In competitive markets, economic profit is driven to zero, however because under this definition an average profit rate is allowed for, accounting profit would remain positive despite achieving "zero" economic profit.

Essentially then, profit is the income received by an individual who has contributed entrepreneurial services, taken risks, and provided direction and guidance for the company. Viewed as a production service that generates income, profit is similar to payments for other income-generating services in the marketplace (wages, rents, and interest). Economists and accountants sometimes classify income acquisition into these four fundamental categories: wages, rents, interest, and profit. The sum of these four items in an entire economy is one way to measure the nation's gross domestic product (GDP). It is important to highlight these distinctions because they form the basis for many of the popular conceptions and misconceptions about profit.

Wages represent the money acquired through physical work, whether the digging of ditches in the searing summer sun or meeting with clients at a five-star restaurant to close an important sales deal. Rent is either the money acquired from the usage of land or more generally by the use of any owned resource, which may include capital equipment. Rent typically describes the money earned by the owner of an apartment or office building, but can also refer to money earned as dividends by shareholders of a corporation. Interest represents money acquired when one person or company lends money to another.

Curiously, in accounting terminology, wages are classified as "earned" income, whereas income from rent, interest, and profit is labeled "unearned" income. This terminology may date to the time when there was wider acceptance of the labor theory of value, which proposed that the value of all commodities was proportional to the amount of labor necessary to produce it. In other words, labor creates value because of the hard work and effort of people, and therefore the money acquired from work is considered "earned." However, when capital or landowners apply their physical property in the production of something, individual physical effort is not required and therefore the income is "unearned."

This terminology is unfortunate since it imparts a negative connotation on some parts of the productive process. The modern interpretation in a capitalist system is that income payments are made to agents that contribute in some way to production. Of course, labor effort contributes to production, and so wages are paid as income. However, in a capitalist economy, individuals own the physical means of production. Resource ownership is sought entirely because land and capital can be applied to a production process, which, in turn, will generate income. If people could not "profit" or benefit from land and capital usage, there would be no incentive to own it (land) and create it (capital).

In the past, land and capital ownership was concentrated in the hands of a small wealthy minority. The image of a capitalist, typified in political cartoons of the late nineteenth century, was once a heavyset, cigar-smoking railroad tycoon, holding bags of money and trodding upon the poor defenseless masses. However, in developed countries things have changed considerably as a larger and larger proportion of the population own their own homes and have retirement plans containing ownership shares in numerous companies. This means increasingly more people are both workers and capitalists at the same time. In the United States today, a typical capitalist is a retired woman supporting herself on the income from her 401K disbursements, plus a supplement from social security. Despite these changes in capitalist composition, the popular image of the capitalist has not changed very much. There remains a strong sense that the owners and management, especially of large multinational corporations, continue to exploit powerless workers.

One other type of income classified as "unearned" is interest income. Just like profit, money acquired as interest on loans has a long negative history. In medieval times, any kind of money lending was known as usury and was condemned as immoral by many religions. Still today, the Islamic prohibition on usury motivates religiously sanctioned financial services known as Islamic banking. In non-Islamic cultures usury is not restricted, but the negative connotation sometimes persists.

The reason interest income is viewed suspiciously is perhaps the same reason it is classified as unearned income. Before modern economics developed, money acquired by lending, was thought to be money out of nowhere. It required no effort and no work, and hence was viewed as pure exploitation of the borrower by the lender. The lender effectively stole money away from the borrower. This image is perpetuated with the stereotype of loan sharks, who lend money to desperate people and use strong-arm techniques to ensure repayment. However, with the development of a modern banking system, and especially with recognition of the concept of opportunity cost, borrowing and lending was less frequently viewed as an evil.

The modern view of interest is that it is a payment for a service. That service is the privilege the borrower receives to use and spend money now instead of later. In contrast, the lender must forgo the current use of his money and what it might purchase (i.e., his own current consumption) when he lends it to another person. The opportunity cost to the lender is the forgone consumption, while the interest payment is the fee that covers that cost. Borrowing and lending, when done responsibly (which is not always the case), has been a significant contributor to the expansion of output and the raising of living standards around the world.

Thus, a more reasonable view of income from interest, rent, and profit is as money "earned" because of a contribution to the productive process, in a similar manner to a wage payment for a labor service. Production requires workers to combine with capital, land, and natural resources to produce the goods and services demanded by households, governments, and other firms. When money is unavailable to pay for labor and capital, it can be financed by borrowing from someone who prefers to save his consumption for a later time. In this case, interest payments will be paid that also contributes to production.

A More General Definition of Profit

A more general application of the term profit, then, is as a synonym for the term net benefit. To profit from an activity means to receive a net benefit. That benefit might be measured in monetary terms as with the money earned in an endeavor, or it might be measured in terms of the utility (a.k.a. happiness) acquired by an individual. Although in economics we typically assume that utility is derived from the consumption of goods and services, in more general terms utility can also arise from interpersonal relationships like friendship, or from one's perception about oneself (self-image) or one's perceptions about the activities of others. For example, an environmentalist may receive a psychic benefit when learning that a whaling ship has been prevented from pursuing its intended mission. Under this very general definition, we would say the environmentalist has "profited."

Clearly this usage of the term profit is much broader than its typical use. When social justice supporters express outrage at the high profits of multinational oil companies, they are using the standard, more-narrow definition. Nevertheless, by broadening the definition, we will be able to recognize the source of complaints by those who worry about high profits (as typically defined) and also to see that these same complaints have a much wider domain.

Returning to the four main sources of income in an economy—wages, rents, interest, and profit—we may note that each of these corresponds to an individual benefit received in excess of the costs of generating that benefit. For example, the cost of work to a worker is the value of his next best opportunity, more than likely that is the benefits he would have experienced with leisure. Alternatively, the cost may be conceived as the disutility, i.e. the hardship, associated with the work activity.[3] The net benefit, or "worker profit" associated with work is the wage minus that individual's opportunity cost. In a free market, if the wage exceeds the value of the next best opportunity (leisure, with no income), then a person accepts the job.

For the capital owner the opportunity cost is to leave the equipment unused, in which case he would earn nothing. Thus the rental payment itself is the net benefit or "capitalist profit" associated with the rental of his equipment. For a lender—envision a financial institution—the cost of the funds is the interest paid to depositors. A bank functions by paying depositors a lower rate of interest than is charged to borrowers. The difference between the two rates corresponds to a net benefit, or "lender profit."[4] Finally, we return to the entrepreneur. This is the person, or group of people, who organize workers, capital, and, potentially, borrowed funds in a productive activity. The entrepreneurs anticipate that the revenues earned on sales of the final product will exceed the wage, rental, and interest costs, in which case they will make a net benefit, or "entrepreneurial profit."

Alternative Sources of Profit

Once we broaden the definition of profit to include any benefit received by an individual in excess of costs, we might inquire into methods, other than those described above, by which a person might profit. One obvious alternative is theft. Thieves accost people on the street, hit them over the head, and run off with their wallets and purses. Bank robbers pursue larger prizes by going directly to the primary money storage facility. Con artists get people to give them their money by tricking them into thinking they will receive something of value in return—when in fact they will not. When money, or other things of value, is acquired via theft, it is not appropriate to call it income since it is not a payment for the provision of anything. However, the thief does benefit by an amount in excess of his expected cost of engaging in thievery. Therefore it is appropriate to say the thief has "profited" from the activity under our more general usage of the term.

Another alternative way a person may profit, besides theft, is through the receipt of a gift. The cost to the gift recipient is zero but the gift itself generates a positive benefit. Therefore, applying the general definition, it is valid to say the person has "profited" upon receiving the gift.

One final unique profit situation occurs when individuals produce benefits for themselves. For example, if a hunter shoots and kills a deer and brings the deer back for his family's consumption, then his family benefits. The cost is the opportunity cost of foregone leisure, perhaps watching a football game on a Sunday afternoon. As long as the benefits, which include the psychic benefits, or pleasure, from hunting exceed the opportunity cost, the hunter and his family profit from the activity.[5] Note, that because only one person or household is involved in this activity, there would be no recorded market activity. Thus, in some instances, profit arises outside the formal marketplace.

Finally, the suggestion of psychic benefits in the hunting example opens the door for other types of nonmarket profit opportunities. Thus, when a group of people protests in the streets to demand democracy, their actions are not a market activity. Nevertheless, they protest to achieve an outcome, such as freedom of speech and the right to elect their own leaders, which has value to them. Clearly, they expect the benefits of obtaining these freedoms will exceed the costs they might incur from their protests. In other words they expect to "profit" from the activity. These types of nonmarket benefits, like freedom and democracy are very difficult, if not impossible, to measure. However, inability to measure does not mean we must ignore them since people's behavior clearly demonstrates they are very important profit sources.

Self-Profit, Voluntary Exchange, and Transfer Profit Defined

This classification scheme is not a new idea. Henry George, in his book *Protection or Free Trade* (1949) wrote, "is it not true, as has been said, that the three great orders of society are 'working-men, beggar-men, and thieves?'" In a similar vein, using this broad definition of profit, we will distinguish between, not three, but four unique methods by which individuals obtain profit. In later chapters it will be shown that any type of profitable activity one might imagine can be identified as belonging to one, or a combination of several, of these profit-seeking methods. Secondly, it will be shown that in terms of fairness or justice criteria, several profit-seeking methods are universally regarded as preferable to others. In the end, these profit-seeking methods will be used to identify compromise principles that can guide policy choice.

Self-Profit

Self-profit corresponds to any benefit an individual receives based solely on his own independent activity and without interaction with any other person. Simple examples include a primitive hunter-gatherer who kills game and picks berries for his own sustenance, or collects branches to build himself a shelter. A modern example would be a runner enjoying a morning run, or a naturalist who walks through the forest to observe bird and animal species. Washing dishes and cooking one's own dinner are examples of self-profit.

In a modern economy, because people are so interconnected, it is difficult to find many examples of pure self-profit. In most cases an individual's own benefit is dependent on the use of land, capital equipment or information. If that land, equipment or information is owned or provided by someone else, as when exercise takes place in a health club, or because running requires the purchase of appropriate shoes, then self-profit is intermingled with voluntary exchange.

Voluntary Exchange

Profit by voluntary exchange corresponds to the benefit an individual receives after engaging in a mutually voluntary exchange with another. Most exchanges consist of bilateral trade, where two people exchange one object for another. In a barter economy, we might imagine two people exchanging apples for oranges, or labor services for a meal and a place to sleep. In a money economy, people exchange objects for money; apples are sold at the market for money; labor services are offered in exchange for a wage.

When exchange is voluntary (not coerced or forced in any explicit or implicit way) we can reasonably conclude that both traders expect to benefit from the exchange, for if not, why trade? In a barter economy, an apple grower seeks out trades with an orange grower because a combination of apples and oranges in his diet is more satisfying than consuming only apples. The orange grower is likely to feel the same way, preferring diversity in his diet as well. This implies that after the trade, assuming each party received what was expected, both traders are happier than without the trade. Because each trader benefits from the exchange, it is reasonable to say that each has "profited" through exchange. This is the classic economic story about the mutual benefits that arise from exchange.

Indeed, since both traders go away happier, we can claim that there is surplus value created because of exchange. Recognize that each person derives some happiness from consuming only apples and only oranges. After exchange, each person derives even more happiness with a combination of apples and oranges. Total happiness rises, which is why economists call this a positive sum game.

If we take this one step further, we will realize that people are not naturally endowed with a continual supply of apples or oranges to trade with others. To make exchange possible, people need to produce the apples or oranges or other desired goods or services that other people seek. Production, in turn, requires the combination of labor, capital, land, and natural resources. When the final products are exchanged on the market, they generate income to all the workers and owners of capital, land, and resources, who contributed to the production. Thus, via market exchange, everyone who contributes to the production process will profit. This is the market story related by Adam Smith when he wrote about the butcher, brewer, and baker seeking to profit via production and exchange.

Transfer Profit

Transfer profit corresponds to a benefit received by one agent as a direct consequence of a comparable loss to another. With transfer profit, there is no surplus value like there is with voluntary exchange. Nothing new is produced. Instead, one person's gain is another's loss.

There are two variations of transfer profit. Involuntary transfers occur when the transfers are made unknowingly or without consent, as with theft. In contrast, voluntary transfers arise when the transfers are made willingly, as with gifts, charity, and philanthropy. These differ because, with involuntary transfers, the transfer is caused by the profit recipient, whereas with voluntary transfers the transfer is caused by the giver; the person who does not receive the profit.

When critics of globalization complain about the evils of profit seeking, when they argue that large multinational corporations are controlling the decisions of government institutions, when they openly worry about harmful labor market practices in developing countries, they are reacting to different manifestations of involuntary transfers. Similarly concerns about involuntary transfers arise among free market advocates as well, albeit directed at different situations. For example, when people complain about the vast power of the government to transfer money away from people and control the decisions they can make, they too are reacting to a manifestation of involuntary transfer profit. Also, when we study the ravages of war throughout history and react with sorrow at the death and destruction, we are reacting to perhaps the most notable example of involuntary transfers.

In his famous treatise, "The Law," first published in 1850, Frederic Bastiat emphasized the problems associated with the widespread tendency for people to engage in involuntary transfers; what he referred to as "plunder." Bastiat wrote, "...man may also live and enjoy, by seizing and appropriating the productions of the faculties of his fellow men. This is the origin of plunder. Now, labor being in itself a pain, and man being naturally inclined to avoid pain, it follows, and history proves it, that wherever plunder is less burdensome than labor, it prevails; and neither religion nor morality can, in this case, prevent it from prevailing."[6]

Egoism and Altruism

A controversial issue that affects the debate about profit-seeking behavior concerns the acceptance, or the perceived morality, of egoism and altruism. Economists, among others, have generally accepted egoistic behavior as a natural characteristic of people. Furthermore, following the teachings of Adam Smith, they argue that egoism can actually lead to socially beneficial outcomes in the marketplace. To many, egoism, greed even, is a good characteristic.[7]

Nonetheless, most people seem to regard egoism as a character flaw at best. They see self-interested behavior as the source of problems, even a source of evil, in our society. To most people, greed is something we should all strive to extricate from our personal behavior. The suggested alternative is to act altruistically: to give rather than receive; to do good things for others without demanding or expecting anything in return.

Figure 6.1 illustrates a series of transfers between two people to highlight different viewpoints concerning egoism and altruism. The rows signify the three main types of interactive profit realization: involuntary transfers, voluntary transfers, and voluntary exchange. The shading in each box indicates whether the person gains (gray) or loses (dots). Also depicted is the person responsible for initiating each transfer, that is, the chooser.

In the case of involuntary transfers, Person 1 chooses to initiate a transfer that makes himself better off while causing harm to Person 2. If

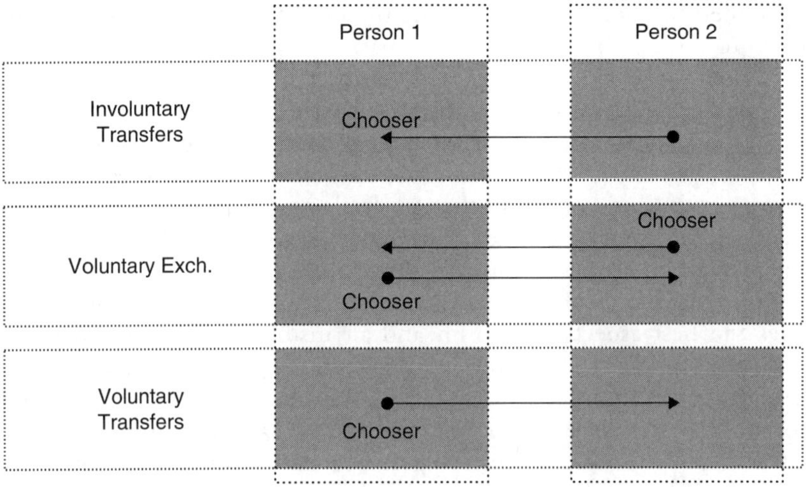

Figure 6.1 Alternative Transfer Scenarios.

Person 1 is egoistic, then he may believe it is acceptable to take any type of action that causes self-benefit, even if it causes direct harm to someone else. However, to most people, this kind of behavior is condemned because of the involuntary losses to the victim. In addition, egoism, the sentiment that leads to this negative outcome, is often faulted as the culprit. When people criticize egoism they very likely have this type of activity in mind.

Many believe that the moral alternative to egoism is to act in ways that are altruistic, to give of oneself selflessly. Note that this is precisely the situation described with voluntary transfers. In that case, Person 1 chooses to give to Person 2. Person 2 receives a benefit while Person 1 suffers a comparable loss. But even though one person gains at the other's expense, just as with involuntary transfer profit, it is clearly superior since the person who loses, chooses to make the transfer. It is difficult to find fault with this.

The moral controversy seems to be whether an effective society requires the promotion of altruism to overcome the negative consequences of unbridled egoism. Fortunately, there is a moderate alternative that stands between the two extremes. That compromise is voluntary exchange. In this case, Person 1 chooses to give something to Person 2 while simultaneously receiving something back in return. From the principles of voluntary exchange each person gives up something of less personal value than what they receive, leading to gains to both people.

Whether exchange-transfer-actions are egoistic or altruistic depends on one's perspective. In Adam Smith's butcher-baker story, he emphasizes the egoistic aspects of exchange; that each person exchanges because they expect to benefit. However, one could just as easily focus on the giving side of the exchange. Each person produces something that will be given to another, thus generating benefits. From this perspective each person's actions are altruistic.

Since the effect of exchange is a benefit to both people, it stimulates the best aspects of egoism and altruism. Notice that voluntary exchange consists of two simultaneous actions precisely like the altruistic voluntary transfer case—each person chooses to give something to another. In this way voluntary exchange can be thought of as an altruism pairing. Also, since each person benefits from the giving of the other, people may be willing to partake in exchange because they are egoistic. However, egoism in this exchange case is not the same as the application of egoism in the involuntary transfer case because neither person chooses to take something from another; instead both sides of the transaction are voluntary.

The point of this diversion into egoism and altruism is to make the following claim: most of the presumed evils in the world arise because of reactions to involuntary transfers, not because of the egoism or greed inherent in the individual chooser. Those who argue that we need to squash human egoism and promote altruism are partially correct but partially misguided. Egoism and greed are definitely associated with the negative outcomes arising out of involuntary transfers. Altruism is also clearly associated with the positive outcomes arising with voluntary transfers. However, to disparage egoism in favor of altruism also condemns the positive interactions that arise out of voluntary exchange, and, as will be suggested in the next section, it is the growth of voluntary exchanges that has stimulated most of the advances of modern human society.

At the same time, free market advocates who sometimes seem to suggest, like Gordon Gekko, that greed is always good are also exaggerating their point.[8] Egoism and greed that stimulates voluntary exchange is clearly beneficial, but that same greed is detrimental when it motivates involuntary transfers. Thus, greed is not always good. At the same time, the elimination of greed is clearly bad, since it would incapacitate one of mankind's most important advances: voluntary exchange.

Profit Seeking and the Evolution of the Modern Economy

When scientists discuss the behavior of man in modern society they often recognize that man evolved over hundreds of thousands of years and that many of the traits embodied in man's behavior are those adapted to a much more primitive way of life. Modern recorded society has existed for little more than 5,000 years. In evolutionary terms, that is like the blink of an eye. With this in mind we can inquire into the fundamental evolutionary tendencies of man and animals with respect to the methods used to seek profit (i.e., to benefit themselves) and consider how and why those methods have evolved in modern times.

Consider first the method used by a carnivorous animal, such as a lion, to acquire the food it needs to survive. After taking up a position hidden in the high grass, downwind from where a herd of zebra is grazing, the lion will wait until the herd approaches sufficiently near. Then with a sudden burst of speed and energy the lion will burst into the open and pursue the animal closest and easiest to attack. The victim will often be a younger or weaker member of the herd. After pouncing upon, and bringing down the hapless prey, the lion will brutally bite into the neck of the animal to quickly incapacitate and kill it. Afterwards, the lion and its pride will leisurely devour the zebra.

As the feast progresses, other animals in the vicinity will smell or see the new food source. Rarely will other animals attempt to steal the prey away from the lions since they understand the lions will protect their food with deadly force if necessary. At this stage we might say that the lions effectively own the carcass since they have the power to protect it for their own consumption. Nevertheless, were the lions to leave the carcass unattended, other animals would quickly descend upon it to claim it as their own, in the approximate order of more to less powerful. Thus, this implicit ownership of a food source lasts only as long as the animal remains prepared to defend it.

Once the lions have had their fill and move on, the remains of the carcass become the food source of hyenas, birds, small mammals, and eventually the bacteria that will return the animal's body to the earth.

Every living thing on the earth requires food, air, and water to satisfy its most basic need; to remain alive. In nature, every living thing satisfies this need by taking it from its environment. The plants take the nutrients from the soil where its seed has sprouted and uses the rays of the sun that fall upon it. Animals take the fruits, nuts, and seeds from other living organisms. Carnivores use their speed, power, intelligent instincts, and other evolved traits to take the lives of other living creatures. Every creature on earth survives by taking what it needs to survive. No one asks permission. To the extent that ownership, or a claim, to a food source exists, it is fleeting, lasting only as long as the animal is prepared to defend it.

In terms of the methods of seeking profit described above, the natural state is involuntary transfers between egoistic species. The plants whose leaves are eaten, or whose fruits and seeds are taken by other animals, do not choose to provide these to others. The animals that become a food source for other animals never choose to do so. These actions are always involuntary; the animals that take food to survive never ask permission from the provider. Involuntary transfers are the basic state of nature.[9]

Next, consider premodern humans. Early humans survived like all other animals, either collecting edible fruits, seeds, and plants, or killing animals in the wild. However, as human capacities developed, they also developed the ability to plan for the future. With this came the creation of tools for specific purposes—tools that could be used over and over again for hunting or cooking—capital equipment in modern parlance. With the ability to plan for the future, man also learned to store food that had been collected or killed.[10]

The development of agriculture via the cultivation of grains and the domestication of animals opened up new opportunities for humans. One of the most important features of these new production methods was the reduction of the costs associated with searching for food. In addition, continual experimentation led to the development of more effective tools and cultivation techniques, which increased productive output for a given amount of time and effort. Because costs were reduced and output simultaneously raised, communities began to produce surpluses.

Surpluses in households or communities could be used in two ways. First, they could be stored. Grains could be stored in pots and protected from the elements. Fish and meat could be salted to prevent spoilage. Domestic animals could be bred and kept alive until they were needed for food. Alternatively, surpluses could be traded for other desired items; for example, surplus grain in exchange for fish or tools.

Trade and exchange also developed because of the advances made possible by the division of labor, which allowed individuals to specialize in particular productive activities. Some could become tillers and harvesters, others the caretakers of animals, and others the makers of tools. By specializing in particular occupations, each person would become more knowledgeable about one production activity and accordingly could increase productivity. Because of specialization coupled with the desire of most individuals to consume a variety of goods, surpluses were inevitable. The division of labor enabled each person to produce much more of their specialty item than what they themselves desired of that good. Such a surplus is only valuable if it can be traded for other items whose producers themselves are also faced with a surplus relative to their own desires.

Mutually voluntary exchange facilitates the division of labor and thus is necessary for the success of the agricultural and industrial revolutions. Without trade, the advance of human civilization beyond hunter-gatherer societies is untenable. Nonetheless, although the possibility of trading opportunities can motivate the desire to produce surpluses, which in turn can stimulate the division of labor, the presence of surpluses also has a secondary effect.

As communities become richer, not only will they stockpile grain surpluses and expand the number of domesticated animals, but they will also create a larger stock of tools, implements, housing structures, housewares, and trinkets. This stock of wealth, all of which would be valuable to other humans, accordingly becomes a target for bandits and marauders. Once some communities have some wealth, other groups have choices between two distinct ways to profit; either produce for themselves by exploiting nature directly, or, steal from others.

Taking from nature, although it represents involuntary transfers between species, would be classified as self-profit above, since the hunter-gatherer need not interact with any other human to provide for his own sustenance. However, if the human acquires what he desires by stealing stored, or recently gathered, foodstuffs from other humans, then it becomes an instance of involuntary transfers. Furthermore, one may presume, since throughout evolutionary history humans were used to taking what they needed directly from nature, that taking from other humans instead, either by force or subterfuge, would amount to much the same process. Indeed, one might well argue that it is more natural for man to steal from others, be it nature or other men, than it is to produce and exchange.[11]

Of course, either process involves some cost; taking from other humans can be as difficult and dangerous as taking from nature. However, depending on the circumstances, one or the other will be easier, or less costly, to undertake. One can imagine that early humans would choose whether to take from nature instead of from other humans if either the size of the gain was larger, or the cost, or effort, of doing so was lower. That is, humans would choose the method that generates the greatest net benefits; that is, that which is most profitable.

A community that has not developed the knowledge or ability to produce a surplus itself may find it less costly to create weapons and carry out raids of communities known to possess surplus commodities. Indeed, as the agricultural revolution extends to more communities and as more surpluses develop, we might expect it to become easier for nonsurplus communities to take from others rather than taking directly from nature.[12]

The productive trading communities, of course, will try to defend their possessions from these bandits. Thus, some of their surplus production will need to be diverted to produce weapons for defense and perhaps, in larger communities, defenses such as walls and a security force; all this to protect their "property" or possessions.

This simple story suggests that the evolution of modern human society can be seen as a transition from a state in which humans satisfied their needs entirely via involuntary transfers to a state in which humans satisfy their needs via production and voluntary exchanges. An important lesson of modern economics is that the growth of living standards depends critically on specialization and the division of labor, which in turn depends on the viability of mutually voluntary exchanges. To make the growth of human welfare possible, societies have developed a variety of mechanisms that serve to promote voluntary exchange (e.g., establishment of rules regarding private property) and to ward off the potential for involuntary transfers (e.g., moral dictates like "thou shalt not steal"). However, although the transition to a society with a preponderance of mutually voluntary exchanges and the elimination of involuntary transfers is well on its way, it is neither complete nor inevitable.

Property

The operation of voluntary exchange, involuntary transfers, and voluntary transfers requires an implicit assumption: the items exchanged or transferred belong to the people involved in the transaction. Ownership claims arise in a variety of ways; from a simple assertion that what I possess is mine, to a formal legal title issued by a government carefully identifying the property and the person or entity that owns it. The legitimacy of property ownership claims is a complicated question that has motivated substantial discussion and debate over the centuries.

John Locke argued that individuals own themselves and as a consequence can also claim any products that come from the exertion of one's own effort. Thus, when an individual combines his labor effort with wood from the forest and produces a table, the table can rightly be regarded as his property. Even simple stories like this are fraught with complications, though. Thus, one could ask whether the wood taken from the forest was rightfully his before he applied his labor.[13] Nevertheless, despite the complications, I would expect that if another person steals away the first person's table and claims it as his own, the original producer would surely object. Thus, legitimate or not, the producer believes the table is his. This suggests that the concept of property is prior to any state regulation or philosophical definition. In nature, people will often collect or take whatever they are capable of, and will effectively claim the items as their own. Theft is only considered theft if the original holder of the stolen items believes they are legitimately his own; for if he does not, there can be no complaint.

The fear of losing ones claimed property also inspires efforts to defend that property from being taken by others. One method of defense is the creation of a security force, whose members develop the weapons and expertise needed to protect the surplus from theft. In exchange for these services the defenders can receive a share of the surpluses generated. In this way a benevolent government can develop whose primary mission is to protect the property of citizens in a community.

However, just as weapons can be used to defend, so they can also be used to attack and control. Thus, as mentioned before, as surpluses became prominent in agrarian societies, it also became easier to apply effort to the production of weapons and to establish armies that could effectively steal the surpluses away from the producers. It is in this way that malevolent governments are formed.

In modern societies complex legal practices and institutions have developed to protect claims to private property, especially with regards to land, but also with regards to financial assets, inventions, trademarks, artistic creations, and even radio frequency bandwidth. Formal legal titles to property are regularly provided, monitored, and enforced by government agencies. Nevertheless, not every possible valuable asset is currently titled around the world. Informal or implicit property rights remain an important element in some sectors and in some countries.

Hernando De Soto (2000) offers an excellent survey of informal, or extralegal, property arrangements that persist in many developing countries. Perhaps the most memorable is his suggestion to use the barking of dogs to identify who lays claim to property in rural areas.

He writes: "As I strolled through rice fields, I had no idea where the property boundaries were. But the dogs knew. Every time I crossed from one farm to another, a different dog barked. Those Indonesian dogs may have been ignorant of formal law, but they were positive about which assets their masters controlled" (162).

Following the barking dogs offers a useful metaphor to think about ways to identify other informal assignments of property rights in many different contexts. De Soto's book is an excellent guide to both formal and informal property right arrangements both today and throughout history.

In the rest of this book, we will not take up the complicated issue of property, except to say that it is an important requirement both to facilitate voluntary exchanges and to explain the negative reactions to involuntary transfers. Without property, exchanges will not take place. Without property it is impossible to have something stolen away.

Next Steps

The chapters that follow will elaborate upon the concepts of voluntary exchange, involuntary transfers and voluntary transfers. Chapter 7 will show that involuntary transfers are common in modern society in forms that go well beyond simple theft. With the evolution of a complex society comprised of an equally complex set of operating rules, people have developed clever techniques to transfer benefits to themselves while at the same time justifying these actions as fulfilling a social purpose. Whenever these actions are recognized as involuntary transfers, as they often are by at least some observers, they are roundly chastised. Indeed, I will argue that many of the complaints people have about the way society functions, on all sides of the political spectrum, are inherently complaints about perceived instances of involuntary transfers. Sometimes these perceptions are accurate, but at other times it seems likely that people form false impressions. One objective of research, then, is to determine in which circumstances the perceptions of involuntary transfers are valid.

Chapter 8 will illustrate how an economy is likely to function if it operates strictly on the principle of free, mutually voluntary, exchanges; a principle consistent with a free market competitive economy. The chapter will demonstrate that both positive and negative outcomes are likely to arise in a dynamic free market. The realization of losses, which is a natural outcome when markets function appropriately, is nonetheless sometimes characterized in terms of involuntary transfers. I will contend that this is what leads, in part, to the negative reactions some have about profit seeking and the operation of free markets.

Chapter 9 discusses manifestations of voluntary transfers, or gifts in modern society. These transfers become possible only after a society establishes a surplus in production. It seems natural, in modern times at least, that a compassionate society would share a portion of its surplus with those who are unable to satisfy their most basic needs or who may not be able to achieve a certain minimum standard of living. Sharing is notably encouraged by most moral and religious codes. Some contend that a compassionate society ought to consist of a preponderance of voluntary transfers. Unfortunately, the positive productive incentives, which can raise people's living standards in a free market economy, are likely to be discouraged by an overexpansion of voluntary transfer activity.

The more important implication of this discussion is to suggest that a focus on understanding and distinguishing the three types of profit seeking provides an analytical framework for the choice of public policy. As will be explained, the framework lies squarely in the middle of popular opinions across the political spectrum. As such it represents a true moderate compromise proposal.

The application of this framework is different from current methods. The common analytical framework applied today is to ask whether any proposed policy is "good" in some overall sense. Does the policy raise national welfare? Is the policy economically efficient? Do the positive effects, economic and otherwise, outweigh the negative effects? Is the policy fair? As discussed in earlier chapters, these questions cannot be answered with a high degree of confidence using the available metrics.

The alternative is to consider public policies in light of the degree to which they might stimulate voluntary exchange and voluntary transfers and discourage involuntary transfers. In the end, the overall welfare objective remains the same, except that now, the same objective is sought indirectly by thinking how policies and institutions affect profit-seeking behavior.

CHAPTER 7

Involuntary Transfers

Transfer profit is a benefit received by one agent as a direct consequence of a comparable loss to another. With transfer profit, one party gains, the other loses equally; nothing new is produced. There is no surplus value accruing as with voluntary exchange. There are two variations of transfer profit. Involuntary transfer profit, discussed in this chapter, occurs when the losing party must suffer the transfer unwillingly or unknowingly. In contrast, voluntary transfer profit, discussed in chapter 9, arises when the losing party makes the transfers willingly, as with charity or philanthropy.

Numerous types of economic activities and behaviors are manifestations of involuntary transfers. Some examples are obvious. However, many others become recognizable only after searching for it. In some instances involuntary transfers occur in isolation, while in other cases they are confounded with other interactions such as voluntary exchange. Sometimes involuntary transfers are abhorred by society, at other times they are defended as necessary to secure a fair economic or social outcome.

This chapter provides numerous examples of involuntary transfers to demonstrate that they are widespread throughout society and that its presence, whether actual or perceived, is the source of many economic and social complaints across the political spectrum. For example, when critics of globalization complain about the evils of profit seeking, when they argue that large multinational corporations are controlling the decisions of government institutions, when they openly worry about harmful labor market practices in developing countries, they are reacting to manifestations of involuntary transfers. Similarly, when free market advocates complain about the vast power of the government to transfer money away from people and control the decisions they can make, when they support management over labor unions, or when they support competition policies, they too are reacting to manifestations of involuntary transfers. Even the disdain for the ravages of war represents a negative reaction to involuntary transfers.

This chapter will highlight several distinct forms of involuntary transfer profit including theft, cheating and dishonesty, military conquest, exploitation, government transfers, anticompetitive practices, and externality effects. Some examples overlap with the globalization debate; those that do not will serve to illustrate the pervasiveness of involuntary transfers.

The presence of involuntary transfers has prompted the development of a variety of defenses. Often the defenses appear as moral codes that individuals are taught as they grow up. In many cases these same principles are codified into public law with proscribed penalties if violations occur. Finally, some defenses involve protections in the form of police and military forces. The chapter argues that all of these features of modern society are in place to defend individuals from becoming a victim to involuntary transfers.

Finally, this chapter will evaluate involuntary transfers in terms of the fairness principles discussed in chapter 4. It is shown that involuntary transfers are unfair with respect to most of the principles. The one noteworthy exception is with respect to distributional fairness. Nonetheless the argument made here is that the concerns that pro–free trade groups have about some policies have the same fundamental foundations as the concerns of social justice groups have about other policies; both sides are reacting to perceived injustices, that is the unfairness of involuntary transfers.

Thievery, Cheating, and Corruption

The clearest example of involuntary transfers is theft. Whenever one person takes something without assent from another, the first person benefits at the direct expense of the other. Transfer profit via theft is always involuntary. This is the reason a thief will take property secretly, as with burglary; or will steal the item unexpectedly and quickly flee, as with purse snatching; or will threaten or resort to violence as with armed robbery. In the latter case, the use of force is intended to convince the property holder that resistance will lead to a much greater harm.

In the modern world, there are many creative methods used to transfer money from one person to another. For example, sometimes a person devises a way to electronically transfer money from one bank account into another. Other times someone offers to sell a good or service, but after receiving payment does not provide the promised item. Scams of this sort are commonplace around the world.

Theft via Imperfect Information

In other instances, thieves manipulate information in market dealings in ways that transfer money in their direction. In order for a competitive market to function the way it does in textbook examples, agents need good information. Accurate and complete information is important to consumers who need to know the prices as well as the quality of the products they purchase. For many products, a consumer can easily learn the price and quality; for other products, they may be difficult to observe. Consider the consumer dilemma that arises with automobile repair.

When an individual's car begins to malfunction it is brought to an auto repair shop. The service the consumer wishes to purchase is a well-functioning car at the lowest possible price. Initially neither the buyer or the seller knows which parts must be replaced and how much labor will be required to produce the intended result. Once the repair shop identifies the problem, an estimate for the total cost is typically provided to the consumer who can either accept or reject the offer. However, the consumer rarely knows the true nature of the problem or what it should cost to repair. Thus, the consumer is at the mercy of the seller because the seller has better information about the product than the buyer. Economists refer to this as a case of asymmetric information.[1]

It is easy to see how asymmetric information can lead to bad outcomes. If the auto repair shop is honest, there is no problem. It will provide accurate information about the source of the malfunction and will repair the problem at a price that covers the cost of production plus a reasonable profit. However, one can never be sure if the mechanic is honest. The best way for the consumer to be sure what is the true problem and a reasonable price for repair is to take the car to a second mechanic for another opinion (and hope the second mechanic is honest). Unfortunately, this step is time consuming and incurs an opportunity cost. Therefore most consumers will usually accept what the mechanic suggests unless the estimate seems outrageous. Clearly, the mechanic has better information, and it would not be difficult to add additional time and services to the customer's bill in order to increase his own profit at the expense of the consumer. In this case, a dishonest mechanic can transfer extra money, or profit, from the consumer. Part of the transfer is for legitimate services, but some fraction is a pure involuntary transfer. In this example involuntary transfers are confounded with voluntary exchange.

A more significant example of using false information to generate involuntary transfers is the Enron scandal of 2001. In this case, a company that was touted as one of the most successful businesses in the country for five straight years by *Forbes* magazine suddenly turned out to be hiding behind a mountain of false information. The scandal involved continual misreporting of company profits in part by using creative accounting methods and in part through outright lies. As a result Enron was able to promote a rising stock value because a steady stream of investors were eager to participate in the good fortunes of a seemingly successful company. The success of the company during years of deception maintained the high incomes of the management team involved in the cover-up, but also contributed to rising wealth for the employees with retirement funds invested in company stock. However, the income generated and the wealth acquired was based on a lie. When the cover-up became known and it was learned that the profits were little more than creative accounting, investors rapidly divested leading to the collapse of the stock price and ultimately the company itself. Those most hurt were the employees who had most of their savings invested in company stock. Many were left with nothing.

The Enron incident is another example in which involuntary transfers are confounded with voluntary exchange because at the same time the cover-up was occurring, Enron continued to produce legitimate goods and services that generated revenues used to pay wages and profit to the stakeholders of the company. Thus, only a fraction of the profit generated by the company's operations was illegitimate; the rest arose from market exchange.

Bribery

In many countries, corruption in the form of bribe taking is rampant. In many cases bribery takes the form of involuntary transfers. In some instances, government officials may be empowered to grant licenses for certain privileges; for example, to obtain a building permit, or to import a good. By withholding these licenses, or forcing license seekers to wait, officials can extract money for procedures as simple as stamping a document. In this and many other situations government officials who act as gatekeepers can prevent certain activities from taking place unless involuntary transfers (bribes) are made to them.

Easterly (2001, 241–52) takes his readers on a tour of bribery and corruption around the world. He writes of the U.S. beer owner who had several associates appointed to the Environmental Protection Administration (EPA) who thereafter eliminated restrictions allowing the beer company to legally dump toxic waste; Japanese businessmen who offered extravagant entertainment to government officials in return for a favor; the Ecuadorian president who had his agents obtain $3 million in currency for him from the Central Bank as his term expired; the Chinese businessman who allegedly diverted as much as $2.2 billion in public funds as kickbacks on construction projects; and the U.S. company that allegedly paid the Philippine president $80 million to secure the contract to build a nuclear power plant.

Baker (2005) emphasizes that widespread cheating, tax evasion, and corruption takes place in international business and within many governments. One example is cited in which IBM provided a bribe to top officials of Banco de la Nación, the largest national bank in Argentina. For a $250 million contract to provide computers and services, IBM transferred $27 million dollars to foreign bank accounts held by these Argentinean decision makers to secure the business contract. Examples like this are extremely common and surely occur every day around the world.

Worker Exploitation

One major concern of many social justice advocates is the perception of widespread exploitation in the economic marketplace. Typically, multinational corporations are viewed as the principal exploiters, while the workers are the individuals being exploited. Exploitation is difficult to define and often seems to be in the eye of the beholder. However, true economic exploitation represents situations in which money is being involuntarily transferred from one person or group to another. This occurs for one or more of several reasons; if someone receives a lower economic return than is justified by his contribution to production; if the person is not free to voluntarily choose to participate in a market activity; or if a person is forced to endure degrading or harmful situations in an economic activity. In order for exploitation to occur there must be some degree of involuntariness. If not, one would need to explain why individuals would "choose" to be exploited.

One frequently cited example of worker exploitation occurs when someone receives a lower economic return than justified. What is "justified" is often a subject of debate, however. Some people argue that workers have a right to a "living wage," loosely defined as a wage sufficiently high to help a worker provide for himself and his or her family. To advocates of a living wage, market wages often appear unjustifiably low.

For example, many contend that large multinational corporations generate large incomes for the corporate elites and celebrity sponsors while simultaneously exploiting the vast majority of their workforce by paying abysmally low wages. Evidence of exploitation is the fact that the ratios of CEO salaries to average worker salaries within U.S. companies averages over 500:1.[2] For many, this is sufficient to show that the powerful elites in the company are benefiting off the backs of the working poor.[3]

However, before jumping to the conclusion that there is exploitation, we should look more carefully at the reasons why the wage differential is so high. Economists typically argue that the "justified" wage is the value of the worker's marginal product (VMP), defined as the value each worker contributes to production. This is the additional revenue the firm would earn if the worker works one more hour. In competitive markets, when firms maximize profit, a wage set equal to each worker's value of marginal product defines the profit maximizing and thereby the market-justified wage. Because of the very large supply of unskilled workers, it is possible that in some countries worker productivity is low enough to generate a low market wage. In economic theory, there is no requirement that the wage be sufficient to satisfy any particular standard of living. Many people appreciate this argument, but usually not to the degree of a 500:1 difference in CEO/worker earnings.

If workers are paid less than the value of their marginal product, then it is reasonable to claim economically that they are being exploited.[4] There are numerous stories from developing countries about unskilled migrant workers being underpaid by withholding a percentage of wages from each paycheck. Sometimes workers will be promised a wage, but have substantial amounts withheld at payment time, or employers will postpone payment until long after work has been completed. If the worker quits the job because of the unfair treatment, he loses all hope of being paid. For the employer, there are usually other eager unskilled workers hopeful for an opportunity to work and who are unaware of the deceitful practices. Court systems in these countries are usually ineffective so that enforcement of contracts is weak at best and legal remedies rare. In addition, poor workers have few resources to engage in legal battles anyway. Thus, employers may be able to maintain a system of exploitative underpayment for a considerable period of time.

Another reason some observers see low wages as obvious exploitation may be a presumption that wages should be related to effort. Most everyone accepts that work requires effort and can cause disutility—work is usually no fun! If people could acquire income without any work effort, most would give up work in a minute. The main reason to work is because it provides much-needed income to buy goods and services. Thus, wages compensate for the disutility caused by working.

To illustrate this point, imagine the average day of the CEO of a company like Nike Shoe compared to the average day of a worker on the production line of a Nike shoe factory in Indonesia. The CEO will spend his day in chauffeured limos, catered meetings, riding aboard corporate jets, dining in swank restaurants, most likely at the company's expense. This does not sound like there is much disutility from work at all. Of course, this does not consider the worries, concerns, anxieties, pressures, and heavy responsibility felt by the CEO, but those issues are also mostly ignored by critics of the system. In contrast, during a typical day, a factory worker will awaken early, eat simple homemade meals, commute via bicycle, bus or on foot, and spend the day in a hot noisy factory.

Clearly, the factory worker works every bit as long as the CEO. In terms of effort—the "hard" part of work—the factory worker might be thought to work even harder than the CEO. The amount of stress the worker faces may be as high or higher. And yet, the factory worker might receive only $4 per day for his efforts while NIKE's CEO Mark Parker received $4.16 million annually in 2006, which amounts to $13,800 per day.[5] What can explain this kind of inequity? This enormous gap in wages seems grossly unfair to many observers. If you do not accept that marginal productivity explains all of this difference, then you are left believing that the CEO is being paid way too much relative to the worker.

Exploitation is claimed largely because high incomes accrue to top management and shareholders while the poor factory workers, who, prima facie, appear like they are the one's mostly responsible for producing the "shoe" that's being sold, live in squalid conditions.[6] Furthermore, the working conditions of the factory worker are sometimes unsafe, unhealthy, and dramatically unpleasant in comparison to the corporate elites. On the basis of these assumptions, it would seem the top salary earners in the company are taking a disproportionately large share of revenue and leaving a disproportionately small share for the factory workers. It is as if they are "stealing" money away from workers. Indeed, it is widely believed that the corporate elites are "profiting" at the expense of low paid workers.

Which account is accurate is not important for the point being made here. The point is merely to argue that the prime objection to the actions of multinational firms in this situation is really a concern about involuntary transfers. Critics of multinationals believe that owners and managers are exploiting poor workers by taking too much of the revenue for themselves. Concerns about worker exploitation are simply a manifestation of a more fundamental concern about profit via involuntary transfers.

Private Anticompetitive Practices

Competition in the market prevails when firm's owners, workers, and others engage in mutually voluntary exchanges. This point will be discussed in detail in the next chapter. However, when owners or workers act to restrict competition, it also represents a manifestation of involuntary transfers. There are many different methods economic agents use to keep competition at bay; frequently it will involve government intervention.

Cartels

One method to restrict competition that does not require government help is the formation of a cartel. A cartel occurs when a subset of firms in an industry decide to coordinate their output and pricing decisions. Their objective is to restrict output and raise the market price, thereby allowing firms to achieve something closer to monopoly profit.

Firm owners, and many other stakeholders in the firm, will achieve higher incomes. However, consumers of the product will face a higher price. All of these consumers will reduce their demand; some of them to such an extent that they drop out of the market altogether. The higher prices paid by remaining consumers and the effect on consumption will cause each of them to suffer losses. When economists compare the gains to the firms with the losses to consumers, the losses exceed the gains leading to a reduction in overall economic efficiency. In other words, overall national economic welfare falls as a result of cartel formation.

Most notable for our purposes here is that cartel formation causes a transfer of income to occur from one group of people (consumers) to another group (producers). But is the transfer voluntary or involuntary? Two interpretations are possible. First, one could argue that the natural state of an economy is perfect competition and therefore the cartel arrangement involuntarily transfers income from consumers to the producers relative to the natural state. Alternatively one could recognize that in any voluntary transaction, both parties receive some surplus benefit. However, there may be no proper or natural distribution of the surplus between the traders. If this indeterminateness is accepted, then the cartel formation simply enables one party to capture a greater share of the surplus generated by trade. Since trades continue to occur voluntarily between producers and consumers, the new distribution of income does not represent an involuntary transfer.

Mergers

When two firms in the same industry merge to become a larger firm, it is a step in the direction of monopoly and as such is an anticompetitive practice. There is a large literature in economics about mergers and much of it points to the potential for efficiency improvements that can arise because of fresh management, elimination of redundancies, and other reasons. However, in some cases mergers are clearly an attempt by one firm to eliminate a formidable competitor. Even if the two firms together are too small together to employ monopoly pricing, the merger will still temporarily reduce competition and improve the outcome for the acquiring firm.

Milton Friedman (2002, 26) discusses two possible interpretations for the term free enterprise. "What meaning is to be attributed to "free" as modifying "enterprise?" In the United States, "free" has been understood to mean that anyone is free to set up an enterprise, which means that existing enterprises are not free to keep out competitors except by selling a better product at the same price or the same product at a lower price. In the continental tradition, on the other hand, the meaning has generally been that enterprises are free to do whatever they want, including the fixing of prices, division of markets, and the adoption of other techniques to keep out potential competitors."

Mergers and firm acquisitions (M&As) occur all the time. In recent years, some major combinations included JP Morgan and Bank One, AT&T and Bell South, Glaxo Wellcome and SmithKline Beecham, and America Online with Time-Warner. As these company names reveal, some of them had also merged previously, such as Time Inc. and Warner Communications. Although there are numerous rationales for M&As and while improved efficiency is one possible outcome, M&As raise suspicions that the prime motivation is to prevent competition. In many countries, M&As must be reviewed by a government agency to ensure the combined company does not violate antitrust legislation. However, even though an M&A is approved, it is hard to imagine that the acquiring company will not be achieving at least some reduction in competitive pressures. Whether improved efficiencies that may result from the merger compensate for the temporary reduction in competition is something that would have to be evaluated case by case. Whether the anticompetitive effects of M&A are significant or whether they are relatively minor is also something we do not know. Nevertheless, regardless of the long-term effect, any reduction in competition may lead to higher prices for consumers of the product and thus may represent involuntary transfers from the consumers to producers.

Labor Market Practices

Actions to prevent competition through the formation of cartels is not limited to output markets; similar practices are also undertaken by workers, arguably in response to unfair or exploitative practices by owners and managers. The formation of labor unions to engage in collective bargaining raises the bargaining power of workers vis-à-vis the owners. Just like before, one reasonable interpretation is that collective bargaining simply allows workers to obtain a greater amount of the surplus that arises in every voluntary exchange. For example, suppose workers are willing to work for a firm for any wage greater than $8 per hour; at a lower wage they would walk away and look for other employment. Suppose the firm is willing to pay workers a maximum of $12 per hour. Anything higher and the employer would stop hiring. This means that there is a range of wages that would make both parties willing to enter into exchange. A labor union will attempt to bargain for a larger amount of the surplus. The result may be a contract with a wage at $11.50 per hour rather than $8.50.

However, this example is not an instance of involuntary transfers. Instead it is simply a story about effective techniques to establish distribution of the surplus. However, collective bargaining techniques can become anticompetitive and lead to instances of involuntary transfers.

Consider a case of a labor union that forces workers to be members and pay dues. The inability to opt out of the union creates an involuntary element to the arrangement. Also, since restricting union membership also reduces firm labor supply, the union could effectively force the wage up. This action is analogous to cartel behavior by firms in the output market; only here the action occurs in the labor market. In this case, by artificially restricting supply, the union members are able to shift a greater amount of the surplus away from the owners. Involuntary transfers occur because the losers—the firm owners and the workers who cannot gain access to the union—are made worse off involuntarily.

In a similar vein, consider professional licensing requirements. These are put into place ostensibly to maintain higher quality standards for workers in these professions. For example, the legal profession requires lawyers to pass a very difficult bar exam in order to practice law. The medical profession requires doctors to pass a series of tests in the United States to be qualified to practice medicine. Of course, these standards ensure that the best test takers will become qualified to practice law and medicine, and it is quite likely that on average the better test takers know more and will perform a higher quality service. However, at the same time, it is clear that if standards are kept high enough, they can also serve as an effective barrier to entry in these professions. If this occurs, then voluntary exchanges are prevented, prices are pushed higher in the marketplace and the certified professionals gain transfers at the expense of consumers.

These practices are often controversial. Some people are opposed to labor unions and to strict licensing standards. I suggest that these objections arise from the suspicion or belief that the activities are allowing organized groups to take advantage of others by achieving involuntary transfers. Once again, determining the appropriate policy prescriptions can be difficult because voluntary exchange (providing quality services to consumers) is confounded with involuntary transfers (restrictions on open competition to sustain higher quality). For now, the purpose here is only to suggest that, to the extent that labor market practices such as labor unions or licensing standards are anticompetitive, they represent examples of involuntary transfers.

Government Sponsored Anticompetitive Practices

Private attempts to restrict competition via cartels, mergers, or unionization often fail. This is because the presence of additional profit either stimulates cheating by the participants or the entry of new firms and workers. Some believe that this market response is sufficiently strong that there really is no need for competition policies because the market itself will automatically and eventually revert to free competition. Perhaps because of this reality, firms also recognize that while private actions to restrict competition may fail, government interventions to restrict competition can often be very effective. There are numerous ways this can occur, some of which are discussed below.

Indeed as Epstein (2003b) notes, "the creation of the state poses risks of the very evil that it is supposed to negate.... governments are not only good at protecting the goods and services produced by ordinary individuals. Often they are adept—too adept—at shifting opportunities, advantages and property from one group to another, especially by allowing political majorities to control the destinies of the minorities that live under their rule." Frederic Bastiat (1850) wrote more forcefully, "It is impossible to introduce into society a greater change and a greater evil than this: the conversion of the law into an instrument of plunder."

Import Tariffs

Consider the case of an industry facing competition from foreign imported products. When imports flood in, domestic firms must adjust quickly to the new circumstances or face decline and possible closure. A common response by the import-competing industry is to lobby for increased protection in the form of higher tariffs.

In a simple model, a tariff will protect the domestic industry by raising the local price, thus helping the industry to maintain output, profit, and employment. If not too high, the higher tariff will also increase government revenues. Thus, the workers and owners in the protected industry and the government budget will gain from the tariff. However, the domestic consumer of the product will have to pay a higher price. Consumers will reduce purchases, pay the higher price, and subsequently have less money to spend on other things. In other words, their real income will fall because of the tariff.

Government interference in the market in this case is clearly an anticompetitive practice; a tariff reduces foreign competition. Indeed, the action is called protection because it protects the earnings of the import-competing firms. Since the industry seeks higher income than is possible without government intervention, the solicitation is known as rent seeking. In a broader sense, the effects of a tariff amount to money being taken away from some people and given to other people, albeit not directly. Some individuals in the industry and some government programs receive more income, while all domestic consumers of the product receive less. Since those who lose from the policy are unaware of the losses they incur or have little to no ability to influence the decision or both, the action is a form of involuntary transfer profit.

Agricultural Subsidies

Another example of government intervention with an anticompetitive effect is the use of agricultural subsidies and support programs. These payments, made by governments to support farmers, reduce the effective cost of production and make it possible for many, otherwise inefficient, farms to remain viable. For efficient firms it provides a boost in income as well. The policies cause the domestic price to increase effectively transferring money away from the consumers of agricultural goods and taxpayers who must pay for the subsidies, toward the farmers. For the same reasons outlined above, it is arguable whether these transfers are involuntary, but given that taxpayers and consumers are not allowed to opt out and since there is widespread opposition to these subsidies, clearly many people view the subsidies as involuntary.

Several arguments are used to justify these policies. Most notable are the desire to maintain secure domestic food supplies for national security reasons. Income supports also help to smooth out the price fluctuations that are common in commodity markets and thus fulfill an insurance role. Finally, it is argued that because foreign agricultural industries are heavily supported, domestic interventions are necessary to level the playing field. Nevertheless, the relevant question is whether these concerns justify the involuntary transfers generated by government intervention.

Market Externalities

Although most economists tend to believe in the benefits of an unfettered marketplace, most will also accept that government interventions are justifiable in certain circumstances. One such circumstance is when market externalities are present. As explained in some detail in chapter 3, an externality arises when the economic activity of one agent, be it a firm or a consumer, has an impact on the well-being of another person external to the original market activity itself. The classic example is pollution. When an industrial firm pollutes the air and water in the vicinity of its factory, the people who breathe the air in the local community and use the river downstream may be negatively affected. However, these negative effects are not a part of the production and consumption activities in the market for that product. If firms that pollute do not take into account these negative effects on others, economic theory teaches that firms will over-pollute relative to what would be best from a wider social perspective. In this case, government implemented restrictions on the firm can serve to reduce the negative external effects and raise economic efficiency and social well-being.

Many other types of externalities are well known. Although many arise from production activities, some arise from consumption too. For example, the consumption of gasoline in consumer automobiles causes air pollution in the community, a negative effect upon others. Some externalities are positive in their effect. Thus, when a firm conducts R&D, some of the knowledge it acquires for its own use may nonetheless spillover into applications in other industries. External industries may acquire the useful knowledge via channels as simple as bar room conversations between researchers from different firms.

Positive externality effects transfer benefits to another individual or group and as such are not objectionable. Nevertheless, the creator of the externality, because there is no monetary return for the positive effects, is likely to under produce the product relative to what is optimal from a social perspective. In these cases, government subsidies can be used to achieve a more desirable social outcome.

Negative externalities, however, ARE objectionable to the person or group that is negatively affected. These effects are unintended byproducts of production or consumption activities. Typically, the creator of the external effects is not maliciously trying to harm others in order to benefit himself. However, the creator may be reluctant to prevent the external effects for several reasons. First of all, the negative impacts may not be felt immediately. If an industry dumps toxic chemicals in a nearby field, it may take years before it begins to affect the groundwater. Secondly, it will be costly to prevent the negative effects. Installing pollution abatement technology can be very expensive. If these costs are high enough, and especially if the negative effects become known only much later, the firm would not wish to suffer a reduction in profit to produce in a cleaner manner.

Nonetheless, because the polluter's costs would be higher if the product were produced in a way that caused no negative external effect on others, it is reasonable to claim that a part of the polluter's profits are related to the losses incurred by others. As such, negative externalities like pollution are an example of involuntary transfers.

Military Conquest

Offensive military actions can be thought of as theft on a grand scale since it involves one group forcibly taking control of the possessions and even the individuals from another group. As mentioned in the last chapter, when prehistoric societies began to produce surplus food and valuable tools, it became possible for other human groups to acquire what they needed to survive by forcibly taking (i.e., stealing) from other people rather than taking from nature and producing things for themselves. As human civilization grew, so did the resources devoted to build weapons rather than tools. Thus, military conquest is a notable and historically widespread example of involuntary transfers.

Historical writings sometimes celebrate the accomplishments of great military leaders. But, consider the economics of military conflicts. In particular, think about all of the individuals involved fighting these battles and wars; they all require food, clothing, shelter, and military equipment to support and sustain them. As populations grew, the sizes of the armies also grew. Alexander the Great's army had as many as 40,000 men. Genghis Khan had an army of over 100,000 men. Napoleon invaded Russia with over 500,000 troops. During these campaigns, the soldiers are not actively engaged in any productive activity that creates food, clothing, shelter, or military equipment. Thus, to sustain themselves, armies require resources that must be taken from somebody else. In ancient times, the conquering armies demanded tribute, or simply raided the stockpiles of food, clothing, and equipment from the towns and villages that were overrun. Armies were notorious for taking other things besides goods, including taking people into slavery or servitude and the rape of women and children.

When supplies ran out, an army could simply move on to another town or village whose surplus supplies had not yet been plundered.

In modern times, armies are supported by government expenditures, which is available because it has been transferred from taxpayers. Taxes come from the incomes of people who have produced something. Had taxes not been paid, these individuals would have spent the money on other goods and services. Instead, when taxes are paid, this consumption is shifted and used for military purposes. Thus, in these situations, goods, services, and other benefits are transferred from one group of people to another. Thus, offensive military endeavors are clear examples of profit from transfers.

Whether the transfer is voluntary or not depends importantly on one's perception of government programs. In a democracy, are taxes paid voluntarily because the populace has voted for representatives who in turn have collected taxes to pay for the military? Or, are the taxes involuntary because a refusal to pay may land one in jail? This issue is discussed later in this chapter and in chapter 9.

Defensive Responses to Involuntary Transfers

Examples of involuntary transfers, including the simple and obvious ones like theft, to more obscure examples like negative externalities, highlight the many ways that one group of people can benefit from the losses of others. In most instances, the losers, or victims, of these actions do not generally sit back and endure the losses unless the effects are well hidden. Instead, a sizeable number of defenses have arisen to protect people from the losses arising from involuntary transfers.

For example, a variety of strategies are used to defend against personal injury. Self-defense techniques provide the wherewithal to repel an attacker. Mace, pepper sprays, and brass knuckles can have a similar effect. The right to bear arms and own guns in the United States has been justified throughout history as a necessary measure to ensure protection for people. Bank tellers, presidents of countries, and the Pope are all protected with bulletproof glass.

To protect personal property from theft, people install locks on doors and windows and place valuable possessions inside safes. Fences and gates are used to prevent entry to personal properties. Security guards are hired to protect businesses, and residential communities. Finally, police are trained and mobilized in communities to protect against loss of property and injury to people. To empower the police, laws have been established allowing police to detain persons suspected of crimes against others and establishing procedures for verification and punishment of those caught injuring others and stealing property.

The threat of attack from other countries creates a demand for a national defense to protect, not only possessions, but also the nation's freedom and culture. Thus, countries maintain standing armies; build tanks, fighter jets, and aircraft carriers; develop nuclear and biological weapons; and establish espionage agencies to monitor the behavior of suspected individuals and countries.

There are a variety of defensive responses to other forms of involuntary transfers as well. States have established numerous laws to prohibit fraud, corruption, and bribery. States attorneys are typically empowered to investigate and prosecute individuals and businesses accused of violating these laws. Punishment, if caught and convicted, may serve as a deterrent.

Laws are also in place to prevent the misuse of information; businesses are not allowed to falsely advertise or make unsubstantiated claims about their products; securities brokers are not allowed to take advantage of insider information; and public companies are not allowed to falsely represent their business accounts and must submit to periodic audits for assurance purposes.

Other laws are put in place to mitigate concerns about worker exploitation. Minimum wage laws, occupational health and safety standards, and even prohibitions against slavery and indentured servitude, are all intended to prevent, at least to some degree, involuntary transfers.

Finally, some involuntary transfers that arise due to anticompetitive behavior also have legislation against it in many countries. Antitrust laws, and the necessary clearance for mergers, both serve to check monopoly formation. Even free trade areas and the agreements reached under the WTO, by helping countries to commit to freer trade policies, also helps ensure a lower amount of involuntary transfers achieved through government policy.

Defensive Responses as Involuntary Transfers

Defense generates well-being because it reduces the fears and anxieties that arise because of the possibility that theft, personal injury or other involuntary losses may occur. Because defensive goods and services are produced and purchased in the marketplace, we could think of these as an example of voluntary exchange. However, defensive goods and services themselves are demanded only because of the threats that are posed by others. In the absence of these threats—that is, in a perfect or ideal world—people would not demand these goods and services. Thus, we can think of the demands for defensive goods and services as being indirectly involuntary.

Using theft as an example, when a thief robs someone at gunpoint in a community, knowledge of the crime within the community raises the possibility in their minds that they too may become a victim in the future. That fear generates the demand for defensive goods and services. Since the thieves create the fear, thieves are also responsible for the existence of this market activity. In other words, the behavior of thieves generates a negative externality effect. For this reason, the demand for defensive goods is ultimately involuntary; people are forced into it by the potential actions of others.

The purchase of defensive goods and services also incurs an opportunity cost that is different than the cost of other goods. If less defense (or, in the extreme, no defense) were necessary, then the time, effort, and resources that went into the creation of defensive goods and services would be available to produce what might be called primary goods and services; that is, goods and services that are demanded because the goods themselves provide well-being. Examples of primary goods are food, clothing, automobiles, refrigerators, and hotel and entertainment services.

Who incurs the opportunity cost, and thus who loses, depends on the way defensive goods are financed. For personal or private protection, individuals self-finance by allocating some portion of their household or business budgets toward alarm systems, security guards, or gun purchases. Consequently, they forgo the purchase of other things. In this way they suffer a loss in comparison to the ideal circumstance in which no defensive activities would be required. Of course, in comparison to the true state of the world, in which fear of involuntary transfers is real, the defensive expenditures are worthwhile and this is why they are made. Nevertheless, even self-financed defensive expenditures qualify as an example of involuntary transfers. The winners in this situation are the successful perpetrators of involuntary transfers (i.e., the thieves), as well as those who benefit from the production of defensive goods and services.

The second method to finance the purchase of defensive goods and services is via the use of public funds. Tax revenues finance law enforcement agencies and provide for a national military defense. Taxes also finance the judicial system and agencies whose purpose is to enforce contracts, protect private property, and prevent anticompetitive monopoly formation. As with private financing, these expenditures incur an opportunity cost. In this case the cost is borne by the taxpayers who must forgo other (primary) goods and services. The redistribution, or involuntary transfers, occurs between taxpayers (who presumably do receive the benefits of protection just as with private financing) and the providers of defensive (secondary) goods and services.

With defensive goods provision there is a notable difference with previous examples of involuntary transfers: the receivers of the benefits are not the agents causing the transfer to take place. While thieves, in the simple example, do benefit from the crime, additional benefits accrue to the providers of defensive goods. This can generate some additional negative effects.

Recognizing that defensive responses to many forms of involuntary transfers are inevitable because the threats will never disappear entirely, the transfers that arise here also cannot be avoided. However, the level of defense that is provided can be affected by manipulating information. If the probability that an incident like theft will occur is perfectly known then, in a private context at least, one could calculate an acceptable amount to spend for defense. However, when the probabilities are unknown, or when taxpayers finance the cost, it is conceivable that defense is overprovided. Here are two plausible examples.

First of all in a private setting, a security firm selling residential alarm services might exaggerate the threat of burglary in its advertisements in order to raise community fears and secure larger sales. Although, the defensive expenditures may be wanted and needed by potential victims to a certain degree, a customer might nonetheless wind up with a much more secure house and have spent much more than true information might have warranted. In this case the security firm is eliciting greater than an appropriate amount of involuntary transfers.

A more extensive problem of a similar nature might be apparent in the size of defense expenditures in many countries. Although a national defense is perhaps worthy of considerable expenditures and while most taxpayers have no problem, in principle, with making contributions, international security threats may be overemphasized by those who stand to benefit from the defense spending. In 1960, U.S. President Eisenhower warned of the growing influence of the "military–industrial complex." Since then, military expenditures continue to grow while many critics regularly contend that defense firms themselves are responsible for a considerable amount of unnecessary spending. To the extent that national security fears are exaggerated, or when defense firms use their lobbying clout to elicit greater than necessary transfers, involuntary transfers are also greater than necessary.

Fairness and Involuntary Transfers

With respect to the fairness principles, involuntary transfers are mostly unfair. Involuntary transfers occur whenever one person or group gains at the direct expense of another person or group. While the most common examples are theft, offensive military incursions, corruption, and fraud, involuntary transfers also occur in the minds of some observers, when governments tax its citizens.

That an involuntary transfer, such as theft, is unfair is easy to see vis-à-vis the fairness principles discussed in chapter 4. First, it clearly violates positive reciprocity fairness since the transfer involves a gain to one person and an equal loss to another. There is no positive reciprocity whatsoever. Second, due to the defense mechanisms that are usually inspired to ward off involuntary transfers, the net effect is more likely to be negative than zero. This implies that involuntary transfers are not fair in terms of maximum benefit fairness.

In terms of the golden rule, involuntary transfers are not something one would wish others to do toward oneself so it is not fair on this basis to transfer or take something away from another. In terms of privacy fairness, the person who has something taken away—the victim—has not done anything to the perpetrator and thus the victim's privacy is clearly infringed. Finally, with respect to nondiscrimination, although the victims of involuntary transfer can be anyone, it is more likely that those who suffer losses are more vulnerable in some respect. The victims are relatively weaker, less educated, older, or more frail. In these situations, involuntary transfers do tend to discriminate and is unfair on this account.

The tendency for involuntary transfers to occur to certain weaker groups often provides a justification to use similar transfers in reverse. Thus, if someone believes that the income inequality in a country is mostly due to powerful groups exploiting its weaker citizens, then one might favor a government sponsored redistributive effort. By using progressive taxes, societies can transfer income from the relatively wealthier to those whose incomes are lower. In this way involuntary

Table 7.1 Consistency of Involuntary Transfers with Fairness Principles

Distributional	Yes and No
Nondiscrimination	No
Golden Rule	No
Positive Reciprocity	No
Negative Reciprocity	No
Privacy	No
Maximum Benefit	No

transfers can be used to equalize incomes in a society and thus might be considered fair from that perspective.

Also, although the laws or regulations calling for punishment of those who commit involuntary transfers will generally conform to negative reciprocity fairness, the transfer activity itself is not fair with respect to negative reciprocity since there is no balanced reciprocal action. Nevertheless, for those who believe that involuntary transfers in the marketplace have created exploited victims who have suffered losses as a consequence, one can argue that causing reciprocal losses to the relatively wealthy via progressive taxation is fair with respect to negative reciprocity.

Table 7.1 offers a summary of the fairness characteristics of involuntary transfers. Note that involuntary transfer profit is mostly unfair with the exception of possible redistribution schemes like progressive taxation that can mitigate distributional fairness concerns.

Conclusion

In summary, involuntary transfers, in its most egregious form, such as with outright theft, is easy to characterize as unfair, and most people would probably accept the interpretation. Involuntary transfers are unfair in terms of privacy fairness, reciprocity fairness, the golden rule, maximum benefit fairness, and nondiscrimination fairness. However, other occurrences of involuntary transfers, as with progressive taxation (which again we could argue as to what portion of taxes is involuntary), can be characterized as fair with respect to distributional fairness and negative reciprocity.

Involuntary transfers appear to be the root cause of virtually all claims of injustice. People react sharply and instinctively against anyone else seen to be profiting by taking something away either from themselves or from someone they care about. One problem we face is that every group sees involuntary transfers in different places and in different intensities.

Some people see involuntary transfers in exploitative wages and horrible working conditions of some workers in some places. They believe that the high income earners in those industries are taking advantage of its often unskilled and uneducated workforce. Other people see involuntary transfers in the taxation policies of governments who take money away from its citizens coercively. Some see involuntary transfers when pharmaceutical companies maintain high drug prices in developed countries and use their political clout to prevent importation of cheaper substitutes. Other people see it when immigrants illegally enter a country and take away jobs from its citizens, commit crimes, or receive government-financed benefits. Some see involuntary transfers when foreign firms purportedly dump their products on foreign markets in order to achieve monopoly advantages in the future. Others see it when some countries violate their commitments made in the WTO and gain an advantage over other countries. Some see involuntary transfers when multinational firms disregard the environment and fail to protect endangered animal species. Others see it when a government writes rules and regulations that give advantages to some firms over others. Finally, some see involuntary transfers when a country engages in military conflict with another.

While the complaints about policy choices on both sides can be attributed to reactions to involuntary transfers, both sides also tend to advocate involuntary transfer methods to correct for other economic problems. This leads to an inconsistency. For example, social justice advocates often promote redistributive policies such as minimum wages and higher corporate profit taxes. For supporters of these policies, government is supposed to regulate markets to achieve more desirable results and thus it is considered acceptable policy. However, free market advocates often see these same policies as infringements on the freedom of private markets.

Some who oppose taxation policies on grounds of inequity, may also accept certain protectionist policies like antidumping that protect domestic firms from so-called unfair foreign competition. They might also accept selected industrial policies to promote national security via farm or technology subsidies and to promote intellectual property right protections. However, these policies also use the power of government to restrict free market exchange and facilitate the involuntary transfers from some groups to other groups.

The next chapter will consider the manifestations of voluntary exchange in market economies and investigate the effects if free voluntary exchange is allowed to prevail, and will consider the fairness properties of voluntary exchange. The chapter will argue that while voluntary exchange will generate some unfavorable effects, it is also shown to be mostly fair with respect to the fairness principles.

CHAPTER 8

Voluntary Exchange and Competition

Mutually voluntary exchange is the best example of a win-win situation. Whenever a bilateral exchange occurs, both parties must profit, for if not, one party would simply have refused to trade. This basic result is sometimes used to argue that a free market economy, consisting of billions or trillions of bilateral voluntary exchanges, must therefore be to the benefit of everyone. In one sense this is true, but upon a more careful investigation, it is also misleading. To clarify the distinction, this chapter will explain in some detail how competitive markets are likely to work. However, the competitive process we need to understand is not the "perfect competition" described in standard economic models. Rather, we need to understand dynamic competition as described by Joseph Schumpeter (1942) when he talked about *creative destruction*. For Schumpeter, the crucial economic dynamic was one in which new businesses rise up in a creative process while existing businesses are simultaneously destroyed. Friedrich Hayek described this same dynamic competition when he discussed *competition as a discovery process* and the free market as a "*spontaneous economic order.*"[1]

This chapter provides a detailed description of dynamic competition in response to one commonly suggested policy change; trade liberalization. It demonstrates that when competition works without impediments or restraints, that is, when it works as envisioned, it is rife with ups and downs, winners and losers. The positives occur as creative, innovative businesses, new and old, improve quality, adjust product characteristics, and reduce production costs ahead of their competition. The negatives occur for all who try, but fail, to realize these same outcomes. These firms are relatively less creative, less innovative, and less lucky than the winners. As a result jobs are lost and painful transitions occur.

Because of the rhetorical necessities described in chapter 5, proponents of trade liberalization will typically emphasize the innovative aspects of competition, the likelihood of economic growth, the raising of "average" incomes and many other positive outcomes. They will also tend to minimize the real strains and pressures associated with well-functioning competitive systems. They even seem to suggest that these "problems" are merely transitory and will disappear in time. But such is not the case. A competitive market will be a continual swirl of changes—a kind of churning—that will regularly act to force some firms out of existence with their employees losing jobs and being forced to adjust and change.

This chapter will emphasize that the fear and anxiety created in the dynamic competitive process is critically important as a motivator for the creative, innovative process itself. This tension and anxiety are *necessary* stimulants to business experimentation and discovery. For this reason, trying to protect those who lose in the competitive process is counterproductive since it will act to stifle creativity and innovation. Thus, these kinds of losses must be accepted as an unfortunate, but necessary, by-product of competition.

Furthermore, suggestions by economists to compensate the losers from trade liberalization with gains from the winners is problematic since compensation will reduce anxieties faced by potentially uncompetitive firms and thereby reduce the overall effectiveness of the competitive process. Although compensation may be suggested as a means to induce political support, its cost is a weakening of the competitive system. As such, compensation, when provided, is an example of objectionable involuntary transfers rather than voluntary exchange.

Free Market Competitive Responses to Trade Liberalization

Consider the impact of a policy change that inspires significant adjustments throughout an economy. The policy change chosen is trade liberalization; however, similar effects can be expected with any policy change that causes numerous prices to adjust. As such trade liberalization mimics the effects of policy changes more generally. Of course, admittedly, markets do not currently operate exactly as described below. This is largely because businesses and interest groups have managed to induce their governments to implement policies and regulations that act to impede free and open competition. Nevertheless, numerous markets remain highly competitive, especially in developed countries, thus the adjustments described below do correspond to real-world processes to a degree I assume firms respond to competition with competitive responses rather than reverting to involuntary transfer mechanisms to protect themselves. In this way, we can examine how a market would work in more ideal circumstances. It is worth noting that this more idealized market process is probably the way most economists imagine markets can work.

A trade liberalization policy change means a reduction of tariffs collected on imported goods. Trade liberalization can also involve the elimination of internal rules or restrictions that previously prevented foreign goods from being supplied freely and easily. In either case, trade liberalization will increase the degree of competition faced by domestic industries.

Import Country Effects

As trade liberalization reduces the prices of imported goods, domestic import-competing industries will be forced to adjust. Consider the clothing industry. Domestic clothing consumers will now face a choice between buying lower priced imported clothing or the somewhat higher priced domestic clothing. If the products are seen as almost identical, a consumer will switch purchases to the cheaper imported product.

As long as some fraction of consumers shifts purchases to the imported good, demand will fall for the U.S.-produced good. Reduced demand for the domestic product will result in lower revenues and an increase in inventory. The domestic firms can respond in several ways. First, to try to maintain sales volume, the firms can lower the price of its clothing. However, even if market share is maintained, revenues will still fall since the same sales volume commands a lower price. Since production costs will remain the same initially, domestic firm profit will fall. Even with a lower price, some firms will not be able to maintain sales volume and will be forced to reduce output or deal with rising inventory. Perhaps the quickest way to respond to reduce costs and output is to lay off workers.

Job losses in import-competing industries are the most noteworthy effect of trade liberalization. In the late 1990s, the United States

Table 8.1 Effects of US Import Competition

		1997	*2001*	*% change*
Textile Mills NAICS 313	Output Value (billions)	$58.7	$45.7	–22.1%
	Employment (thousands)	392	294	–25.0%
	Imports (billions)	$6.3	$6.8	+7.9%
Textile Product Mills NAICS 314	Output Value (billions)	$31.1	$32.0	+2.9%
	Employment (thousands)	235	210	–10.6%
	Imports (billions)	$4.8	$7.6	+58.3%
Apparel Mfg. NAICS 315	Output Value (billions)	$68.0	$54.6	–19.7%
	Employment (thousands)	711	456	–35.9%
	Imports (billions)	$47.1	$62.4	+32.5%

Source: U.S. Department of Commerce: Bureau of the Census; International Trade Administration (ITA), http://www.ita.doc.gov/td/industry/otea/industry_sector/tables_naics.htm (June, 2006).

was eliminating quotas on textile and clothing products as a part of its WTO agreement. The increases in imports affected employment in the import-competing industry. Table 8.1 below shows the changes that occurred in three industry sectors—textile mills, textile products, and apparel manufacturing—during a four-year period as quotas were being eliminated.

In the textile mill industry, imports rose by 8 percent, while the value of U.S. output fell by over 20 percent in four years. The industry reduced employment by over 25 percent during the period, eliminating almost 100,000 jobs. The situation was more severe in the apparel-manufacturing sector. As imports rose over 30 percent, output fell by about 20 percent. Employment was cut by over 35 percent as the sector shed over 250,000 jobs. In the textile products industry, output actually rose slightly while imports increased by a whopping 58 percent. Despite stable production, employment was nonetheless reduced by just over 10 percent shedding 25,000 jobs. The number of jobs lost in just this four-year period in only three U.S. industry sectors was over 375,000.

From an even broader perspective, if we consider all the import-competing industries affected by increased import competition due to the WTO agreement and other free trade agreements, besides just textiles and apparel, we would likely discover job losses numbering in the millions because of the transitions. While this represents a relatively small fraction of the U.S. workforce, it is nevertheless a very big deal especially for the workers who have lost their jobs.

If we expand the perspective and consider all import-competing industries *worldwide* affected by the increased competition due to bilateral and multilateral trade liberalization agreements, we will certainly be able to count total job losses in the hundreds of millions over several years. A reasonable question to ask is; what happens to these workers?

Adjustments to Job Losses

Industries can reduce their workforces in a variety of ways. One method is simply not to hire new employees to replace retiring workers. Thus, a small percentage of these workers are not suffering from their loss of job since they have merely retired from the workforce. Other workers may have independently decided to take a job in another industry. They too may not be replaced. All industries experience a natural attrition of workers and thus can reduce their workforce modestly with very little negative impact since the separations are voluntary. Most industries try to do this whenever the reduction in labor needs is small or can be stretched out over a longer period.

However, many other workers, perhaps most, will lose their jobs quickly and unexpectedly. Some of these workers will find new jobs quickly. Others will remain unemployed for some time. In many countries, workers will receive unemployment compensation for a period of time, however, they will still suffer a loss of income together with the anxiety associated with job loss and job transition. An additional loss is the opportunity cost of lost production since these workers are idle during the transition. Some who find new jobs will not make as much income. Some may take several part-time jobs just to make ends meet. Others will be more successful, perhaps landing a better job in an expanding and prospering firm. In all cases and in all countries, the income effects will be mixed.

Export Country Effects

As markets are opened to international trade and competition, a completely different story emerges among the domestic industries that are able to expand exports. These firms face lower tariffs in markets abroad and can respond by reducing the price they charge without reducing the revenue they receive on foreign sales. The lower foreign price will increase demand allowing them to expand output. Output expansion in turn will require more resource inputs, including new workers.

Salaries and wages of current employees may also rise as rising revenues are spread among stakeholders and as the expanding export firms try to attract and retain higher quality workers.

In the clothing industry example above, the jobs created in the industry are in the foreign countries that have been able to expand exports to the U.S. market. Thus, the increases in imports correspond to new jobs somewhere else. One might conclude, then, that trade liberalization is good for them but bad for the United States. However, this conclusion is true only if we restrict our attention to the employment effects in the import-competing industries. Remember, trade liberalization agreements will also lower the barriers that U.S. firms face abroad, allowing them to lower their prices to foreign consumers and increase exports at the same time. Expanded exports of goods and services, brought about from trade liberalization, will create new jobs in many industries.

Net Effects of Trade Liberalization

International trade analysts sometimes evaluate the effects of a free trade agreement by calculating the net effect on jobs. The simplest way to do this is to calculate the number of jobs associated with every million dollars of imports and exports and then measure how exports and imports change after an FTA. In this way, one can estimate how many jobs are created in export industries and how many are lost in import industries. The Economic Policy Institute applied this method in 2003 to argue that the North American Free Trade Agreement (NAFTA) had led to a net loss in jobs in the U.S. economy. According to their estimates, "between 1993 and 2002, NAFTA resulted in an increase in exports that created 794,194 jobs, but it displaced production that would have supported 1,673,454 jobs... Thus, the combined effect of changes in imports and exports as a result of NAFTA was a loss of 879,280 U.S. jobs."[2] This, they conclude, is the real cost of free trade.

This analysis correctly shows some of the losses and gains in jobs due to free trade but it does not capture everything. There are many more effects of the FTA. One problem with this analysis is that it focuses on trade deficits. Since trade deficits grew larger after NAFTA, EPI concludes that jobs have been lost. It is certainly true that when a country runs a trade deficit, there is more money used to demand foreign goods (foreign import demand) than the money that returns to demand U.S. goods (U.S. export demand). But what happens to the excess money that flows out? This study ignores it; effectively assuming it is lost. But that money, and the demand it generates, is not lost. The excess outflow of money comes right back in on the financial account side of the balance of payments. When the United States runs a trade deficit, there is an inward financial flow, called a financial account surplus. This money does not just sit around. Instead it is lent to U.S. banks, firms or the U.S. government. In all cases, this financial inflow stimulates spending by someone in the U.S. economy. That spending creates jobs that more than likely are not tied directly to trade, as those are already accounted for in the trade statistics. Instead these jobs will be in firms that produce for the domestic market, what economists call the nontraded sector. These jobs in the nontraded sectors would not exist except for the extra spending, which, in turn, would not exist without the borrowing financed by the financial surplus, which would not exist without the trade deficit. This means that by focusing on the trade deficit only, the analysis misses some of the jobs being created (and lost) in the economy. A more comprehensive approach is to focus on the total number of jobs gained and lost in all sectors of the economy after trade is liberalized.

Labor Market Churning

Free market economies are in continual flux, constantly changing. New businesses are opening, older businesses are closing every day. New jobs are advertised and filled, while workers in other jobs retire, quit, move, or are fired. When trade liberalization occurs, perhaps the most important effect is a quickening of the dynamic flux in an economy. The increase in competition with foreign businesses and the expansion of market opportunities for export industries further stimulates the process Josef Schumpeter called "creative destruction."[3] Another way to describe the process is as a kind of "churning," or stirring-up, of the market. Which businesses are operating, which workers work where, and who makes more or less income, all are more rapidly changing after trade liberalization.

One way to see the churning that takes place in an economy is to look at business startups and closures. Since the beginning of the worldwide recession in 2008, evidence of churning is less apparent since most industries have suffered losses and very few have experienced gains. Thus it is more instructive to use a prosperous period such as 2005 to illustrate the natural ups and downs of the economy.

In the United States in 2005 there were about 672,000 new businesses (with employees) created. During the same period about 545,000 businesses shut their doors. The total number of businesses in the United States with employees is about 5.8 million.[4] This means about 10 percent of the business stock is refreshed each year with a small net gain being the norm.[5]

With each business closing, jobs are lost. Sometimes the layoffs make headlines: "IBM to lay off 8,000 to 12,000 workers;" Citigroup to lay off as many as 15,000 workers; Circuit City to cut more than 3,500 store and IT jobs.[6] However, it is very important to put these layoff stories in perspective. First, one should know how many layoffs occur in total in the economy in a typical month. Secondly, the more important trend is not how many occur in one industry, but whether the aggregate trend is significantly higher than usual. Finally, one should also look at the trend in job hires during the month. If job hires are rising as fast or faster then layoffs, then the economic effect is surely less severe.

When a company reports a significant layoff of workers, it is likely to be spread over several months or even a year. Compared to the total changes taking place economy-wide, these reported layoffs are typically a very small share. But, even if it were a large share, this only means that labor market churning has hit one particular sector or firm very hard in this period.

Every month the U.S. Labor Department reports the aggregate employment changes by industry.[7] In the January 2007 report we learned that employment fell in many industries: motor vehicles and parts lost 23,000 jobs, furniture and textile mills both lost 4,000 jobs, and computer and peripheral equipment lost 6,000 jobs. However, in the same one-month period, health care employment rose by 18,000 jobs, professional and business services was up 25,000 jobs, while food services employment rose by 21,000 jobs. The net effect for the month was a gain of 111,000 jobs. This follows a net increase in December 2006 of 206,000 jobs. The total number of payroll jobs in the U.S. economy was 137.3 million.[8]

The point here is that the typical churning of job gains and losses in the entire economy dwarfs most layoff stories. Nevertheless concern about job losses is one of the most powerful and convincing arguments used by opponents of trade liberalization. And, almost certainly, trade liberalization will cause an increase in the number of job dislocations.

In international trade models, labor market adjustments occur smoothly and easily. Workers who lose their jobs in the contracting import-competing industries immediately find better jobs in the expanding export industries. However, in the real world, while it may work out well for some people sometimes, for many others the skills of the newly unemployed—such as textile and sewing machine operators, sewers, and seamstresses—will not match the demands for computer programmers, financial and systems analysts, or health care professionals in the expanding sectors. Thus, these workers will remain, at least temporarily, unemployed. In most periods, expanding trade does not correspond to a rising aggregate unemployment rate. This means that many of the displaced workers are indeed finding new jobs.

Nevertheless, even though trade liberalization may simply add to the already sizeable number of job losses and gains without affecting the overall unemployment rate, the connection between increased trade and job losses will be obvious, especially to those who lose their jobs because of trade. This is why it is especially difficult to argue in support of free trade to the owners of businesses and their employees who expect to suffer these dislocations.

The politically astute supporters of free trade often dismiss these concerns by arguing that they will be temporary and that these same individuals will be better off eventually. Unfortunately the reality is very different. This implies that an honest argument supporting free trade must come to terms with these painful and unfortunate outcomes that will become more commonplace if the world continues its push toward freer trade. A more appropriate way to respond to the realities of labor market churning is to argue, as we will below, that first, churning is a very important and necessary process to achieve rising standards of living, and second, that the process is more fair and just than any plausible interventions would be.

Positive Incentive Effects of Fear

Labor market fears, worries, and anxieties are rarely mentioned by supporters of freer trade, and never measured in empirical assessments. Nonetheless, these effects are clearly a major cause for concern among those workers whose jobs are threatened and a prime reason to oppose free trade.

An excellent description of the extreme anxiety the churning process of trade liberalization will sometimes cause can be found in a *New Yorker* article, "The Churn: Creative Destruction in a Border Town,"[9] which describes what adjustment to open international markets will be like from the perspective of the people living through the process:

> Fruit of the Loom had chosen a few veteran laborers to go, briefly, to Honduras to train the cheaper workers who would replace them. Some of the others would board the meat- and poultry-industry buses that idled outside the county employment office, luring those sufficiently desperate to take short-term slaughterhouse jobs in the Ozarks. But, as Fruit of the Loom's cutting machines and bleaching vats were cranked up on pallet jacks, loaded onto flatbeds, and hauled to the Port of Brownsville, many of the company's workers pocketed a month's severance and filed into Mario's van. They applied for unemployment assistance equal to roughly half their former wages, took aptitude tests, and studied the twenty training brochures that were taped to the van's walls. And thus they joined the Rio Grande Valley's eight thousand other former inseam, watch-pocket, and waistband experts in what economists call capitalism's necessary churn.

However, despite the fear and anxiety that comes with free trade, the increase in competition also has a very important effect upon incentives. This is because fear can affect behavior; fear motivates action. In a separate context, it is fear of a midterm or final examination that motivates students to study and learn; it is fear of embarrassment that motivates a dancer to practice before a performance. In a similar way, it is fear of losses and economic failure that can incite owners, managers, and workers to action. Two types of responses may occur: one a competitive response, the other an anticompetitive response. The anticompetitive response involves attempts to profit, or to prevent losses, via special government protections. These actions were described as examples of involuntary transfers in chapter 7.

The alternative is the competitive response. If firms respond competitively, they must accomplish a few basic tasks: they must lower their costs of production, improve the desirability of their product and preferably, do both simultaneously. Unfortunately, these tasks are not always easy to achieve. Even more importantly, to be successful, a firm must do both of these faster and more effectively than other firms competing for the same consumers.

Faced with falling profit due to foreign competition, managers will seek out all conceivable ways to lower their costs of production. This may mean purchasing more technologically advanced equipment, laying off the least productive workers, or outsourcing some processes to a more efficient (cheaper) external company, perhaps in another country.

But, not all of these steps will necessarily be effective. New technology may be expensive, and it will be difficult to decide whether to incur a larger cost, or borrow to purchase equipment whose effectiveness will be uncertain until tested. Firing workers immediately reduces cost, but also requires a readjustment of assignments of the remaining workers. Finally, although outsourcing, or offshoring, may reduce cost, it too may be significantly less effective. If the effectiveness, or productivity, of inputs falls by more than the cost is reduced, the attempts at cost saving will actually make the company less competitive.

Businesses can also raise their competitiveness by improving the desirability and quality of their product. This may involve changing the colors and design, or adjusting the materials used in production. It may mean devoting more resources to quality control. It may mean hiring a more effective sales team or expanding efforts to place their products in more retails outlets. The firm may also work to enhance their market demand through advertising. Advertising will communicate information about the product to a larger group of consumers, and improve the image and reputation of their product vis-à-vis their competitors.

These adjustments will also be difficult to make. For example, how much more should be spent on design, on quality control, on advertising? What will the return be in terms of increased sales revenue? Should all three be done, or is one approach more likely to be effective than another?

These questions will not have easy answers. Successful adjustment will depend on the creativity and effort of managers and workers. It will also depend somewhat on luck. Because there are so many ways to respond to the increased competition, each firm will respond somewhat differently. Some will further reduce their workforce, and devote resources to advertising. Others will switch to cheaper input sources and adjust the quality and design of their products. Some firms will adjust the mix of products they produce. Each firm's objective is the same; to remain competitive and maintain, or even improve, profit.

Not all firms will be successful. Some will see their sales plummet and will be unable to cut costs fast enough. These firms will close, ultimately firing their entire workforce. Other firms will struggle; sales may fall, then rise, then fall again. Some firms will struggle for a long time, but continue to barely cover production costs and so will remain in business. These firms may wind up with a much smaller workforce.

Worker Responses to Competition

One of the major concerns people have about the competitive process is the effect on workers. When companies adjust to competition they often release workers to improve efficiency. We might ask what the firm's responsibility is to the workers. And how should workers respond to the churning in the market?

First of all, a business consists of a group of owners who put together a plan to produce a product they believe is demanded by consumers. If they do this effectively, they will profit. To produce the product and distribute it they need to hire workers for a variety of tasks in the production process. To attract effective workers, firms must offer terms that are agreeable; after all, workers have the right to refuse. At the same time, when markets are free, firms have the power not to hire someone or to fire a worker if the worker has become ineffective.

Keep in mind that in a dynamic competitive market, consumer demands and the most effective production process are both quite likely to be in constant flux. That means that demands for worker skills will change over time. To remain as flexible as possible a firm must be able to hire and fire workers as needed to maintain the best service to their customers. Restrictions on that flexibility will automatically reduce the firm's ability to satisfy their customers' demands and will reduce its ability to compete effectively; that is, unless all other firms are required to face the same constraints.

Some restrictions may be mutually voluntary. For example, a firm may recognize that it can hire more competent workers if it commits itself to a one-year labor contract. In this case, the contract constrains the actions of the firm, but the firm may do so willingly to attract better workers. In contrast, the implementation of a national minimum wage law constrains the terms of an allowable labor contract. The law means that some freely voluntary exchanges are now prohibited, which in turn may impede the ability of some firms to provide the best product to its customers. It may also prevent some firms from offering jobs that might have been offered otherwise. When all firms in a country must face the same constraint, the minimum wage law might not reduce competitiveness vis-à-vis other local firms since everyone must conform to the same constraint. However, when different countries have different minimum wages, the more highly constrained firms may suffer a loss of competitiveness.

Suppose firms could freely hire and fire workers whenever they desired. How would workers respond? They would likely respond by changing their expectations and their behavior. A worker in a competitive economy would know that the firm has no obligation to provide a job under any conditions different from the terms of the employment contract. For example, a worker who knows she can be fired tomorrow, or at the end of the year, has a much stronger incentive to strive to be as individually productive as possible. A worker will want her boss to know she is a hard worker, that she contributes to the firm's goals, because to do so makes it less likely she will be the one fired if an adjustment occurs.

At the same time the firm knows that any worker can walk away from his or her job at anytime, again also subject to the terms of the labor contract. This a reason why firms have incentives to provide decent working conditions to its workers. Better treatment can motivate higher productivities. If workers feel mistreated, or if they expect that changes in the market may result in the loss of their job, then they are free to look elsewhere for employment. In order to find employment elsewhere, the worker will need to be able to demonstrate his effectiveness. To remain constantly in demand then, the worker should continually improve and expand his skill set.

Thus, workers' freedom to move and firms' ability to fire, motivates both better worker treatment on the part of firms and better efforts on the part of workers. Adding labor market constraints reduces firm and worker flexibility and reduces the ability of firms and workers to compete in a dynamic market.

Competitive Experimentation and Discovery

The firms that succeed will be the ones that choose the right competitive response. However, identifying what the right response should be is almost impossible to know beforehand. Even the owners and managers of the firms themselves will not know whether the adjustments they are making will ultimately succeed or fail. This is one reason competition creates such a high level of anxiety for owners, managers, and workers. There is always an enormous amount of uncertainty and risk.

Economic models typically assume that firms have good, even perfect (!) information about the market and their costs of production.

When imperfect information is introduced, models often assume one agent has perfect information and the other does not (asymmetric info), or, if the information is unknown to all, then the agent at least knows the probability distribution of that information. However, all of these assumptions are unlikely to be satisfied in the real world. It is true that firms know a lot about their own market, but they do not know everything, and they especially do not know what market conditions will be like in the future.

Nevertheless, competitive markets represent an extremely effective way to resolve this uncertainty. The resolution comes through experimentation, through trial and error. In a competitive market, every business enterprise represents an experiment taking place every day as producers offer their products and services for sale and hope that consumers will come along and buy freely and voluntarily. Consumers will consider the price, design, functionality, and quality of the good or service and will buy only if they believe the product fulfills their needs or desires.

Each firm's objective is to fulfill a sufficiently large number of consumer desires, so as to cover their costs of production and return a reasonable profit. In textbook models, the choice problem is simple; simply set output so that marginal revenue equals marginal cost. In real-world businesses, the decision process is much more complex, especially for large companies.

Every product that makes it to the marketplace has a multitude of individual decisions behind it. Consider a simple product like a can of soup. The producer had to decide on the recipe, where to buy the ingredients, the equipment, and labor resources needed to make the soup, the type of can to use, who would produce the can, the color and design of the label, which retailers would stock the product, how much to spend on advertising in newspapers, radio, TV, and the Internet and, finally, what price to charge. In the background the producer also had to decide what type of health care and retirement plans to offer workers, implement quality control procedures to ensure product safety, adhere to government regulations concerning worker safety, manage the payroll, hire new workers to replace recent retirees, fire some workers who were habitually late for work, and throw one of the administrative assistants a birthday party. Decisions like these, and many more, affect the price and the quality of the product for sale, whether it be soup, bread, wristwatches, or life insurance.

Firms will succeed when they can consistently manage the production process in a way that provides a product consumers desire, while also covering the costs of production plus an adequate profit. Unfortunately, in many instances businesses cannot rest even after they have discovered a production process that works because consumer demands are never fixed and immutable. Instead, demands change as incomes, tastes, trends, and availability of alternative products changes. This means that the best business strategy will quite likely be one that continually changes and adjusts as well. It is as if businesses are shooting at a moving target. To make matters worse, as trade is liberalized, the target moves even faster.

Friedrich Hayek (2002) wrote that "The difference between economic competition and the successful procedure of science is that the former exhibits a method of discovering particular temporary circumstances, while science seeks to discover something often known as 'general facts,' ..." Market demand is the *particular temporary circumstance* that is constantly changing and changing ever more rapidly with globalization.

Since no individual firm (and surely no government) really knows what the most effective product and production process really is, the best way to deal with this uncertainty from a systemic perspective is to have many, many firms simultaneously attempting to hit the moving target and satisfy demand.[10] To understand why, consider the alternative for a moment.

Suppose only one or two firms try to satisfy consumer demand for, say, bicycles. With only a couple of firms, consumers will not have many choices. As long as both firms can produce an adequate bicycle, consumers will have no choice but to buy from one of them. The two firms might split the market almost equally and if the firms earn a comfortable profit, possibly neither one would have a strong incentive to change very much.

Next imagine what happens as three, four or ten new bicycle firms are added. The incumbent firms, and all the others, would now have a much lower chance of survival because the expansion of consumer choices may lead all consumers to choose something else. Firms would now need to pay much more attention to their potential customers' needs and desires. Some firms might decide to specialize in certain niche products, for example, expensive racing bikes or children's bikes. Other firms might decide to produce a range of bicycle styles to satisfy many consumer types. Some firms may spend more on advertising attempting to attract new consumers into the market, or persuade consumers to switch to their brand. Other firms may provide better service agreements by offering buyers regular bicycle tune-ups and repairs. Whatever a firm does, it will remain in business in a competitive market only if it satisfies some segment of consumer demand. No single firm may know exactly what is best, but they will all have the incentive to continue to investigate and learn from their customers and the market. This is what Hayek meant when he described competition as a discovery process.

The Objective of Competition

The main objective in competitive markets is the satisfaction of consumer desires. Consumer demands are the primary source of well-being in an economic system. These demands are satisfied through the pursuit of profit. Profit is the extra benefit one obtains above the cost of producing or acquiring something. Producers profit whenever they satisfy consumers demands, which in turn enables them to purchase goods and services for themselves to satisfy their own consumer demand. But, production activity is not the goal; jobs are not the goal; even profit is not the ultimate goal; production, work, and profit are merely the means to an end, the end being consumer demands.

Unfortunately, popular discussion and public policy making is dominated by excessive focus and concern for producer outcomes. This is largely because of the functioning of political markets. Mancur Olson (1965) argued that smaller groups who stand to enjoy relatively larger benefits from a government policy will be able to organize and influence political decisions much more effectively than large groups who have little to lose individually. Even though the net losses to the large groups (consumers) may overwhelm the benefits earned by the small group (producers), the small group often wins. In democratic governments it is interesting to note how many new policies tend to substantially benefit a small group, paid for with small incremental costs to a very large group (consumers or taxpayers).

Furthermore, in many instances government interference in markets tends to reduce the benefits received by consumers. This is largely because of imperfect information. If governments knew how to satisfy consumer demands more effectively than the firms in the marketplace, then they could design policies that would prevent entry by firms with the bad ideas while guaranteeing the markets for the champion firms. This would eliminate all those costs associated with unnecessary market experiments that the government knows will fail. However, if government does not have better information than firms about consumer desires, then market interventions will almost surely inhibit the competitive experimental process. This means consumers will not have as many choices before them. Furthermore, unless the government is lucky enough to inhibit only the least effective firms, consumers will also, almost surely, be made worse off.

Government is also at a disadvantage because the individuals most closely involved in the production process will have better information about consumer demands than the government workers, who are more distant. Thus, when firms compete, managers and workers within the firms themselves will be able to analyze their own sales data, negotiate prices with intermediate input suppliers, and survey their own customers about their desires. They will use all this information to make decisions about which type of product will be most successful to produce. Thus, with free competition, the most relevant and available information is used to make decisions to satisfy consumers.

In contrast, when governments make policy decisions, the information they have about the market has to be worse, not better, than the individual firms' information. If the government attempts to acquire market information to assist it in making better decisions, the best source of that information is the firms themselves. However, the firms have the incentive to provide biased information to the government. Firms prefer to inhibit competition with other firms; ideally they would prefer to be a monopoly. Thus the information they provide government policy makers will often help mold policy decisions to favor their own interests. This kind of lobbying is surely the norm, rather than the exception. Firms have every reason to protect their own interests even if it means tilting the debate in a favorable direction. These actions are also the reason many people are extremely suspicious of, especially, large firm motivations.

Opportunity and Incentives

In a well-functioning free market economy the fear of losses from international competition should inspire owners, managers, and workers to perform with greater effort and skill to increase output, reduce cost, and increase the quality of the product. So, we might ask next, whether these reactions by businesses to the fear of competition will guarantee successful transition of these businesses in the new global economy. Alas, the real answer is a great big, emphatic, NO!!!!

A competitive economic system is *not* a system in which everyone benefits. This is the unpleasant and rarely spoken reality. A competitive system is one that, by its nature, raises fears and anxieties. As the world globalizes and as competition extends its reach to include more markets, there will be an increase in this fear and anxiety in all countries. This is precisely what we are seeing today and it is a primary motivating factor for the renewed resistance to globalization.

Alan Greenspan explains, "The problem is that the dynamic that defines capitalism, that of unforgiving market competition, clashes with the human desire for stability and certainty. Even more important, a large segment of society feels a growing sense of injustice about the allocation of capitalism's rewards. Competition, capitalism's greatest force, creates anxiety in all of us. One major source of it is the chronic fear of job loss. Another, more deeply felt angst stems from competition's perpetual disturbance of the status quo and style of living, good or bad, from which most people derive comfort" (2007, 268).

The fight to preserve the status quo will initially involve pointing fingers and laying blame on others. This is especially easy to do when the blame can be directed at foreigners. People seem to have a natural inclination to look to external sources to explain their own misfortune. Perhaps this is why competition from domestic sources is not looked at in the same way.

However, despite the continual swirl producing winners and losers, a competitive system is one in which is best suited to satisfy the ever-changing and amorphous consumer demands and provide individuals with the best chance to reach their maximum potential. It is a system that provides opportunity. The beauty of the system lies not in the misguided promise that "all good will come to all people." Rather, the beauty lies in the incentive structure that motivates (indeed forces) all individuals to achieve their very best. If you do not, you will fall further and further behind. The system's incentives reward those who work hard and have natural skills and abilities and sometimes those who are simply lucky. It rewards those who succeed in producing that which other people want the system to produce. At the same time the competitive system withholds rewards from those who are lazy, are less fortunate in terms of their natural endowments and in many cases are simply unlucky: it withholds awards from those who produce what consumers do not want.[11]

The longer-term impact of a competitive system will be the provision of goods and services that consumers most want, at the lowest economic and resource cost at the moment. The size of the economic pie will rise over time if the system is allowed to work. This will mean a higher average standard of living for people in all countries, as it is usually measured. However, the distribution of those gains may be quite different from what they would be in a system rife with intervention. Thus, it is not accurate to say that everyone would eventually benefit in a competitive system. This is the reason many people would still prefer a system with government "protections," which as the term implies, *protects* the benefits of some groups.

Costs of Free Competition

Although there are many efficiency advantages in the operation of free voluntary exchange and competitive markets, there are also costs. Some costs have already been mentioned. Many producers and their workers will lose in the competition to other firms who produce a more desirable product. Consumers of the losing firm's product may also lose somewhat. For example, a small number of consumers may feel that the failing firm's product is ideal for them relative to the alternatives. However, if that consumer group is too small, it may not be cost effective for a firm to serve them. When the firm fails due to insufficient demand, these consumers will have to switch to a slightly less desirable product.

Experimentation

Additional inefficiencies arise in a dynamic market because of the wasted experimentation. As mentioned above, failed market experiments represent costs that are not recouped. In an ideal world, with perfect information about consumer desires, only those firms that can succeed would produce, thereby saving unnecessary duplicative efforts. Unfortunately, this represents an unrealizable ideal. Suggestions to fix these problems assume that market participants have accurate information about production costs and consumer demands before beginning production. However, as explained earlier, since market conditions are constantly changing, it is difficult even for firms most engaged in the market to anticipate future changes in supply possibilities and demand potentials. The most effective and direct way to learn is through the competitive process itself.

Winner-Take-All Markets

One other important source of inefficiencies in the competitive process is the presence of winner-take-all markets as described in Frank (1995). He describes situations in which many individuals or firms compete in a market in which there can be only one or several winners, each of whom will realize extravagant profit. Examples include the markets for professional athletes, movie actors, musical artists, and corporate CEOs. Earnings for a small group of people in these markets easily reaches multimillion dollar levels. Think only of Tiger Woods, Michael Jordan, Julia Roberts, Tom Cruise, Britney Spears, Madonna, Michael Eisner, and Warren Buffett, to name just a few.

The inefficiencies in these cases arise *not* because the high salaries are unwarranted. These salaries arise because the added value by these individuals in their respective occupations really does amount to multimillions of dollars. Indeed, it is valid to say that the multimillion dollar salaries of athletes and performers are matched by at least that much surplus value created among the large group of consumers who enjoy their performances.

Rather, the inefficiencies occur because the high salaries attract many people to the competition for these positions, almost all of who will ultimately be unsuccessful. Frank shows that even if people have perfect information about their low chances of winning the big prize, many more people than is optimal will enter the competition. The inefficiency is the lost opportunity of alternative production; that is, the value of the output these individuals could have produced had they not devoted their time to playing basketball, or to voice lessons, or to MBA and law school study.[12]

This example is one of many prisoner dilemma problems in which individual desires to profit and a lack of cooperation can result in aggregate inefficiencies. Another classic example is the nuclear arms race. The first country to develop one nuclear missile that can cause catastrophic damage to a foreign country gains a security advantage over that country, hence there is an individual desire to do so. The rival, however, now has an incentive to develop two nuclear missiles weapons. The first could destroy its opponent's weapon in a first strike, and it would have one more extra giving it extra security against its rival. Of course, once the rival builds two missiles, the first country has an incentive to build three to take back the advantage. And so it can go, and did go, on and on during the cold war era as the United States and the Soviet Union wasted billions of dollars building weapons that, thankfully, were never used.

The solution to a problem like this normally involves cooperation. In the case of the nuclear arms race, the United States and the Soviet Union eventually agreed to a strategic arms limitation treaty (SALT) in which both countries agreed to reduce their nuclear arsenals. The fear that either side would cheat on the agreement necessitated a complex system of verification to maintain the trust that the agreement would indeed be implemented.

Drawing on this example, Frank refers to this kind of agreement in all contexts as a positional arms control agreement. For example, sports franchises, such as Major League Baseball, have cooperated to prevent any one team from dominating a league and to prevent excessively high salaries by agreeing to limit the total amount each team can spend on player's salaries. Similarly, Ivy League universities and MIT *colluded* in the late 1980s with an agreement not to use financial aid as a method to attract the brightest students. The purpose was to stop a positional arms race in which financial aid was being offered even to students whose families were financially able to pay in order to attract them. The cost was that less financial aid was available to excellent students who could not afford the tuition. These are two instances in which collusion to restrain competition can actually have a positive effect.[13]

Innovation and Competition Policy

Another important issue is the relationship between competition and innovation. In the competition story above it is blithely assumed that competition will inspire fear of losses and automatically induce the discovery process. Discovery may or may not involve innovation of new product or process technologies and it may or may not occur. When it does not involve innovation, discovery can mean finding the cheapest and most reliable input suppliers, or learning how to incorporate known technologies, such as internet service provision, into one's business operations. These represent static efficiency effects from competition—in other words, improvements in the allocation and uses of resources that are already available. However, in many industries discovery involves creation of whole new products or services to satisfy a consumer demand that had never been satisfied before. Discovery can also mean designing new machinery that enables the firm to improve product quality or reduce cost. In these cases, discovery involves new innovation. These are known as Schumpeterian growth effects because the innovation in new technology may induce a more rapid growth of the industry and the economy.

Aghion and Griffith (2005, 2) provide a good overview of the issues:

> But are we so sure that competition always favors innovation in developed economies? In fact we often hear the opposite view being advocated by prominent innovators—for example, by Microsoft over the past five years—namely, that tough competition discourages innovation and inhibits productivity growth by reducing the expected rents from innovation. . . . If, as an entrepreneur, I anticipate future antitrust action, or future liberalization of entry in my market, why should I invest so much in new innovations if the rents from these are to be destroyed by new entrants or potential competitors? On the other hand, antitrust practitioners and competition authorities argue that competition is a necessary input into innovation, both because it encourages new entry and because it keeps incumbent firms on their toes and forces them to innovate in order to survive competition.

In part this describes a conflict between antitrust policy and intellectual property policy. Intellectual property protections include, patents on new inventions, trademarks for original labels and designs, and copyrights for literary and artistic work. These protections confer monopoly rights for some firms and individuals in certain prescribed situations, normally for items in which the cost of producing the first unit of these goods (i.e., the fixed costs) is high, whereas the cost of every additional unit (the marginal costs) is very low.

The best example is for a new pharmaceutical drug. The cost to identify a drug that alleviates a particular ailment, can often run into the billions of dollars. However, once it is known what the drug can do, it is easy for others to identify the chemical composition and produce it at a very low unit cost. If an imitator is allowed to reverse engineer the drug, then the imitator can produce and sell it at a very low cost to the consumer. Hence patent protection enables the innovator to recoup its high fixed cost with monopoly profit by preventing competition from imitators at least for some period of time. Without the patent protection, or intellectual property protections, more generally, innovations and, subsequently, economic growth might be decidedly lower.

Aghion and Griffith carefully examine both the theoretical and empirical literature in this area and ask whether one can turn to economists for an answer to the question: does competition inspire innovation. Their answer is no:

> While competition features prominently in the history of economic thought, it is fair to say that economists still have a limited and sometimes contradictory understanding of its economic effects and, in particular, of the relationship between competition and growth. What we have accumulated so far are only bits and pieces:...From this a deep feeling of confusion arises.

Overview of the Costs of Competition

It is important to recognize that support of free markets and competition cannot be justified with some sort of *proof* that it will always lead to the most efficient outcome. Researchers have identified numerous examples of inefficiencies when markets are completely free, including the winner-take-all markets, other prisoner dilemma situations, incentives for innovation and the presence of other kinds of market imperfections described in chapter 2. The key problems in every attempt to correct for these inefficiencies are the lack of sufficient information and the problem of capture by the political system. As discussed in chapters 2 and 3 it is enormously difficult to measure the full impact of policy changes and to determine precisely the right policy lever and policy strength to use to improve economic efficiency. Consequently, policy actions to correct for distortions or imperfections will surely change economic outcomes and the distribution of income, but it will remain *impossible* to know whether these outcomes are *better,* in some clearly defined way, than what would have happened without the corrections.

In addition, once the opportunity to correct perceived problems is available in the political system, parties have incentives to propose policies beneficial to themselves and to cobble together efficiency or fairness arguments to justify them. Unfortunately, we have no idea whether this piecemeal approach to policy making improves overall outcomes relative to free competitive markets.

Compensation

Economists, cognizant of the fact that trade liberalization will cause harm to some groups in the economy, often argue that compensation be provided to those who would lose. This would essentially entail a system of monetary transfers from the winners to the losers. In the event the actual winners cannot be identified, the practical solution is to fund the transfers from general tax revenues. Compensation is also supported for political reasons: if the potential losers from trade liberalization are vocal enough, compensation can be used to quiet the opposition.

The nature of effective competition though, provides an argument *against* compensation. Since trade liberalization will increase the competitive churning in product and labor markets, many of the weaker industries and the workers whose skills are least in demand will be the ones that lose from trade liberalization. If compensation is provided, these firms and workers will lose the incentive to change and adjust. And, if adjustment is incomplete, consumer demands will not be fully satisfied.

Distributional Effects of Trade Liberalization

Competition inspires creative behavior but it does not guarantee success. In fact, in a truly competitive economy, despite noble efforts on the part of some firms and their workers, many will still fail to compete; other firms will produce better products at lower prices. Perhaps this will come because other firms have cheaper, more reliant sources of input supply, perhaps, because other firms introduced more efficient management procedures. Maybe other firms hired a more competent average workforce, or maybe they were lucky enough to choose the style and design for their product that more people wanted this season. For many reasons, some the fault of the management and workers, some just dumb luck, businesses will fail. These failures will cause income losses for employees and will cause anxiety-filled adjustments to other jobs. Once again, the truth about competition is that it is a difficult process for many of the participants.

We might ask whether these adjustment costs will be borne by all people at one time or another. In other words, how will these costs likely be distributed? Unfortunately, here too the answer is unlikely to appeal to those in search of fairness and justice. The cost will almost surely be borne disproportionately by those who are less skilled, less educated, and generally poorer. The reasons should be obvious.

Those workers who are most skilled will be in the greatest demand by many different firms. Every firm would like to have the best managers, the most creative researchers, the most prudent accountants, etc. Those individuals who rise to the top in their profession will face fewer difficulties, first because they will likely be one of the last people fired in a declining industry and second because they will have more alternative opportunities in other industries if they are forced, or decide, to leave a firm. The way firms identify the most-able, the best educated, the shining stars, is by noting their previous achievements relative to others. Thus, those who attend the most elite schools will be identified as having the greatest likelihood of being among the best and brightest. Also, those who have more money or whose families have money will be better able to leverage that to achieve better academic outcomes and will also likely have better connections with people who make hiring decisions.

Fairness and Voluntary Exchange

Voluntary exchange involves the simultaneous, voluntary transfer of goods and services between two individuals. Each person gives away something willingly in order to receive something else that the other person also gives away willingly. If both are free not to trade, then the very fact that a trade occurs must mean that both traders expect to profit from the transaction. This simple exchange process happens whenever a person buys food at the market, when someone pays their electric bill and when a firm pays wages to an employee.

The exchange process requires acceptance of private ownership. We presume that an individual "owns" his own labor services, that the money he uses in a transaction is rightfully his, and that the goods a firm sells are not claimed by another. If no one owns the means of production and the returns to it, or if the state owns it, then the free voluntary exchange process is compromised.[14,15]

Thus, two things are needed to define a free market economy; free voluntary exchange and ownership. Competition arises in this environment whenever a group of sellers with similar products is matched with a group of buyers with similar demands. If all exchange is left free, then competition automatically arises.

Competition is a catalyst that can motivate people to achieve their very best, because to be successful requires that the products you are trying to sell are more desired than the similar products others are selling. This makes competition a process in which, on average, individuals that are smarter and work harder will achieve more economic success than others. Thus, a competitive system with free voluntary exchange will operate as a meritocracy. However, not all outcomes need be based on skill and effort; luck will also play a role. Sometimes a business will sell more items than competitors simply because it guessed correctly what consumers' preferences would be this year.

Voluntary exchange, and the free market competition that arises from its application, is fair with respect to several fairness conceptions described in chapter 4. First, voluntary exchange is fair with respect to privacy fairness, which states that individuals should be left alone when their actions do no harm to others. With exchange both parties to the transaction agree to exchange voluntarily and the process does not cause harm to either party directly involved in the trade. However, voluntary trades by some people may cause harm to others if a person shifts his exchanges from one person to another. Thus if one week a person buys California wine instead of French wine, the French wine seller will be harmed. However, although harm occurs, attempts to prevent that harm would inhibit voluntary transactions and violate privacy fairness itself. It would also force buyers into trades with some sellers over others, thus violating nondiscrimination fairness.[16]

Voluntary exchange is also fair with respect to positive reciprocity fairness; indeed it may be more than fair. Positive reciprocity says that positive benefits given to another should be reciprocated with equal benefits in return. I do something for you with value x, and you should return the favor and do something else for me also with value x. However, when voluntary exchange occurs, each party receives a benefit that is *greater* than the value of what is given up; surplus value is created as both sides in a trade profit. Thus, we might claim that voluntary exchange is not just reciprocity fair but reciprocity-plus fair, or even better than reciprocity.

By similar logic voluntary exchange would also tend to satisfy maximum benefit fairness, because there is a surplus created for both parties to a trade. However, it is conceivable that the perceived losses that accrue to parties left out of the exchange (e.g., the French wine merchants) may be larger than the surplus benefits accruing to the two traders. In this case maximum benefit fairness is violated. This result is in line with the more general point raised earlier: free trade, and hence free exchange, does not guarantee that all people will benefit, or that the sum of the benefits, measured broadly, will exceed the sum of the losses.

Voluntary exchange is fair with respect to golden rule fairness. The golden rule requires that each person take actions that they themselves would encourage others to take. With reciprocal trade, the parties to the trade can surely not object to the behavior of the other. Sometimes rules or laws are implemented that restrict voluntary trades. For example, the United States prohibits sales of supercomputers to certain countries deemed potentially unfriendly to the United States. If a firm violates this rule and trades voluntarily with a restricted country, one could argue that the voluntary trade, by breaking a law, violates golden rule fairness. However, the unfairness in this case applies strictly to the rule, not to the exchange itself. Nonetheless this example shows the application of the fairness criteria is sometimes ambiguous, or at the least, subject to multiple interpretations.

In terms of nondiscrimination fairness, as long as all of the policies, procedures, and institutions used to encourage voluntary exchange apply equally to all, then nondiscrimination fairness is realized. If, in contrast, some transactions are restricted, perhaps to guarantee continued profitable trading by another market participant, then these restrictions would violate nondiscrimination fairness.

By itself, voluntary exchange has very little or nothing to do with negative reciprocity, which states that a negative effect caused by someone can be reciprocated with a similarly valued negative response. With voluntary exchange, both sides of the transaction are positive.

Finally, one can also argue that voluntary exchange can sometimes result in unfair outcomes, most notably with respect to distributional fairness. Distributional fairness involves perceptions of the equality of outcomes such as the realizations of income and wealth of individuals. As suggested by Nozick (1974), if thousands of individuals agree to pay, say $5, to see Wilt Chamberlain play basketball, then Chamberlain's income increases significantly, whereas each of the sports enthusiasts' wealth falls slightly. The resulting distribution of wealth becomes more unequal as a result of numerous voluntary exchanges.[17] If we only accept movements in the direction of income equality as our measure of fairness, then voluntary exchange is potentially unfair with respect to this fairness conception.

In summary, voluntary exchange is consistent with privacy fairness, reciprocity fairness, golden rule fairness, and nondiscrimination

Table 8.2 Consistency of Voluntary Exchange with Fairness Principles

Distributional	No
Nondiscrimination	Yes
Golden Rule	Yes
Positive Reciprocity	Yes
Negative Reciprocity	n.a.
Privacy	Yes
Maximum Benefit	Yes

fairness. It may or may not be consistent with maximum benefit fairness and is unlikely to be consistent with distributional fairness. Thus, although we cannot claim voluntary exchange is always fair regardless of how one classifies fairness, we can argue that it satisfies many of the fairness criteria and thus might be deemed "mostly fair."

Table 8.2 offers a summary of the fairness characteristics of voluntary exchange. Note that voluntary exchange is mostly fair with the exception of distributional fairness and the nonapplicable case of negative reciprocity.

Conclusion

People engage in voluntary exchange because they seek to profit. They wish to improve their own well-being, to make themselves happier. To be ready to trade, one must have something other people want. Generally these items do not come to us like manna from heaven; instead we must work at it, we must make it, create it. One thing we all can give is our labor services. However, if we wish to exchange our time and hard work with an employer, we must have skills an employer will demand. If we wish to sell a product instead, then we must produce that product first. Production may require our own effort as well as the effort of other workers. Production will also require the input of capital and natural resources. An owner's task is to purchase those inputs, manage their activities, and produce a product that can be sold to willing buyers at a price that covers the costs of production. If that entire process is managed successfully, the owner will profit.

This kind of profit is laudable. When we match this process to the fairness criteria it is straightforward to show that voluntary exchange is mostly fair and just. Indeed, as suggested in chapter 6, trading something of value to another can even be viewed as altruistic since part of every transaction involves giving something that another person values or desires. Successful trading requires one to discover peoples' wants and needs and to satisfy them through your own efforts. If a person or business can do so, they will also benefit themselves, thus trade has both an altruistic and an egoistic aspect combined.

The desire to benefit oneself—to profit—is natural. When profit arises by benefiting others, that is when it is matched with the altruistic component, then we should support and promote that activity. Indeed, it is accurate to say that those who profit the most in a free market are those who have given the most to others. In contrast, when profit is obtained via involuntary transfers from others, as discussed in chapter 7, then profit is not laudable. In the case of transfers, there is no altruistic giving, only taking. Profit from involuntary transfers is what gives profit seeking a bad name.

The key to a new understanding is to separate these two ways to obtain profit. When we do so it becomes clear why some view profit making so negatively. Many people believe that businesses will do whatever is necessary to make more money. When they see businesses achieve that profit by cheating its customers, promulgating misinformation, selling dangerous products, exploiting or mistreating its workers, or by using its power and influence in government to restrict competition, then they are reacting to a clearly objectionable type of profit via involuntary transfers. Thus, these negative reactions to profit are all reasonable since all profit is not good profit.

Another source of confusion is that the sources of profit, even for a particular firm, are confounded. Some firms produce products that are desired by their customers but at the same time obtain special regulations from government giving them a competitive edge. Some firms produce products that are desired, like car repair, but pilfer a little extra income with a small dose of dishonesty. Some firms produce products that people want, but at the same time mistreat or even imprison their workers to reduce their costs and raise their own profit. What a person believes about the profit incentive will depend on what part of a business activity seems more prominent. Those who look favorably upon profit tend to see more of the market activity, while those who view profit negatively tend to see more of the involuntary transfers.

Friedman (2002, 112–13) makes this same argument about the confusion over profit and tries to clarify by distinguishing between two types of harm; positive harm (involuntary transfers) and negative harm (voluntary exchange induced):

> [There is] a serious confusion about two very different kinds of harm. One kind is the positive harm that one individual does another by physical force, or by forcing him to enter into a contract without his consent. An obvious example is the man who hits another over the head with a blackjack. A less obvious example is stream pollution discussed in chapter ii. The second kind is the negative harm that occurs when two individuals are unable to find mutually acceptable contracts, as when I am unwilling to buy something that someone wants to sell me and therefore make him worse off than he would be if I bought the item.... There is a strong case for using government to prevent one person from imposing positive harm, which is to say, to prevent coercion. There is no case whatsoever for using government to avoid the negative kind of "harm." On the contrary such government intervention reduces freedom and limits voluntary co-operation.

Thus, we should not disparage profit, per se, or believe that all negative outcomes indicate examples of involuntary transfers. Instead we need to disentangle the actions of businesses and individuals to identify the method used to acquire profit. A moderate compromise seeks policies that accept and promote profit via voluntary exchange while restricting or prohibiting profit via involuntary transfers.

This is especially important because not only is the desire to profit natural, but it is an absolutely necessary motivating factor for voluntary exchange. Voluntary exchange, in turn, was absolutely necessary to enable the division of labor, which was needed to achieve the increases in productivity that has propelled the human race into a modern and wealthier era. As will be argued in the next chapter, the absence of profit seeking could relegate our fate to a much lower average standard of living, especially if the alternative is a society motivated by primarily by altruism.

Although the promotion of voluntary exchange has many positive features, this chapter has also emphasized that a free competitive market consisting of a myriad of voluntary exchanges will be fraught with ups and downs for its participants. While proponents of free markets often try to put a positive spin on the process by suggesting that eventually all people will benefit, the actual experience of market participants will be quite different—that is because competition is hard. It is very difficult to adequately satisfy the needs of a group of consumers, especially when there are other businesses trying to do the same thing.

Successful firms must first discover what people want. Even this may be difficult since consumer demands will continually change as incomes, tastes, and knowledge about alternative products changes. But even if a firm correctly identifies consumer desires for the moment, it must also be able to satisfy those desires more effectively than its competitors. When it does so it will profit. But those profits may be fleeting since profit making by one firm will attract other firms to step in and try to grab some of that profit away. The result is a competitive system replete with fear and anxiety.

In all cases, success today may disappear tomorrow. Firm owners will worry their profit will dissipate; workers will fear being fired. However, this fear and anxiety can actually be a good thing *if* it motivates the correct behavior: the positive responses to competition. The positive response is when firms react to the pressure by continually adjusting its product features and production process to better satisfy its consumers' needs. Workers must react by continually preparing themselves for adjustment. That can involve everything from showing up to work on time and working hard (i.e., prove to your employer that you are valuable), to investment in new up-to-date skills (perhaps to prepare for another job).

Unfortunately, many firms and workers will respond to the fear and anxiety by seeking involuntary transfers instead. Firms do not like to compete and regularly and actively attempt to reduce competition either independently (e.g., with mergers) or with government intervention. Workers also resist competition by demanding unionization and pressuring companies not to adjust to competitive pressures by laying off workers. Along the way the company—seeking profit—is sometimes demonized. Suggestions for compensation are also widespread, especially when groups lose because of changes in government policy, as with a reduction of trade barriers. These responses, however, all represent calls for involuntary transfers to improve the well-being of losing groups by transferring money from others.

An additional problem arises because in pursuing involuntary transfers, firms must devote resources (employee time and energy) that are diverted away from product improvements. This process of rent seeking is a directly unproductive activity; the more resources devoted to rent seeking, the poorer a society will be (all else equal).

But what is society to do about the hardships caused by competition? This chapter does not suggest, like many people do, that the hardships will be small and temporary. Instead, it is argued the hardships may sometimes be severe, persistent, and somewhat arbitrary. On average, especially if good and bad luck is equally distributed, those individuals who are physically less capable, have fewer skills, or suffer from other impediments, such as poor health or disabilities, are more likely to suffer hardships in a competitive system. Concerns about outcomes like this are one reason supporters of free markets are typically lambasted for being heartless and uncompassionate on the mild side, to being downright evil at the extreme. In the midst of these kinds of attacks, it can explain why free market supporters also tend to underemphasize the extent of the negative effects.

An honest argument supporting free competitive markets cannot ignore these negative effects or act as if they are unimportant. Fortunately there is a solution; it is possible to respond to these negative outcomes in competitive markets in a compassionate way. However, the solution is not the one typically provided by those suspicious of free markets. Policies that tax the rich and redistribute to the poor, although well intentioned, are nonetheless applying involuntary transfers to correct for these problems. A more equitable and reasonable solution can be found in another type of transfer, *voluntary transfers*. Examples are discussed in the next chapter.

CHAPTER 9

Voluntary Transfers

A competitive free market economy, absent involuntary transfers, will lead to higher incomes for whoever is able to provide the greatest benefit to others. Some successes will arise because the person works long and hard, others successes will accrue to those who are smart or clever, while still other successes will arise by sheer luck.

Low incomes will accrue to those less fortunate. Some may earn less because they are not willing to work hard, some will not have the skills or abilities needed by others, and some will have low incomes because of bad luck.

In the natural animal world, the weakest animals are generally left to fend for themselves, which in most circumstances results in early death. The stronger animals simply do not have the resources and capacity to care for the infirm without jeopardizing their own survival or the success of their more resilient offspring. As a result, the weak are left to an unpleasant fate.

A personal example of the cruelty of nature occurred one day as I was hiking near Washington DC. A mother goose was walking along with several goslings following her closely. One gosling was obviously crippled, limping with great difficulty to try to keep up with its siblings and its mother. To add insult to injury, every time this poor gosling caught up to the group, the mother goose would viciously attack the crippled offspring and chase it away. Clearly, this young goose was being abandoned by its mother and by Mother Nature. It would not live long with its limited capabilities and lack of support from its mother.

As humans, we might evaluate the behavior of the mother goose in terms of our common moral codes and suggest that perhaps she is evil; however, we normally do not attribute moral behaviors to animals. Clearly the mother goose is acting according to her nature. Instinctively she abandons her weak offspring. Biologically this makes sense since extra time and devotion to the weakest member would reduce the resources she can provide to her healthy offspring, thus giving the healthy ones a lower chance of survival. By abandoning the weak she provides extra support for the strong. Of course, she is probably not thinking this nor is she concerned about what other geese think. Instinct and nature are often cruel, but are also natural.

In contrast, human society has achieved the ability to produce much more than is necessary for the mere survival of the species from generation to generation. That surplus has also arisen naturally via the successful expansion of the voluntary exchange mechanism; what Hayek called the spontaneous economic order. However, as demonstrated in the previous chapter, that mechanism does not ensure that everyone will thrive. Such a system could leave weaker members behind, much like the poor gosling.

The presence of a surplus in human society makes it possible to act with compassion to those less fortunate. A sufficient surplus enables some to transfer resources to the less fortunate to allow them, at the minimum, to survive, where otherwise they may not, and at a maximum to enable them to achieve a level of well-being comparable to those with much better natural endowments.

Today, in a rich society, there is no reason why a competitive economic system cannot be compassionate to the less fortunate at the same time. The wealthier and the more fortunate can afford to forgo some consumption, some profit, to transfer resources to the less fortunate, and help ensure that everyone, even those in dire circumstances, can enjoy some of the basic pleasures of life.

There are two ways to achieve the necessary transfer. First, society can force individuals to transfer benefits to others involuntarily. All governments are capable of achieving this with taxation and transfer programs. Alternatively, society can inspire people to give voluntarily to others in need. The latter method seems preferable to the former.

Probably this is the main reason voluntary transfers, or giving, is highly praised. John D. Rockefeller, who made his fortune in the oil industry and later established the Rockefeller Foundation, said, "Think of giving not as a duty but as a privilege." Winston Churchill said, "We make a living by what we get, but we make a life by what we give." Maya Angelou, the well-known novelist, said, "I have found that among its other benefits, giving liberates the soul of the giver." Talking about government's responsibility toward others, former U.S.

President Jimmy Carter said, "Government is a contrivance of human wisdom to provide for human wants. People have the right to expect that these wants will be provided for by this wisdom." Marian Wright Edelman said, "Service is the rent we pay to be living. It is the very purpose of life and not something you do in your spare time." Finally, John F. Kennedy said, "Ask not what your country can do for you, but what you can do for your country."[1]

Each of these statements highlights the high regard most people have for giving, service, and charity. For many, charity is a moral imperative. Christians are taught the story of the Good Samaritan from the Book of Luke in the New Testament. In the parable, Jesus tells of a traveler who is robbed, stripped, and left for dead. Two people pass him by and leave him in distress. Later a Samaritan stops and provides assistance. Similarly, the Koran encourages Muslims to "give food out of love for Him to the poor and the orphan and the captive:... only feed (them) for Allah's sake;... desire... neither reward nor thanks." In both cases, giving to others, especially those in greater need, is considered morally righteous. One is encouraged to give, and to expect or demand nothing in return.

In modern societies voluntary transfer activities are widespread and have developed in a variety of ways. They occur whenever one person receives a benefit, transferred from someone who gives voluntarily. Perhaps most voluntary transfers occur person to person, or family to family, as with gift giving for holidays and birthdays. Some voluntary transfers occur via private organizations that have been created to fulfill a larger charitable purpose. Finally, a considerable amount of voluntary transfers occur as a result of government activities, also designed to fulfill some social purpose.

In this chapter we will highlight the many different ways voluntary transfer profit manifests itself in modern societies. Afterwards we will assess how voluntary contributions can be stimulated to alleviate the hardships expected in a free market competitive economy.

Household and Community Transfers

Perhaps the most significant voluntary transfers occur every day within individual households. Consider a family with a husband, wife, and several children. By earning wages from work during the week, the adults in the family generate income to provide for the food, shelter, and other needs of the entire household. The children do not typically contribute to the income of the family, until they are older, and thus all of the benefits they receive come as a voluntary transfer from their parents. To make this arrangement possible, the parents need to make income in excess of what is needed to provide for themselves. In other words they need to produce a surplus.

In some families the surplus is used to provide for elderly family members: parents or grandparents who are unable to work and provide for themselves. Sometimes one families' surplus is given to more distant relatives: an aunt, uncle, or cousin who has fallen on hard times.

Families also transfer goods and services to each other in the form of gifts. Gifts are given to one another on special occasions like birthdays and weddings, and holidays such as Christmas and Passover. Sometimes gifts are given simply as a sign of love or friendship.

Clearly, families give to each other enormously and it is perhaps the most important form of voluntary transfer that exists in human society.

Civil Society

What is broadly known as civil society has grown in prominence in recent years. Mostly these organizations arise because the organization's founders recognize a need or demand in a community or in the world that is not being adequately satisfied. Because the needs are widely varied, so too are the organizations themselves. Even the labels given to these types of organizations are diverse. They include charities, nonprofit organizations (NPOs), foundations, nongovernmental organizations (NGOs), the "third," the social economy, and, of course, civil society.

The Johns Hopkins Comparative Nonprofit Sector Project provides a workable definition for civil society (Salamon, Sokolowski, and Wojciech 2004). First, an organization must have some structure and regularity to their operations, but need not be constituted as a formal legal entity. Second, the organization must be private rather than public, especially in their operations and decision making, although they may receive substantial funding from a government. Third, the organization does not distribute profit to shareholders, instead reinvesting any profit back toward the prime objectives. Fourth, the organization must be self-governing and not controlled by an external group. Finally, membership and participation is voluntary. No coercive measures are used to obtain funding or to solicit labor assistance.

Civil society organizations have been created to support numerous special causes, including cultural interests, education, research, health and social services, environmental concerns, development and housing issues, civic advocacy, and religious congregations. The organizations collect donations from individuals, companies, or governments and use these funds to finance assistance for a group of people in need.

There is a bewildering array of organizations. Some charities focus on a particular local need. For example, Miriam's Kitchen in Washington DC provides regular meals to the homeless in the community. Other charities are national in scope, such as the American Red Cross, which is well known in its role to collect blood donations and provide numerous others forms of health emergency assistance. Finally, some charities have become truly global, such as Doctors without Borders, which offers emergency medical assistance to people affected by war and natural disasters, especially in less developed countries that cannot cope with these emergencies.

Some charities are run by religious organizations, such as Christian Charities or Islamic Relief. Some focus on health issues like the San Francisco AIDS Foundation. Others provide "Freedom from Hunger." Some organizations perform essentially *expressive functions.* These include advocacy groups like the Save Darfur Coalition, environmental groups such as the National Wildlife Foundation, and human rights groups like Amnesty International.

Philanthropic foundations are usually the best funded since they typically have a primary contributor whose name is attached. These foundations provide grants for research and social projects using the investment income from a large stock of assets that make up the initial contribution. Since the asset stock remains in place, it can support operational expenditures and giving for an indefinite period of time. Foundations also solicit additional contributions to help maintain their program levels or to expand. The three largest foundations in the United States in terms of total historical giving are the Gates Foundation at $2.8 billion as of 2006, the Ford Foundation with giving of $532 million, and the Robert Wood Johnson Foundation with giving of $346 million.[2]

Corporations also establish foundations to promote social benefits for others and to generate a certain amount of goodwill for themselves. The largest corporate foundations in terms of total giving over their histories are the Aventis Pharmaceuticals Health Care Foundation ($217 million), the Walmart Foundation ($155 million), and the Bank of America Charitable Foundation ($123 million).[3]

Communities have also established foundations to provide assistance for individuals in need locally. These provide vehicles for individuals and local businesses to contribute to an endowment they know will be reinvested for people in need in the local community. Among the largest of these is the New York Community Trust with total lifetime giving of $157 million, and the Greater Kansas City Community Foundation with $140 million.[4]

The size of the civil society sector around the world is large, important, and growing. Overall, the Foundation Center estimates that in 2005 total giving by all U.S. foundations amounted to just over $10 billion. This is just a fraction of what takes place around the world. The Johns Hopkins Comparative Nonprofit Sector Project estimated that in the 35 developed and developing countries they studied, civil society contributed around $1.3 trillion in expenditures per year in the late 1990s, employed approximately one million workers and engaged about 190 million volunteers.

Although many activities of nonprofit and civil society organizations represent examples of voluntary transfers, not all the activities of nonprofit organizations can be classified as such. For example, some nonprofits operate much like a business in that they provide goods and services to customers who themselves contribute money to finance those services. Examples are hospitals, universities, and religious organizations. A nonprofit hospital, for example, receives a substantial amount of its operating revenue directly from its patients or the patients' insurance companies and provides services to those same individuals. A nonprofit university collects tuition from students to fund its educational services to those same students. A church that collects donations from parishioners uses some of the contributions to build facilities such as the church itself, which in turn provides services to the same group of contributors. Thus, despite classification as nonprofit organizations, a substantial portion of these institutions' activities are better classified as voluntary exchange rather than voluntary transfers. In each case above, individuals give money in exchange for the medical, educational, and spiritual services that are offered in return.

Of course, some portion of these institutions' activities do correspond to voluntary transfers. Hospitals collect donations and receive government funds to help defray the costs of uninsured patients. Universities use tuition and contributions to provide scholarships to especially bright students who may not be able to afford full tuition. Finally, religious organizations use some of their donations to provide essential goods and services to poor families in the community and around the world.

Other civil society organizations, especially those performing an expressive function, are also not obvious examples of voluntary transfers. This includes organizations like soccer clubs, opera companies, fraternities and sororities, book clubs, and the girl scouts. For most of these groups the purpose of the "club" is to organize activities that will most benefit the group itself rather than individuals outside the group. For this reason, contributions to these groups, too, more closely resemble voluntary exchange activity rather than voluntary transfers.

The point to emphasize is that while much of what civil society organizations do correspond to voluntary transfer activity, much of it does not. The distinction can raise several tangential issues. For example, one might ask why a nonprofit organization that receives contributions from customers and provides services to them is not responsible to pay taxes like other businesses that also provide services in exchange for money. I have no answer for this, but it is a question worth considering further.

Government Taxation

Government expenditures are typically put into two categories: (1) spending on goods and services and (2) transfer payments. How to characterize government in terms of the three profit mechanisms is difficult and likely to be evaluated differently by different observers.

The first issue involves the way in which government collects revenues and whether it is deemed voluntary or involuntary. In authoritarian countries without democratic representation, one can easily argue that government revenues are involuntary. In contrast, if a democratically elected legislature implements excessively high taxes, many members could lose the next election to candidates vowing to reduce taxes. Thus, in representative democracies, the people have some power over the actions of its government and thus government revenues might be called voluntary.

In the writings of libertarians and other staunch free market advocates taxation is sometimes described as theft or robbery. On its website, the Ludwig von Mises Institute posts an excerpt from Chodorov (1962) titled "Taxation Is Robbery" that begins with an *Encyclopedia Britannica* definition of taxes as "that part of the revenues of a state which is obtained by the compulsory dues and charges upon its subjects."[5] The fact that taxes are compulsory supports his claim that taxes are robbery.

Chodorov continues with an account of the origins of government taxation:

> A historical study of taxation leads inevitably to loot, tribute, ransom and the economic purposes of conquest. The barons who put up tollgates along the Rhine were tax-gatherers. So were the gangs who "protected," for a forced fee, the caravans going to market. The Danes who regularly invited themselves into England, and remained as unwanted guests until paid off, called it Dannegeld; for a long time that remained the basis of English property taxes. The conquering Romans introduced the idea that what they collected from subject peoples was merely just payment for maintaining "law and order." For a long time the Norman conquerors collected catch-as-catch-can tribute from the English, but when by natural processes an amalgam of the two peoples resulted in a nation, the collections were regularized in custom and law and were called taxes. It took centuries to obliterate the idea that these exactions served but to keep a privileged class in comfort and to finance their internecine wars; in fact, that purpose was never denied or obscured until constitutionalism diffused political power.[6]

Taxation clearly can support the lifestyle and the military activities of an elite ruling class. And given that the ruling class invariably finances an armed force that can, if needed, also threaten its own subjects, it is surely possible to classify taxation as involuntary transfers.

Nonetheless, the fact that legal sanctions are in place to ensure tax compliance and also that tax avoidance is commonplace in most democratic countries may suggest that not all individuals are willing to pay their full tax obligation. Alternatively, it could just mean that individuals are attempting to free ride. If many people avoid taxes such that it leads to an increase in tax rates for the nonavoiders, then tax avoidance can reasonably be seen as an involuntary transfer, fueling the anger and resentment that is frequently aroused in political discussions.

It is difficult to know the specific government programs to which citizens of a country would voluntarily contribute. It may depend on the nature of the spending that the taxes are used to support. Some programs might only solicit support from a fraction of the citizenry. Some might solicit voluntary support only up to a particular funding level, but not beyond. Thus, for any particular government program, different individuals with different preferences and beliefs about government's role, would voluntarily contribute different amounts. This makes it impossible to know what proportion of government to count as voluntary and what to consider involuntary. Certainly, some people in the United States feel the taxes they pay are not overly burdensome because they recognize the valuable services that are being provided. At the same time, there are others who decry the confiscatory nature of taxation and feel the government sector is much larger than it should be.

Government Spending

Taxation used to support government expenditures on goods and services is more like voluntary exchange rather than transfer profit. For example, consider tax revenues used by a local government to finance the town fire department. Protection from fire damage is a service that most households and businesses would be willing to pay for on a private market. However, due to the public good characteristics of fire protection service and the difficulties with preventing free riding, it makes sense to provide this as a government service.

Many other types of government spending provide for public goods that are desired by a substantial portion of the population. This includes expenditures on national defense, road construction, upkeep of parks, police protection, and education. Most of these expenditures should perhaps be classified as voluntary exchange activities since the goods and services are demanded by and provided to the taxpayers. Nevertheless one problem with this classification arises because of the degree of the good or service provision.

Take national defense as an example. Surely, most everyone believes that government should provide for an adequate national defense. No village, city, or country has ever been completely safe from the threat of conquest by other groups. Although we might argue that defense expenditures themselves are technically involuntary, because they are forced upon us by those who threaten us, we can also accept that realistically, we cannot simply wish those threats away. Thus, given the reality of threats, people will voluntarily pay for protection. However, while most everyone wants protection, not everyone desires the same degree of protection. In the United States today, many people believe that national defense spending is excessive. They do not think the United States needs so many nuclear weapons, aircraft carriers, or nuclear submarines. At the same time these individuals have little direct control over how the taxes they pay are used. Consequently they are likely to feel they are being forced to pay more for defense than necessary.

To illustrate, suppose a person calculates that the portion of his taxes that goes to national defense is $4,000. Suppose further the person believes that an adequate national defense could be provided if defense expenditures were 25 percent less. In this case, the individual would voluntarily contribute $3,000 of taxes toward defense, but also believes that the additional $1,000 is excessive. The $3,000 portion of his taxes is certainly voluntary exchange activity, but the remaining $1,000 is an *involuntary transfer*. Because defense is a public good, the provision of the additional $1,000 benefits other people who prefer a higher level of security. The extra $1,000 may also benefit individuals working in the defense industry. Thus, this component of the spending involuntarily transfers benefits from one person to others.

Government Transfers

The second type of government expenditure is known as transfer payments. As the name implies, transfer payments involve money that is simply transferred from taxpayers to selected recipients; the government does not receive a good or service in exchange for the expenditure. Examples of transfer payments include social insurance programs, unemployment insurance, welfare programs, medical programs for the poor or elderly, and government subsidy programs.

As with government spending, some transfer programs, or some portions of programs, are reasonably considered voluntary while some, or some portions, are involuntary. Judgments will vary from person to person and program to program.

With respect to social insurance, taxpayers contribute to programs during their working years and receive benefit payments after retirement, or in the event of disability. The programs are like pension plans. Contributions are a form of saving for the future, while the benefits received later are the returns from that saving. However, in most countries, the transfers go directly from today's working population to today's retired population; there are no savings that accumulate and no return on investment to finance the future benefits. Instead, future benefits will be paid out of taxes collected from future taxpayers. In countries where taxpayers sufficiently outnumber recipients, individuals are mostly content with the system. In these cases social insurance can be thought of as voluntary transfer programs.

However, in many developed countries the number of retirees is rapidly increasing while the proportion of working contributors is falling. This will lead to considerable strain on the system especially if taxes must be increased substantially to pay for the larger group of future retirees. In the United States, many young people believe they will not receive social security payments in the future if the system continues as is, because it may ultimately fail. If this were to occur, or if the pressures of maintaining these systems become difficult, the voluntary nature of these programs may become increasingly involuntary.

In the case of welfare programs, many countries have implemented programs designed to improve the well-being of the nation's poor. An underlying concern motivating these programs is the inequality of income that arises in free market systems. To mitigate these inequalities countries often implement progressive tax systems that require higher rates of taxation for higher income households and lower, or even negative taxes, for low income households. In these ways, using the taxation system and welfare programs, income can be equalized to some degree across the population.

Whether these programs are voluntary or not will depend greatly on the individual views about inequality and progressive taxation. Surely there will be mixed sentiments both within and across countries. Thus, while a substantial proportion of these transfer payments will surely be deemed, by taxpayers themselves, as voluntary, some unknown percentage is likely to be involuntary.

Finally, in the case of government subsidy programs, perhaps only a small percentage might be viewed as voluntary. The recipients of these subsidies, such as the agricultural industries in many countries, would surely favor the transfers. However, the subsidies they receive are much greater than the extra taxes they must pay, so there is no surprise here. In addition, many people are convinced of the importance of supporting family farms and agricultural traditions, or to maintain agricultural production for national security reasons. These individuals might voluntarily contribute to support these programs. However, for many others who recognize the higher costs of food that result, the regressive nature of these subsidies, and the damaging effect the subsidies have on poor farmers around the world, they would clearly prefer not to contribute to these subsidy programs. Since they have little direct control, their tax portions can be considered involuntary.

A Voluntary Transfer Industry—Insurance

Voluntary transfer activity is not restricted to the nonprofit and government sectors. Insurance is one service industry that plays a critical economic role by applying the principle of voluntary transfers.

Insurance is a method to reduce risk. It is also another example of a voluntary transfer program. Insurance services are offered to a group of people who face a positive probability that a catastrophic event will occur. The event will either cause severe financial losses, as with home or business destruction from a tornado, or will require a substantial expenditure to prevent a catastrophic outcome, as with a heart transplant operation. For an insurance program to be effective it is necessary that the catastrophic event occur only to a subset of the pool of people seeking protection. This enables the insurance company to use the sum of the contributions from those who do not suffer a loss to be used to cover the claims of those who do suffer a loss. Since the participants in the insurance pool voluntarily contribute their money, which in turn is transferred to others who suffer a catastrophic loss, insurance is an example of voluntary transfers.

Note that the voluntary component of insurance only corresponds to the value of the claims that are paid. An insurance company will also collect additional contributions to pay for the services provided by the company. These include the financial management of the funds that are held in escrow to be used in the event that claims are submitted, the actuarial services to assess the probabilities of insured events within its client pool, and the work involved to verify the validity of the claims. Monies used to pay for these actions should be classified as voluntary exchange since they represent payment for services rendered.

Fairness and Voluntary Transfers

Voluntary transfers refer mostly to charity and philanthropy. It involves a unilateral transfer in which the giver voluntarily gives to a recipient. Voluntary transfers are easily justified as fair with respect to most conceptions of fairness.

First, since any harm that is caused, is caused to the person voluntarily making the transfer, there is no infringement of privacy fairness. Neither party has reason to object. Perhaps one exception would be if the recipient of the gift feels belittled because of the gift. For example, some poor households may hold a moral conviction that one is supposed to provide for oneself. In this case, a gift of food and clothing, that may seem necessary to the giver to raise the family up out of poverty, may nevertheless undermine the recipient's self-esteem. Acceptance of the gift could make the recipient worse off in these circumstances, although it would be unintentional.

By a similar logic voluntary transfers should also conform to the golden rule. If a person wants others to give to them when in a condition of dire need, then it makes sense to give to others in need when a person can afford to do so. However, one problem with voluntary transfers, and the golden rule more generally, is that sometimes the recipient's preferences are not the same as the giver's preferences. For example, a giver's donations of food and toys for the holidays may not match the recipient's desires. This problem has inspired an alternative version of the golden rule called the Silver Rule, which says, "do unto others as others would have done unto them." In essence the Silver Rule encourages the giver to put himself in the position of the recipient and imagine the recipient's preferences. If this can be accomplished effectively then voluntary transfers are also more effective. If it is not achieved then at worst the giver gives and the recipient receives little that is desired.

In terms of maximum benefit fairness we might at first blush argue that voluntary transfers are neutral since the value of what is given is equal to the value of what is received. However, it may be incorrect to think that the giver only suffers a loss equal to the size of his gift. Because voluntary transfers are generally considered praiseworthy, the giver may receive psychological benefits. If the giver is sufficiently wealthy, these psychic benefits may even exceed the loss of utility caused by the transfer. Since the recipient also benefits, voluntary transfers can produce a net gain. This is the argument that altruism may actually serve one's self-interest. In these circumstances, the transfers are fair vis-à-vis maximum benefit fairness.

Since in most instances voluntary transfers tend to be made by those who are wealthier and received by those in greater need, when transfers occur, the distribution of wealth and income shifts toward greater equality. Thus, voluntary transfers tend to be fair in terms of distributional fairness.

With respect to reciprocity fairness, either positive or negative, voluntary transfers are neutral at best. Although one could argue that because a person gains at another's expense it violates reciprocity, this argument is muted because of the voluntary nature of the transfer. Also with respect to nondiscrimination fairness, voluntary transfers

Table 9.1 Consistency of Voluntary Transfers with Fairness Principles

Distributional	Yes
Nondiscrimination	Neutral
Golden Rule	Yes
Positive Reciprocity	Neutral
Negative Reciprocity	Neutral
Privacy	Yes
Maximum Benefit	Neutral

are clearly discriminatory. However, here again, although one can argue that it violates nondiscrimination fairness, most observers would be reluctant to do so since the discrimination tends to favor the less fortunate.

Table 9.1 offers a summary of the fairness characteristics of voluntary transfers. Voluntary transfers are mostly fair except for several categories for which violation of the principle is neutralized because of the voluntary nature of the transfer.

Conclusion

This chapter has demonstrated how voluntary transfers are manifested in a variety of ways; from the activities of a typical household, the basic functions of charities raising money to be used for people in need, to the operation of basic insurance markets, voluntary transfer activities are widespread. In many instances voluntary transfers occur in the private sector as with household transfers, nonprofit organizations, and civil society. However, transfers made by the government sector are much more significant in magnitude and importance.

One problem with identifying and classifying voluntary transfer activities is that it is sometimes confounded with involuntary transfer profit. This is especially true with respect to government transfers. The need to implement sizeable penalties in the event individuals or businesses do not pay their legally required share of taxes means that some percentage of people must be forced to comply. Different observers clearly see things differently. At one extreme are some libertarians who contend that all taxation is theft. For them perhaps all government activity is involuntary. At the other extreme are those few who would be happy to pay higher taxes in order to foster a more equitable distribution of income.

The chapter has shown that voluntary transfers are mostly fair mechanisms largely because of the freedom of choice. This lies in contrast to the unfairness of involuntary transfers highlighted in chapter 7. Thus, whether the mechanism applied to alleviate harm caused by a free market mechanism is voluntary or involuntary is a very important distinction.

The moderate compromise position is to encourage and promote voluntary transfers but to discourage or prohibit involuntary transfers. In some cases this is easy to identify. For example, household transfers are perhaps the best way to provide for unmet needs because members of a household have the best information about what others in the family need most. However, this solution only works to the extent that the family has an adequate surplus to satisfy the needs of other members. When that surplus is insufficient, a person may need help from outside the household or family.

That help can come from civil society organizations. These groups typically form because members of a community recognize an unmet need and work to satisfy those needs by soliciting contributions from others who have both a surplus and a willingness to contribute for the cause.

When civil society is inadequate to ameliorate hardships, people can and do turn to government. Here the issue of voluntary versus involuntary contributions becomes critical. Certainly there are some government programs that are widely popular. Many people are willing to contribute some amount of taxes for social insurance for example. However, what often begins at a level that most will accept, often ends up at a level that many find excessive.

In the United States, social security began in the 1930s. Initially, the amount of money collected from each working participant was small, and the ratio of workers to retirees remained very high for a long time. This made it possible to offer generous retirement benefits that were paid out of the much larger contributions. However, as the number of retirees rises relative to the working population, to maintain the promised benefits may require a substantial increase in per person contributions. Thus, what began as an acceptable transfer program may require substantial involuntary contributions to sustain.

Another feature of government is that benefits from involuntary transfers are usually concentrated in the hands of a relatively small interest group, with the costs being dispersed across the entire tax base. This contributes to a substantial amount of rent seeking that can slowly increase the size of government. For example, many people, evaluating just one transfer policy, may feel that the benefit to a disadvantaged group is worth the small cost. If in each legislative session, only a small number of transfer requests are made, then again taxpayers may feel that the total cost of several programs is worth it. However, after many years of individually inconsequential transfer programs, taxpayers may suddenly realize one day that the sum total of all the small effects over many years actually has a major effect. Along the way the transfer programs shift from being voluntary to involuntary. Thus, while there may be early acceptance of government intervention when the government is small, support begins to wane as the size of government grows. But once policies are in place it is very difficult, politically, to change them.

In his memoirs Alan Greenspan (2007) writes about a disagreement he had with Ayn Rand over voluntary contributions to fund the activities of government:

> According to objectivist precepts, taxation was immoral because it allowed for government appropriation of private property by force. Yet if taxation was wrong, how could you reliably finance the essential functions of government, including the protection of individuals' rights through police power? The Randian answer, that those who rationally saw the need for government would contribute voluntarily, was inadequate. People have free will; suppose they refused? (52)

Thus, concerns about free riding are valid, as are concerns that, with government, involuntary transfers may get out of hand. The moderate compromise can involve government but it is important to establish mechanisms to prevent government from becoming too large. How large is too large will vary from society to society, as will the extent of assistance to provide to others.

CHAPTER 10

A New Guide to Policy Choice in an Era of Globalization

One of the most important questions in economics and politics is what sort of laws, institutions, and policies a society should implement. A country's constitution defines the basic rules and procedures determining how a country will be governed and what rights and privileges its citizens will enjoy. Each country's legislature establishes rules, regulations, and laws that its citizens must follow. Within each country's constitution a process is defined for changing these laws. Government policy is concerned with the following question: what is the best set of rules and laws for a country to implement? One thing seems clear from the political debates and the continual discussion about how policies ought to be further changed and adjusted; nations have still not reached any sort of "policy equilibrium."

How we choose policies is critically important for everyone. It will determine how rapidly incomes will grow, how many people continue to live in poverty 50 years from now, whether children in the next generation will do better and live happier than their parents' generation, what freedoms and privileges people will enjoy, and what constraints they will face.

The current method of economic policy choice appears to be terribly ineffective. For example, in the debate over trade policy and globalization issues, very little has changed in the past 25, 50, and even 100 years. Despite some dramatic movements toward trade liberalization in the past half century, economic arguments supporting free trade and globalization are presently being strongly countered with interventionist prescriptions by new groups suspicious of the previous trends. In addition, while the debate rages on and with accumulating new evidence supporting one side or the other, the weaknesses of the current analytical methods used to assess policy have been quietly muffled. The reasons for the persistent impasse and for the obscuration are manifold.

One reason is that any policy change will have positive and negative effects nationally and internationally. These impacts, by themselves, simultaneously ensure both support and opposition to any policy proposal. The economic solution of compensation to offset the expected losses is impractical as discussed in chapters 2 and 3; first because it is impossible to accurately identify who gains and who loses how much, and second because there is no way of knowing whether the gains from any prescribed policy change will exceed the losses.

The fact that positive effects from policies like trade liberalization, is possible theoretically, and empirically demonstrable, is not sufficient to prove that these policy options are best in some overall sense. This is because it is always possible to provide theoretical and empirical support for the opposing policies. Although different sides to the debate will contend that their investigative methods are superior to that of their opposition, a more objective observer should conclude that neither side's methods come close to answering the questions: which policy is most efficient (using a *broadly defined* measure of well-being), who are the likely winners and losers, and can we implement a compensation scheme to ensure all will benefit?

Another issue exacerbates the problem: although we cannot realistically identify all the winners and losers from policy changes, some groups will recognize that they would either gain or lose from any proposed policy change. These groups have the incentive to promote or protect their own interests. Often this leads to new policy proposals; proposals that immediately inspire opposition by other groups who recognize they are likely to lose if that policy is implemented. What ensues is a rhetorical battle as each side tries to accumulate as much information supporting their cause and present it to all the other participants in the policy decision; sometimes there are appeals to voters, sometimes to members of a legislature. Thus, there is always a demand for information attesting to the positive and negative impacts of every policy, even though as argued here, that information is incapable of indicating whether the policy choice is good or bad from an overall perspective.

The result is numerous policies that tend to favor some groups at the expense of others. The groups more likely to win are those who can most effectively exert influence within the process. The winning groups will sometimes be those with more money to spend on a campaign to bolster support, sometimes the groups will be ones who have personal connections to a large network of decision makers, sometimes groups will win because they transfer or bribe enough people to support their cause, and finally sometimes groups will win because they have disseminated information effectively enough to convince a sufficient number of people to choose their preferred policy.

Unfortunately, this sort of decision procedure is unlikely to lead to policies that are ideal in any overall sense, except by sheer luck. We can never measure the outcomes adequately enough to know for sure. Instead the process will lead to continual policy changes and adjustments driven largely by changes in the ability of different groups to influence others over time. In other words, as some groups become more influential, their policies will be adopted while the policies preferred by groups with falling influence will be overturned. This approach leads nowhere but in circles.

An alternative approach to policy evaluation is to consider whether a policy is fair or just. However, here too, the choice criteria are incapable of providing a definitive guide to policy. That is because there are at least seven distinct fairness conceptions that evaluators can choose from and these principles contradict each other when used to evaluate particular policy choices. Given the added problems that each fairness conception can be applied either narrowly or broadly and that different variables can be chosen for the fairness evaluation, and we get a situation where virtually any policy can be considered fair. By picking the appropriate fairness conception and its application, a policy can be reasonably deemed fair by one group but simultaneously argued to be unfair by another group.

A New Way Forward

Of course, unless or until we conceive of a viable alternative, it is impossible to change the way we evaluate policies. For any alternative to be broadly acceptable, it must recognize the concerns on all sides. Any alternative must also be relatively simple to understand and implement; complex ideas have little chance of appealing to a mass audience.

The policy proposal in this book suggests a new way forward by applying a simple heuristic mechanism for policy choice. The mechanism represents a moderate compromise between what are often seen as the two extremes in policy options: policies promoting a free market versus policies promoting social justice and fairness. The compromise mechanism has the potential to garner broad support among a diverse group of people because it identifies a single root cause of concern shared by observers on opposite sides of the policy spectrum. Although the mechanism described here will be described primarily with reference to globalization policies, the compromise mechanism is general enough to apply to all public policy decisions.

Simply stated, the mechanism involves choosing policies, procedures, and institutions in light of three basic principles, which individually and together serve to promote five goals:

a. Efficiency: Enable and promote mutually voluntary exchanges
b. Security: Discourage, restrict, or prohibit involuntary transfers
c. Compassion: Enable, and encourage, voluntary transfers
d. Freedom: promote voluntary actions but prevent involuntary actions.
e. Justice: adhere to all three principles simultaneously

Efficiency

Economic efficiency is achieved by allowing and promoting voluntary exchanges whenever, wherever, and with whomever, people wish to make them. Voluntary exchange generates surplus value that benefits both parties in every exchange, thus because of trade something less becomes something more. That is the definition of rising efficiency: creating something more out of less. Voluntary exchange is also necessary to take advantage of the division of labor, which enables greater individual output (economies of scale) via specialization. Without free voluntary exchange (i.e., trade) afterwards, specialization has no value.

It is not an exaggeration to say that the source of the world's prosperity, the reason for the dramatic increase in so many people's standards of living in recent human history, is the enormous expansion of the division of labor and the voluntary exchanges that sustain it.

Efficiency is promoted in another way, too. Billions of voluntary trades occurring together in a market represent the operation of a free market competitive economy. Competition arises because in a market with thousands or millions or billions of trades, many people will be offering to sell similar products. Buyers will have more than one seller to choose from. As a result sellers will win the competition against other sellers only by offering a product that is more desirable to the consumer. In other words, the "competitive market" creates an *incentive* to satisfy consumer desires and demands. This is the ultimate goal of an economic system. The greater the competition, the greater are these incentives, and the greater is the potential surplus generated out of the process. Thus, a competitive market promotes the incentives that result in greater economic efficiency.

Security

Security is achieved by discouraging, restricting, or prohibiting involuntary transfers. Complete and total security is impossible since, in the presence of a surplus, and when individuals store that surplus in the form of property and goods, theft will always be a possible method to profit for some people. In addition, violence between individuals or between countries seems unlikely to disappear anytime soon. For these reasons, defense of one's person and property is necessary.

In one sense, defense is a wasteful activity since all resources devoted to protection are unavailable to produce other directly useful goods and services. In a perfect world individuals would not need locks and safes and guns for security; businesses would not need security guards; communities would not need a police force; and countries would not need a standing army. If all of those resources were devoted to producing food, clothing, movies, and vacations, a substantially greater amount of goods and services would be available. However, because involuntary transfers in the form of theft and violence are always present, we do need to prevent it as best we can. Defense is an unfortunate necessity.

Government can play a role in providing for a community's and a nation's defense. Most important are laws prohibiting personal violence and property theft and punishments for those found guilty of these transgressions. However, involuntary transfers occur in many more diverse ways than just theft and violence. They also occur if workers are exploited and mistreated, when people take bribes, when people lie or cheat to gain an advantage over others, and even when government policy is used to restrict competition and give some groups advantages over others. Thus, government is not only the solution; it is also the problem. Distinguishing between what government can do to promote security and what it must stop doing because it inhibits security is critically important.

Security is also very important as an incentive for voluntary exchange. If a person or business fears that some of their surplus will be taken away by force or by government intervention, they are likely to either reduce the amount of time and effort devoted to creating the surplus (if what you produce is taken away, why do so much of it?) or to build up defenses to prevent the transfers (invest in fences and locks or hire tax lawyers to reduce tax liability, etc.). In contrast, if people and businesses feel more secure, then greater exchanges and fewer defensive responses will arise, thus enabling greater economic efficiency.

Compassion

Enabling and encouraging voluntary transfers promotes compassion. Compassion involves helping those who are least able to help themselves, or giving to those who are most in need. One may classify those less fortunate, or those who suffer from terrible maladies, as victims. Probably everyone has been a victim at least one time in their lives. People are victims anytime they are injured or killed. People are victims anytime someone steals or defaces their possessions or property. Sometimes people are victims when they suffer losses in a natural or manmade disaster, such as a hurricane or a chemical factory explosion.

It is common for people to rally around to support those who suffer from serious losses. Families help each other every day. People contribute to their churches, to charities, and other nonprofit organizations, all of which devote time and resources to helping people in need. These are all examples of compassionate voluntary transfers.

Governments too make transfers to those in need. These come in the form of social insurance, welfare, food stamps, and unemployment compensation. Whether these government transfers are voluntarily provided by the taxpayers, or what proportion is voluntary, is arguable, as discussed in chapter 9. Nevertheless, some portion of government transfers surely corresponds to compassionate voluntary transfers.

Voluntary transfers also provide a solution to the losses that some individuals will face in a competitive market economy. However, this common suggestion to provide compensation is problematic because it generally would require the use of involuntary transfers to be fully effective. In addition, automatic compensation is likely to reduce the incentives to adjust to changing market conditions and act to reduce efficiency effects. Voluntary transfers can alleviate the losses to those who are most negatively affected; not automatically, but out of compassion by those more fortunate toward those less fortunate.

Freedom

Individual freedom is promoted whenever voluntary decisions are allowed and involuntary transfers restricted. Freedom is epitomized in the opportunity to exchange freely any items one owns, or any service one can provide, with whomever one wishes. Any restrictions on voluntary exchanges or any action that forces a change in the terms of exchange (as, for example, with a tax) must necessarily reduce the freedom of the individual traders. Freedom is a feature of all voluntary transfers. People should always be allowed to give whatever is theirs to whomever they wish, for whatever reason they wish.

However, freedom to do whatever one wants is not absolute. It is subject to one important restriction: people are not free to take possessions involuntarily from another. A classic example of something someone should *not* be free to do is to shout FIRE(!) in a crowded auditorium (when there is no fire, of course). Why not? The reason is that shouting fire amounts to an involuntary transfer. Although the motivation to shout fire may seem senseless to outside observers, the shouter must be doing so to achieve some personal benefit. However, to achieve that benefit, the shouter takes away (transfers) the security and well-being of the rest of the crowd involuntarily.

It is sometimes stated that people should be free to do anything as long as it does not harm someone else. However, this is not the appropriate principle either. When a new trader enters a market with a more desirable product, a consumer may stop purchasing from a previous seller and begin to purchase from the new seller. As a result, the previous seller is harmed by the presence of the new seller with a better product. However, the harm caused in this circumstance is a by-product of the voluntary exchange process with multiple sellers and buyers. The harm comes from the consumer's voluntary choice to exchange with someone else. Since this is not an example of an involuntary transfer, these actions should be unimpeded. Thus it is not appropriate to claim that people should be free to do anything that does not harm another. The distinguishing criterion must be *the reason* harm befalls another. People should be free to give whatever they own to another either in exchange or unilaterally for whatever reason. People should not be free to take something involuntarily away from another.

Security in one's person and property also enables maximum freedom. When someone feels threatened by another, fearful that he may suffer bodily harm or theft of his possessions, he is forced by that fear to invest in security measures. Security requires the use of resources (e.g., money must be spent to purchase safes, fences, and guns) that detract from what a person might otherwise prefer to do. In this way, even the threat of involuntary transfers affects the terms of exchange and the choices individuals make. If, by magic, one could eliminate the threat of involuntary transfers, then people would be free to pursue fully that which they most desire at no additional cost to themselves. However, because the prospect of eliminating all involuntary transfers is idealistic, security comes at a cost. Devising a method to inhibit involuntary transfers in the least costly way, while promoting all other voluntary activities, is the path to maximum individual freedom.

Justice

In the debate about globalization it is common for people to argue in support of fairness and social justice. But what exactly do people mean? Chapter 4 argued that there are multiple fairness principles, all of which are individually reasonable, but which conflict with each other when applied to specific public policy issues. Despite that conflict, now, we can respond with a simple definition of justice.

Justice prevails with the simultaneous application of the compromise principles: promotion of voluntary exchange, promotion of voluntary transfers, and the restriction of involuntary transfers. If a society can apply these principles, individual opportunities will abound, economic efficiency will be enhanced, security in one's person and property will be maximized, and those least fortunate will be the recipients of compassionate voluntary outpourings. Individual freedom will be maximized as well.

How such a society will look is anyone's guess since whatever arises will be the result of innumerable individual decisions, not the result of control at the top. The economy and people's lives will go where the individuals themselves want them to go and not where a government, or a group of influential people, prefers.

One thing missing from these principles of justice is any discussion of the distribution of income. Adhering to these principles says next to nothing about how unequal the income distribution will be and provides no centralized control over the outcome. Nevertheless, adhering to the principles will ensure that people who give the most to others, via the voluntary exchange process, will be the ones who earn the highest incomes. To repeat, those who give the most, receive the most! Adherence to the principles will also mean that high incomes will not accrue to those who have taken advantage of others using involuntary transfers. Hence the income distribution that does arise will be merit-based. Finally, although low incomes will accrue to those who are less lucky or less fortunate, a compassionate society can choose to reduce any inequities and provide for a safety net to ensure that no one suffers unconscionably.

Lastly, achieving justice, as defined here, does not require an outpouring of altruism and the diminution of egoism. Egoism and the pursuit of profit is a characteristic that is necessary to promote true justice. Without individual desire to promote one's self-interest, there would be little motivation to engage in voluntary exchange and without exchange would come a dramatic reduction in productive efficiency effects and a drop in a society's average living standards. However, this definition of justice does not condone *every* individual action to promote self-interest since benefits arising out of involuntary transfers are soundly discouraged. Thus, true justice requires egoism to be directed appropriately; the right application being a necessary condition to achieve greater prosperity, while the wrong application being responsible for many of society's perceived problems. Finally, altruism is not the antidote to egoism as often suggested. Instead altruism provides a compassionate mechanism to relieve the suffering of those less fortunate, not as a substitute for appropriate egoism, but as a complement to egoism.

Policy Recommendations: Applications of the Heuristic Mechanism

The compromise mechanism is a method to evaluate policies. With these principles in mind we can now discard the traditional techniques that try to measure who wins and who loses. Instead of asking what the benefits and costs of different policy choices will be, we can now ask: what do the justice principles imply for trade policy, for immigration policy, for environmental policy? How do they change our perceptions of the role of government? When are taxes appropriate and how should they be collected? What is the role of the judiciary? How can a system best be devised that simultaneously promotes efficiency, freedom, security, compassion, and justice? Below I will apply the principles to a collection of issues relating to globalization. In many instances we need only to enforce laws that are already in place. In other instances there may be a need to adjust the laws or regulations slightly. Finally, sometimes the principles call for a complete dismantling of current policies.

The list of polices considered below is a selected sample that are prominent in the globalization debate. However, the principles apply to every public policy discussion. Readers and researchers are encouraged to use and apply these principles to a much broader class of issues.

Finally, the policies that follow from the principles should be regarded as goals to be achieved in the future. I say this fully cognizant of the fact that implementation of these policy options is likely to be very difficult. Resistance to change will be strong since complete implementation will cause some parties to knowingly lose relative to the status quo. Nevertheless, it is important to identify goals to strive for and justifications for those outcomes. Currently we seem to be going around in circles with respect to globalization policy and public policy more generally; sometimes choosing to be more liberal and other times choosing to be more restrictive. In all of the discussion it is hard to identify an ending point. The purpose of the next section is to suggest simple and definitive policy objectives together with clear rationales for the choices.

Goal 1: Choose Free Trade

Freer trade in goods, services, and international investment, together with the technological changes, like the advancement of telecommunications, are perhaps the most important changes that have inspired the mad dash toward globalization in both economic and social contexts. Still, free trade remains a widely contested policy. Both supporters and opponents of freer trade and globalization make their cases by analyzing the effects of various policies and asking whether each policy would make the people of a country better or worse off. Both sides assess the effects using different measures of well-being and different norms of justice and fairness. Unfortunately, these approaches do not provide convincing answers.

The compromise mechanism suggested here offers a new way to make judgments about policies, based not on imperfect measures of individual and global effects, but rather based on simple principles. With regard to the issue of trade policy, the mechanism clearly supports free trade, without exception.

Free trade means the removal of impediments to free voluntary exchanges between residents of different countries. Free trade is clearly procompetitive and thus can be thought of as an international extension of antitrust motivations. As such, it is the extension of voluntary exchange to an international context.

A free and competitive system provides an answer about what to do in the face of great uncertainty. Not only are the overall effects of government policy changes unknowable, so is knowledge of what consumers really want. In a dynamic ever-changing world economy, even firms themselves will not know for sure how to best provide products for their customers in the future. What sells today, may not sell tomorrow. Thus, the most effective way to discover consumer demands and desires is for numerous firms to freely compete with each other. In the process, an economy will experience a continual churning of creative destruction. The creative destruction process itself is like a grand experiment, constantly being run and rerun to determine how best to serve the primary interests in society; that being the pursuit of individual happiness, as the individuals themselves define it.

Note that this recommendation for free trade is not based on the argument that free trade is most efficient or even that we can know that it is *best* in some overall or aggregate sense. The inability to measure the overall effects of any policy means that we have as little chance of verifying the superiority of free trade, as we have of verifying every other policy ever proposed.[1] Instead free trade is supported on the basis of simple principles—the moderate principles. In turn, those principles were derived by asking what we might do to design policies if we accept the premise that we know so little.

Alan Greenspan (2007) highlighted the promise and the problems of the free market system:

> The problem is that the dynamic that defines capitalism, that of unforgiving market competition, clashes with the human desire for stability and certainty. Even more important, a large segment of society feels a growing sense of injustice about the allocation of capitalism's rewards. Competition, capitalism's greatest force, creates anxiety in all of us. One major source of it is the chronic fear of job loss. Another, more deeply felt angst stems from competition's perpetual disturbance of the status quo and style of living, good or bad, from which most people derive comfort. . . . "creative destruction"—the scrapping of old technologies and old ways of doing things for new—is the only way to increase productivity

and therefore the only way to raise average living standards on a sustained basis. (268)

Any restrictions to international trade represent impediments to voluntary exchange, while simultaneously promoting involuntary transfers. For example, a tariff or quota is known to cause a redistribution of income. Some people lose income because of the tariff while others gain, both at home and abroad. Those who lose, have money, or benefits, involuntarily taken away. In light of this, it is the impediments to free trade, typically justified on the basis of self-serving interests, that conflict with the moderate principles, not free trade itself.

The alternative to free trade is what we might call selected protectionism. These are trade policies implemented to correct for certain perceived problems. Among the most important are trade remedy laws, agricultural protections, and infant industry protections. We will consider these exceptions to free trade next, and evaluate them with respect to the moderate principles.

Goal 2: Dismantle Trade Remedies

The WTO-sanctioned trade remedy laws—antidumping, antisubsidy, and safeguards—are available to provide protection from foreign competition for import-competing firms in certain situations. In antidumping and antisubsidy cases, the justification for protection is unfair foreign competition. Antidumping actions are allowed if foreign firms sell their products too cheaply in the domestic markets and cause economic injury to domestic competitors. Antisubsidy actions are allowed when the foreign government subsidizes exports thereby causing imported products to be sold too cheaply in the domestic market and causing injury to the domestic firms. Finally, safeguards are implemented when a sudden increase in imports of a product occurs, causing injury to the domestic import-competing firms.

In all of these cases, trade remedy actions involve raising the import tariff to correct for (or remedy) the perceived trade problem. The protection granted does just that; it *protects* the domestic firms from foreign competition. It does so by restricting the free voluntary exchanges between domestic consumers and foreign firms at mutually agreeable prices.[2] The effect of the protection is also to transfer money involuntarily from some consumers and foreign producers toward the domestic firms. As such the remedies themselves violate the compromise principles because they restrict voluntary exchange and use government regulations to instigate involuntary transfers.

The fact that domestic firms welcome such policies is no surprise. Firms are always eager to find mechanisms that enable them to restrict competition. In this case it is the government actions themselves that facilitate an anticompetitive outcome.

Of course, the justification for antidumping and antisubsidy is the purported unfair actions of foreigners. In antidumping cases, foreign firms may be using a monopoly position abroad to enable them to underprice their product in their export market. That monopoly position represents an involuntary transfer process abroad. Similarly, in antisubsidy cases, the foreign government subsidies represent an involuntary transfer process that provides competitive advantages to the foreign firms. Thus, domestic firms are injured because of foreign government use of involuntary transfer policies.

In the safeguards case, the remedies do not protect against unfair actions but instead offer temporary protection in circumstances of extreme competition (a sudden surge of imports) and market churning. Thus, safeguard actions are pure involuntary transfers that do not counter foreign involuntary transfers. As such they are a prime example in which industries have used the power of government to implement regulations that restrict competition in difficult situations. The prime losers are the domestic consumers who must pay higher prices and for whom free voluntary exchanges with foreign firms have been restricted.

The ideal policy outcome in terms of the compromise principles is clear: the complete elimination of trade remedy laws. This means, paradoxically, that to be more fair, we should eliminate the trade laws purportedly protecting against unfair trade. The problem with trade remedy laws is that they correspond to a manifestation of involuntary transfers—some groups in the economy benefit at the expense of others who have little to no say in the matter.

In instances when foreign monopoly positions exist or when foreign government subsidies enable dumping, a more appropriate and efficient response is either to directly eliminate the foreign involuntary transfer process or to accept the cheaper foreign products. Although trade remedies can be thought of as inflicting harm upon foreigners, because of the harm they have caused us (an application of negative reciprocity fairness), one can argue that two wrongs (i.e., two instances of involuntary transfers) do not make a right. Better to work toward the elimination of foreign monopolies and subsidies in order to achieve a more truly competitive international economy, rather than pile more involuntary transfers on top of existing ones.

Indeed, such advice is consistent with the theory of the second-best described in chapter 2. Second-best theory says that the best policy options are always the ones that attack the market distortion or imperfection most directly. In this example, one would classify the foreign involuntary transfer policy as a distortion because the action involves the taking of property, mostly from the import-competing firm. However, the trade remedy action by the importer government also represents a distortion since it involves another involuntary transfer action, effectively taking property back from the foreign firms.[3] While it will always be true that correcting one distortion with another can raise the well-being of some participants, the better policy overall is the elimination of both distortions; that is, foreign firms do not acquire monopoly positions or receive subsidies from their government, and importing countries do not use trade remedies.

Goal 3: Dismantle Infant Industry Protections

Developing countries often use the infant industry argument to justify protection. According to this argument, firms in developing countries cannot compete in head-to-head competition with firms in developed countries and thus need to be protected until they can become more efficient. Although in theory, infant industry protection, appropriately implemented, can improve the well-being of a country, the argument suffers from the serious information problems described earlier: it is impossible to know which industries to protect, at what level to protect, how long to protect, and whether the protections will really have a net positive effect. Consequently, the use of this policy is like a shot in the dark at a moving target.

More importantly, infant industry protection clearly discourages both voluntary exchange and the competitive discovery process. This means that firms and the country would be less likely to foster the dynamism that would be achieved with more competition. Nevertheless, infant industry protection draws wide support, largely because the involuntary transfers that result from protection, transfers primarily from domestic consumers to domestic firms, make conducting business decidedly easier for the import-competing firms. These firms engage loudly in domestic policy debates and use rhetorical methods to convince their own governments to implement or maintain these policies.

Bear in mind that the proposal to dismantle infant industry protections is not based on some empirically determined guarantee that freer trade will automatically improve the well-being of the nation. Just like we cannot know whether infant industry protections will have positive overall effects, we also cannot know if freer trade instead will have positive effects. Thus, the proposal to eliminate protection is based on the positive aspects of the compromise principles themselves in the face of imperfect knowledge about which policy is best.

Goal 4: Fight Corruption and Bribery

For a developing country a critical factor affecting a movement to freer trade is the number of other market imperfections and distortions that remain in place. Perhaps the most worrisome are those representing egregious forms of involuntary transfers. For example, among the key problems facing developing countries are inadequate legal protections for private property; or when protections do exist, inadequate enforcement of those rights. These institutional problems can result in widespread corruption. Corruption, such as bribe taking, government favoritism, or outright theft, not only inspires contempt within society, but is also likely to discourage voluntary exchange activity. After all, if one cannot secure ownership of one's property, or if one's hard-earned profit is whittled away by the bribes one must pay to stay in business, or if profit is stolen away by corrupt officials, then where is the incentive to produce? Or, as is more likely, why not give up hard work and productive activity entirely and redirect one's efforts toward corruption for your own benefit? If everyone else is corrupt, why not engage in corruption oneself, especially when it is easier to do so?

If free trade is implemented in a country with weak legal institutions and widespread corruption, it is not at all clear that the promotion of *international* voluntary exchange activity will inspire more *domestic* voluntary exchange activity. If instead, the international exchange merely provides greater opportunities for involuntary transfers, or if opportunities for corruption expand in some way, then free trade alone will not offer an adequate solution.

Essentially, this is why the advice of Western economists to implement free market shock therapy in the former Soviet republics failed miserably. Russia and most of the other newly independent states simply did not have the appropriate institutional mechanisms in place to prevent the widespread theft of state resources that occurred once state control was eliminated. Instead of promoting a free and open environment for voluntary exchange, shock therapy initiated large-scale involuntary transfers leading to widespread corruption.

This is not to say that there are exceptions to the compromise principles; instead this is an argument that the sequencing of a transition to freer trade is important. The advice remains to eliminate as many involuntary transfer activities as possible and to promote voluntary exchange. For developing countries however, it may be necessary to solve the domestic involuntary transfer problems before free trade and the promotion of voluntary exchange can become effective. These policy guidelines merely identifies the goal and the justification for that goal, it does not yet offer a guide to the sequencing of changes, or the best transition path.

Corruption is not a developing country issue entirely. In every society, corruption, bribery and other nefarious practices are common. All such practices are examples of involuntary transfers deserving of legislative prohibitions and enforcement. Although it may never be possible to eliminate these practices entirely, the establishment of a strong judicial system capable of prosecuting and punishing corruption can serve as a deterrent.

Goal 5: Dismantle Agricultural Supports

Most of the developed countries in the world, and many others as well, support their domestic agricultural industries. In some cases this involves high protective tariffs on imports, but more notably, interventions involve domestic price supports and other income maintenance programs. Agricultural subsidies measure in the hundreds of billions of dollars annually around the world. The arguments used to justify these policies range from the need to provide insurance from fluctuating prices, to the need to provide for self-sufficiency in food in the event of a national security crisis.

Although these justifications have some validity, they also mask the fact that these same support programs raise food prices thereby inhibiting voluntary exchanges, reduce competition for domestic agricultural firms, and transfer money involuntarily, largely, from consumers and taxpayers to producers. Agricultural industries are strong supporters of these programs because they effectively reduce competition and make their business easier. Unfortunately, the cost of business security is borne by domestic consumers and taxpayers. In light of the compromise principles, agricultural support programs should be dismantled in order to promote voluntary exchange and the dynamic competitive effects in the agricultural industries, and to eliminate the involuntary transfers that support programs engender.

Goal 6: Allow International Factor Mobility (Including Immigration)

Factors of production, both capital and labor, often move to other locations to take advantage of profitable opportunities. When a company decides to move an assembly plant abroad, it is because they expect to be able to reduce production costs, lower the price of their products to their customers and improve their competitiveness. When workers move to another country, they expect that the job opportunities available are better than the ones at homes. That may be because the opportunities at home are nonexistent or meager, or because the available jobs abroad pay substantially more. The profit opportunity in working abroad in the United States and Europe is so great that many people are willing to emigrate illegally and risk prosecution to achieve their goals.[4]

The debate over immigration is often intense. Numerous studies have been done to assess the effects of immigration. Does immigration reduce wages, raise or reduce economic growth, raise or lower poverty rates, increase crime rates, or increase social conflict? No matter how many studies are done, we will never know with much confidence what the overall effects of immigration are. Clearly some groups will recognize how greater immigration will increase competition in their own industry or their own labor market, making it more likely they will suffer adjustment costs. Others, especially firms that hire immigrant workers, recognize that they will benefit from greater immigration. Due to the inherent uncertainties, the rhetorical political debate is unending. The alternative is to set immigration policy on the basis of the compromise principles rather than attempting to convince people using conflicting benefit-cost analyses.

The application of the principles is simple. For both companies and workers, factor movements like immigration are merely examples of mutually voluntary exchanges. Immigration restrictions and impediments to capital mobility are policies that restrict these voluntary exchanges from occurring. They serve to reduce competition for some domestic firms and workers and as such provide involuntary transfers to those protected. In light of the compromise principles the appropriate policy goal is the removal of impediments to international factor mobility. That means free capital mobility and freedom to immigrate.

Of course, immediate and complete factor mobility, especially for workers would certainly cause tremendous adjustment costs as workers from poor countries might be expected to flood into developed country economies. Thus, from a practical perspective, it makes sense to increase immigration and capital infusions gradually over an extended period. Nonetheless the long-term goal should be a world in which workers and companies could move freely to whatever location they expected to profit the most by participating in allowable voluntary exchange activities.

There are several other problems to deal with, especially with respect to immigration. One problem is the potential for immigrants to profit by taking advantage of social services in the host country. In this case their profit arises from the "voluntary" contribution to the social safety net by domestic taxpayers, who may not be happy to see their taxes spent on noncitizens. In other words, host country taxpayers would reasonably view this as an involuntary transfer. One solution to this problem might be restrictions on immigrant claims to social services for a period of time. If migrants knew they could not profit via transfers in a host country, they might be discouraged from migrating unless they expect to find work. Second, social services for poor jobless immigrants could be provided for with voluntary contributions to NGOs designed to fulfill these needs. For example, working individuals in a community of immigrants might be willing to contribute to a fund that would offer assistance to social service support to others in the community. In this way, a local safety net would be provided via voluntary contributions and not at the unwelcome expense of a larger and disconnected set of domestic taxpayers.

Although this discussion merely scratches the surface of the issues arising in the immigration debate, the suggestion here is to apply the compromise principles to each of these issues. The guidelines implore one to ask whether a policy proposal enables or restricts voluntary exchanges, whether it introduces or restricts involuntary transfers, and what role voluntary transfers can play in the solution.

Goal 7: Provide a Generalized Safety Net (Not Targeted Protections)

Since an economy in free trade will be filled with stress and anxiety as agents struggle to compete, a compassionate society will undoubtedly wish to provide a safety net for those agents who, for any reason, suffer continual and persistent losses or who simply do not have the capacity or good fortune to achieve some minimal standard of living.

The minimal standard deemed appropriate will surely vary from country to country but will likely be higher the higher the average income of the country. The larger the surplus a society can generate, the greater its ability to give up some of that surplus to benefit those in need.

The need for a safety net is apparent when we understand the true nature of a competitive system. Despite claims by free trade or pro–free market advocates that everyone benefits in a free, open, and competitive economy, the truth is that competition is likely to cause persistent losses for the weakest agents in the economy. The weak will be those who on average have lower skills, do not work as hard, have physical or mental disabilities, or simply suffer from persistent bad luck.

The compromise principles require that (a) a safety net does not eliminate or reduce competition within the economy (i.e., does not restrict voluntary exchanges) and (b) the safety net provides for transfers voluntarily (i.e., does not force people to help others via involuntary transfers).

For example, consider a government welfare program that transfers income to those individuals with incomes below some prescribed poverty line. To conform to the blueprint, the taxes used for these transfers should be taken from a group of willing taxpayers. If taxpayers are not willing, nonprofit institutions funded by voluntary contributions or donations could provide such a safety net. Alternatively, individuals could use private insurance to protect themselves from temporary losses.

These voluntary transfers should act like a general insurance policy for anyone who suffers persistent or unconscionable losses. Programs could target anyone whose income falls below a certain level and who has no wealth to draw upon. Or, programs might target those who suffer from medical or health problems that prevent them engaging in the market economy. Finally, programs might target the elderly poor who would not be expected to engage in market activity.

In contrast, many protection programs, such as trade adjustment assistance, provide support only for workers who lose their jobs because of one particular problem; increased imports. These policies are discriminatory because they do not cover all individuals who might suffer similar negative competitive circumstances. For example, why do workers in import-competing industries deserve more protection than workers who lose jobs because of technological change?

Safeguards legislation is another example of protection for industries that suffer from a surge of imports. This protection can be thought of as a type of safety net since it will help preserve the jobs in the import-competing industry. However, in this case, protection for some agents is possible only by reducing competition in the import-competing industry, thereby restricting voluntary exchanges. Thus, this policy is not consistent with the compromise principles.

A discussion of how to most effectively maintain competition and simultaneously provide a social safety net is beyond the scope of this study. The point here is to argue that a safety net provision is consistent with the mechanism but that the best design for a safety net is one that promotes voluntary transfers rather than relying on involuntary transfers. Indeed, it may not even be necessary for government to be the main provider of a social safety net. Ideally, families, neighbors, and communities could provide support for people in need. The establishment of numerous NGOs, each fulfilling a different community purpose, and financed via local voluntary community contributions could form the basis for a substantial portion of the social safety net. President George H. W. Bush referred to these organizations as a "thousand points of light" to suggest that when the impacts of many small organizations are cumulated, they can actually have a very significant total effect on a nation. Encouragement of these types of NGOs, serving community needs, is fully consistent with the compromise principles.

Epstein (2003b, 59) points out that voluntary activities are often extensive, and it is a mistake to think that laissez-faire "stifles the expression of individual compassion." However, he also cautions that "(m)odern political institutions have dulled many of those charitable impulses. When the state takes responsibility for the care of the needy, it crowds out private benevolence with public coercion."

Goal 8: Allow Voluntary Alternative Trade: The Fair Trade Movement

Some groups concerned about low wages and worker exploitation in developing countries have decided to take matters into their own hands. Concerned about the low wages of workers in developing countries, these groups have introduced a unique new way to empower consumers who may prefer to purchase goods they know have been fairly produced.

The Fair Trade product market was established by several NGOs. Products such as coffee, tea, bananas, rice, and cocoa that bear a Fair

Trade label can be purchased in developed countries. The label attests to participation in a verification system guaranteeing that the farmers producing the primary product were paid a fair wage. The system uses funds paid by the developed country merchants to operate a monitoring system to ensure that the nonprofit agency's rules are followed. The rules typically require a minimum price be paid per unit to the poor farmers regardless of market conditions, and that basic labor standards be observed. The system offers developed country consumers the opportunity to pay slightly more for their coffee and other products to acquire not just the product but also the knowledge that their purchase does not exploit developing country workers.

The Fair Trade product system is perfectly consistent with the compromise principles primarily because it is voluntary. The system is run by NGOs. Consumers choose whether to pay more for goods with special characteristics. Firms are also allowed to choose whether to participate or not. Although this system may seem to alter the "free market" prices for inputs, it does not because the higher price satisfies a latent consumer preference for particular product characteristics. To the extent that additional money is transferred from consumers to the farmers, the transfer represents a *voluntary* transfer. Also, since none of the businesses are forced to change their behavior, the system does not hinder voluntary exchanges. Of course, this consistency with the compromise principles would change if governments were ever to step in to enforce and expand the process.

Prior to the Fair Trade product movement a similar consumer demand drive was undertaken with regard to sweatshop labor in the clothing and apparel industry. Students and others were encouraged not to buy products from companies or countries where there was evidence of sweatshop labor conditions. One product line especially targeted was college-labeled sportswear and shoes. Among the most prominent targeted company was Nike. For several years, outcries, especially by students on college campuses, not to buy Nike and other products led to careful examination and widespread press coverage of the working conditions in many less developed countries whose factories were producing products to be sold in the developed world. Of course there were numerous problems with interpretation of the evidence. What to one observer was the gross violation of human rights, was to another observer the normal working conditions in developing countries, offering workers a chance to slowly work their way out of poverty. Nonetheless the sweatshop labor movement was largely consistent with the compromise principles, at least in the early stages.

The revelation of any type of consumer preference, even if it relates to the manner in which a product is produced, is perfectly consistent with voluntary exchange. One effect of the movement was to inspire companies like Nike to evaluate and monitor the working conditions of its workers in less developed countries. Although these efforts did not assuage all objections, it was clear that Nike believed it was in their interests to respond to this consumer movement. Eventually, the movement extended its reach by pressuring college administrations to cease purchases of certain product lines in their campus stores. Although a request for these changes is unobjectionable, the implementation of this request would begin to infringe on individual's free voluntary exchanges. Some college students, those who did not particularly care about the sweatshop characteristics of their garments, would be slightly restricted from purchasing freely if the university restricted certain sales. I say *slightly restricted* because these students would not be completely prevented from purchasing similar products elsewhere, albeit with higher search costs.

However, if this same type of request were expanded to the national level with government involved, the intervention would become much more objectionable. For example, if the movement convinced the government to implement import restrictions on egregious products, then everyone in the country would be forced to adhere to the preferences of one special interest group. Legislation such as this would inhibit voluntary exchange activities. Also, because the import restrictions would generate automatic redistributions of income, the action would involve involuntary transfers. Thus, although a consumer driven sweatshop movement is consistent with the compromise principles, a government-sponsored response is not because it shifts the process from voluntary to involuntary.

Goal 9: Prevent Worker Exploitation via Competition

There is an alternative free market process consistent with the compromise principles that could conceivably work to mitigate the problems associated with low wages and sweatshop working conditions. Recall that all transactions are meant to be mutually voluntary which includes the hiring of workers by a business. Consider a company that mistreats its workers, either by paying unusually low wages or with poor working conditions. If the exchange is truly free then workers who believe they are mistreated have no need to continue: they can simply walk away from the job. If they do so, the firm will begin to lose those workers who have better opportunities elsewhere, which will also be the more productive workers. As better workers flee, productivity will fall, and the firm will have difficulty maintaining output. In the extreme, it may be forced out of business. In contrast, if a firm treats its workers better, it will attract and retain the more productive workers. The firm's efficiency will rise and it will have a better chance to succeed.

In a developed country context, Costco is an example of a company that employs this strategy effectively. Costco pays its workers considerably more in both wages and benefits than its major competitors. As a consequence they have an extremely dedicated and loyal workforce, which they mobilize to produce a superior product for their customers. Of course, the fact that a system can work for a firm like Costco does not imply that the same process can work with the market conditions in a developing country.

Undoubtedly, many workers in developing countries are exploited. Some workers arrive in cities from the countryside with an imperfect understanding of how the economic system works. Sometimes they are enslaved by trickery or threats of violence. Although the mechanism does not offer an immediate solution to these problems, it can inspire us to investigate policies that move closer to the idealized free market solution; that which promotes voluntary exchanges and transfers while restricting involuntary transfers.

As discussed in chapter 2, the best solution to any market inefficiency is to be found with a policy that comes closest to fixing the inherent problem. In the case of worker exploitation, the problem is often related to imperfect information on the part of poor workers, inadequate legal protections from violence and fraud, and inflexible labor markets. Other proposed solutions, like the Fair Trade product movement, attempt to convince consumers that they should be concerned about the well-being of distant workers and need to monitor the production processes of the products they buy. However, since consumer indifference in the developed countries is not the real source of the exploitation, it seems unlikely to be very effective in changing the system.

Effective free markets may require a good understanding by the market participants of how a market is supposed to work, including knowledge of legal protections for contract enforcement and other such matters. An NGO that provides legal services to workers can offer valuable information to help smooth the workings of the market. If the funds for the organization are collected from independent donors, like philanthropic foundations, then it represents a voluntary transfer response that can help promote voluntary exchange activity. Paradoxically, if an NGO helps workers to organize unions to force up its wages collectively, then its activities may encourage involuntary transfers. Although many people accept unions as a necessary worker right, it is important to recognize how the empowerment of unions can also inhibit mutually voluntary exchanges. As such, this type of response represents an involuntary transfer solution to involuntary transfer exploitation and does not conform to the compromise principles.

Goal 10: Accept Outsourcing and Offshoring

The issue of outsourcing offers a prime example of the usefulness of the compromise principles in making policy judgments. Outsourcing is a business practice in which services previously provided by in-house employees are now provided by a separate firm. For example, a business might decide to hire another company to provide janitorial services. When the external firm is another domestic firm, outsourcing raises few complaints. However, when the external firm is a foreign firm then the outsourcing is known as offshoring and it often raises vociferous objections.

In recent years offshoring has developed as a highly contentious issue in the United States and European Union as multinational firms have been able to take advantage of the falling cost of telecommunications to shift certain types of jobs to countries like China and India. Whereas traditional trade with these countries may threaten jobs in labor-intensive industries, offshoring has begun to affect the job prospects of highly skilled professionals like computer programmers and medical technicians. That has inspired a dramatic change of heart among many who have been traditional supporters of freer trade. People now claim that the world is different than ever before. Some contend that the traditional economic theories no longer apply. That things are changing more rapidly, there is no question; that the old theories do not apply is simply hogwash!

The compromise principles provide a simple answer of what to do about offshoring: do nothing, allow it to happen. Offshoring represents attempts by companies to lower their costs of production and provide a better service for their customers. Offshoring arises because of the dynamic competitive process and is a clear manifestation of voluntary exchange activity. The only thing new is the ability to outsource abroad, something that has not been readily available to firms previously because of the higher international costs of service provision.

Offshoring is also a manifestation of the creative destruction process. Once firms realize a cost-reducing possibility they should be allowed to take advantage of it because by doing so they are better able to fulfill their fundamental purpose, which is satisfying their customer desires. The firms that do so most effectively will remain in business, while those that do not will ultimately be destroyed. That workers will suffer losses is expected in a dynamic economy and is not a sufficient excuse for policies to protect these jobs.

Every worker in a dynamic competitive economy faces a potential adjustment. A lost job, either from outsourcing; or because of imported goods; or because a superstore opens up down the street; or because an export firm loses out to its other competitors and begins to downsize; all are a part of a dynamic competitive economy. The reasons for job losses are multifaceted and ever changing and they can just as easily affect a production line worker as a top executive. There is nothing special or different about lost jobs because of offshoring.

It makes perfect sense for those who suffer losses from offshoring to construct rhetorical arguments to support protective legislation. It makes sense for them to argue that the world is new and the old theories no longer apply. By building these arguments, workers everywhere may begin to fear job losses and lawmakers may more likely respond with legislation regulating this "new" phenomenon. However, these responses are clearly anticompetitive. They will result in involuntary transfers between consumers and the protected workers and they will be highly discriminatory since the laws will differentially protect those who might suffer a job loss from offshoring but not from other competitive adjustments.

Goal 11: Encourage Worker Preparedness

So then what are workers whose jobs are threatened supposed to do? The best response is an individual one to prepare for the worst. A competitive market will function most effectively if workers understand the vagaries of the system and if they realize that calls for protection, meaning calls for involuntary transfers, will go unanswered. A prepared worker is one who is continually improving his education, constantly in search of better opportunities and resilient enough to persevere in the event a job loss occurs. Opportunities for protection, unfortunately, can act to redirect worker efforts away from what is necessary to land a better job, toward attempts to save one's current job. These efforts are wasteful since they represent activities to secure involuntary transfers rather than efforts directed at useful production.

Tony Blair, the former prime minister of Great Britain, did an excellent job in describing the appropriate worker and societal attitudes that are necessary to maintain these compromise principles:

> The character of this changing world is indifferent to tradition, unforgiving of frailty, no respecter of past reputations. It has no custom and practice. It is replete with opportunities, but they only go to those swift to adapt, slow to complain, open, willing and able to change. Unless we "own" the future, unless our values are matched by a completely honest understanding of the reality now upon us and the next about to hit us, we will fail.... In the era of rapid globalization, there is no mystery about what works—an open, liberal economy, prepared constantly to change to remain competitive.[5]

As Blair suggests, we need a completely honest understanding of reality if we expect to succeed and thrive in the new global economy. But complete honesty and the rhetoric of politics do not mix well. This is the first important obstacle to overcome.

The second thing Blair's remarks highlight is the nature of the global competition that is upon us. Competition is "indifferent to tradition, unforgiving of frailty, and no respecter of past reputations." A competitive market is "replete with opportunities," and these opportunities will go to those who are most adaptable and least resistant to change.[6]

Change is inevitable. Competition inspires change. With change comes many of the good things that we seek for society. However, to promote the opportunities that will come with change, requires acceptance of the painful effects, both immediate and ongoing, of a dynamic competitive system. The pain associated with the competitive process will never disappear. Nor should we want it to disappear, because competition and the fear and anxiety it engenders serves as the prime catalyst for firms to discover what consumers really want. Ultimately, many of the benefits will go to those who are not traditionalist, not frail, and who are most amenable to change itself. This may imply that wealthier, better educated, harder working people will more likely succeed. Although even this generality may not always be true as evidenced by the high-wage jobs lost to offshoring; in other words, no one is immune from the process. Losses in the adjustment process will more likely accrue to the poorest, weakest, frailest, and least educated. The response to these losses should not be the targeted protections to the industries most affected but rather the application of a generalized and voluntary safety net as described above.

What about Income Distribution?

One of the major policy debates over the past few centuries has been the debate between equity and efficiency. Equity generally refers to the equality of income or well-being. Efficiency refers to the productiveness of the economy. Indeed, one of the major concerns about the effects of trade liberalization is the effect on income distribution. As globalization proceeds, many people are concerned that incomes are becoming less equally distributed both internationally and nationally. A common claim is that the rich are becoming richer and the poor poorer.

Numerous studies have been done to assess the income distributional impacts of various types of policies. Not surprisingly, the results are mixed. There are enormous difficulties even in identifying what is the proper instrument to use to assess inequalities. Although measuring income is standard, income is used largely because it is regularly measured rather than because it is the best way to denote individuals' well-being. Assessments of the psychological impacts from policies, impacts such as cultural or environmental effects, are primitive at best. Consequently, it seems highly unlikely that we could ever come to an agreement about what the ideal distribution of well-being should be and whether a nation or the world is close or far from that ideal.

Despite the uncertainties, policies to redistribute income are in place in most countries. The motivation to assess progressive taxes, so that the wealthy individuals pay a greater share of income than poor individuals, is largely based on the desire to redistribute from richer to poorer.

But why redistribute; on what basis? Should the redistribution result in a complete equalization of income across individuals, across households, or across states? What about the equalization of other happiness factors, like health, freedom, or opportunity? Can these be achieved merely with redistributive taxation? It seems that after the failure of socialist economies to achieve adequate productive efficiencies in the pursuit of greater equality, few people today seem to insist that incomes be completely equalized, perhaps because there are clearer indications of an equity/efficiency tradeoff.[7] But that begs the question: how equal must incomes be to be acceptable? And what methods are appropriate to achieve greater equality? These are all difficult questions to answer, but some guidance is provided by applying the compromise principles.

Promotion of free voluntary exchange results in a competitive market economy. In a free market economy there is no clear indication of what the distribution of income will be. Milton Friedman (2002, 161–62) wrote that "The ethical principle that would directly justify the distribution of income in a free market society is, 'To each according to what he and the instruments he owns produces.'" In other words, the more one produces, the more one earns. Individuals who achieve higher incomes will be those who have organized capital and labor effectively to produce the goods and services that other people most desire. The greater the surplus generated for others the greater the return for oneself.

Perhaps if everyone believed that the high incomes in today's market economies were directly related to individual productive efforts there would be less outrage about income inequality. Instead it seems likely that people believe that others' high incomes arise not because they have produced much for others, but rather because they have effectively transferred money to themselves from others, involuntarily. In other words, people may desire policies to redistribute income because they believe that the rich are benefiting at the expense of the poor.

To offer one example, many people have a negative impression about lawyers. Lawyers are often regarded as dishonest, and many people seem suspicious about the legitimacy of their higher average incomes. A common joke law firm name known as "Dewey, Screwem, and Howe" facetiously expresses this sentiment. Notice that the same sentiment does not seem to apply to doctors who also receive very high average incomes. Most likely that is because people recognize the value in the services provided by surgeons, pediatricians, and family doctors, whereas it is much more difficult to see the value lawyers are providing. Although many lawyers are engaged in judicial activities that are absolutely essential to the functioning of our market economy, other lawyers are surely engaged in involuntary transfer activities. For example, involuntary transfers arise when deceptive billing practices are used or when dubious liability claims lead to handsome settlements and high lawyers fees. While all lawyers do not earn income in this manner, that impression is certainly strong enough to have created the popular stereotype.

The same impression may account for the low regard many people have for the very high salaries earned by CEOs, especially when those CEOs oversee a failing business or bank. It is difficult to justify a golden parachute package provided to a CEO that has run a business into the ground or that benefits largely because of government bailouts. Instead what seems obvious to most people is that the wealthy management must be effectively *stealing* money away from others in the organization or from the taxpayers.

These impressions, that the high incomes achieved by many individuals are achieved by nefarious means, surely motivate some of the demands for income redistribution. Nonetheless, several other rationales for income redistribution via progressive taxation are worth considering.

Frank (1985) argues that the desire by individuals for relative status creates a market imperfection. For example, human nature may be such that utility is derived simply by being of higher status (or income) than others in one's community. In this case, income redistribution from higher to lower income individuals can actually raise well-being of the entire community. In a separate work Frank (1995) suggests that winner-take-all markets, in which large returns accrue to a small number of people, leads to an inefficiency because too many people will compete for these limited positions. He argues further that these markets are becoming increasingly widespread. Thus, progressive taxation, can provide an effective mechanism to reduce the inefficiencies.

Nonetheless, the compromise principles suggest the importance of distinguishing between the two different reasons high incomes arise. High incomes occur either because of successful voluntary exchanges or as a result of involuntary transfers (or a combination of both). The compromise principles support the high incomes of the former group but not the latter.

In winner-take-all markets, the high incomes obtained by the winners are justified because they are the outcome of a voluntary exchange process. The high incomes are the return for a comparable surplus generated for others; these individuals gain much because they have given much to others.

A redistributionist income tax policy used to promote greater efficiencies in this case is itself an involuntary transfer mechanism and as such does not conform to the moderate principles. One of the problems with using redistribution involves measurement issues as discussed in chapter 3. Although in principle progressive redistribution can raise economic efficiency, in practice it would be very difficult to implement in a way that only affects winner-take-all markets and to set the income redistribution rates at the level appropriate to ensure that an increase in efficiency actually occurs. Thus, in the end this proposal for income redistribution suffers from the same problem as all of the other legitimate theoretical efficiency arguments for policy: what is good in theory is extremely difficult to implement in practice.

Although a majority of people may favor progressive taxation, for this and other reasons, the people whose incomes are being highly taxed may not share the same sentiments. For these reasons, progressive taxation does not conform to moderate principles, unless it has the widespread support among those who are more heavily taxed.

If it did have their support, then the taxes would fall into the category of acceptable voluntary transfers, which is not an implausible outcome. A society may choose to use the power of government to provide for public goods such as national security, roads, and parks as well as to provide for the needs of some of the weakest members of society. If widespread support for progressive taxes were a part of a society's goals, then the outcome conforms to the moderate principles. However, if the outcome is obtained via bare majority support driven by those who stand to benefit most from the redistribution, the outcome would appear more like an involuntary transfer.

Furthermore, it is important to take account of the behavioral effects of redistributionist tax policies. Since taxes discourage the activity being taxed, taxes on voluntary exchanges would surely reduce incentives to produce more for others. That would reduce economic efficiencies and thereby reduce average living standards. Additionally, both voluntary exchange and transfer profit earners would have incentives to defend themselves against the confiscatory taxes. That may involve identifying ways to reclassify income so it is taxed differently, or lobbying the legislature to include some exceptions to the general rules. Individuals may also hire tax professionals to ensure that legal tax avoidance is maximized. These activities redirect resources toward directly unproductive activities making the taxation doubly wasteful. Also, to the extent that higher income individuals are able to pay more to engage in legal tax avoidance, they would have an additional advantage over lower income earners.

Finally, the compromise principles may provide an answer for how much income inequality is acceptable. Complete adherence to the principles would create a result in which high incomes arise exclusively because of individual contributions in satisfying the desires of others. To reiterate, those who earn the most would be those who have given the most to others in the voluntary exchange process. Income would be based on merit. Lower incomes would accrue to those who have contributed less. Thus although incomes would not be equalized, any disparities would arise for justifiable reasons. In the event that low contributions in the economy result in an uncomfortably low income and standard of living for some people, compassionate voluntary redistributions would surely arise to alleviate the suffering of those with the greatest need.

The Role of Government

Bastiat (1998, 3) wrote,

> [N]othing can be more evident than this: The law is the organization of the natural right of lawful defense. It is the substitution of a common force for individual forces. And this common force is to do only what the individual forces have a natural and lawful right to do: to protect persons, liberties, and properties; to maintain the right of each, and to cause justice to reign over us all.... If a nation were founded on this basis, it seems to me that order would prevail among the people, in thought as well as in deed. It seems to me that such a nation would have the most simple, easy to accept, economical, limited, nonoppressive, just, and enduring government imaginable—whatever its political form might be.

Milton Friedman (2002, 27–28) wrote that

> the role of government...is to do something the market cannot do for itself, namely to determine, arbitrate, and enforce the rules of the game. We may also want to do through the government some things that might conceivably be done through the market but that technical or similar conditions render it difficult to do in that way.

He goes on to say that "there are two general classes of such cases: monopoly and similar market imperfections and neighborhood effects" (28). The compromise principles are perfectly consistent with these views.

Many policies and institutions suggested by the compromise principles are already operative in modern economies and have contributed to the economic success and prosperity of nations. For example, one critical and necessary institution is a judicial system that sanctions and discourages harmful involuntary transfer activities. Among the most important sanctions are laws prohibiting violence against others and the theft of personal property. These laws, and the punishments levied if someone violates them, not only help to prevent involuntary transfers, but by providing security to one's person and property, helps to stimulate voluntary exchange.

Another important inducement to voluntary exchange is the provision and enforcement of property rights and contracts. By establishing formal and verifiable titling procedures, traders can be more confident that the exchanges they make are with others who have clear ownership rights to the products they are trading. For example, when a real estate transaction is made in the United States, there are formal procedures and institutions involved to ensure that the seller of the property has title to the property and that any lien holders are properly identified before the transaction is completed. These procedures are costly and are included in the closing costs of major transactions. Nevertheless, these procedures contribute to the legitimacy of the trading system and thereby promote voluntary exchange. In countries where these procedures are not as explicitly formalized, real estate trades are on average more costly because of the increased potential for fraud. Thus, procedures and institutions such as these are an absolutely necessary part of a competitive free market system.

However, merely having a judicial system is not sufficient. Some judicial systems work more effectively in some countries because the procedures are applied equally to all, and all citizens have equal access to its protections. In some countries, crime rates are very high because judicial protections and sanctions are weak. Consequently involuntary transfers occur much more frequently. At the same time, because protection from personal injury or theft is higher, voluntary exchange activity is likely to be discouraged.

Some laws are intended to stimulate competition and thereby conform to the principles. For example, antitrust legislation is designed to prevent the formation of monopolies that can raise business profitability at the expense of their consumers. If antitrust achieves this goal, then it is consistent with the guidelines. However, some economists, such as Milton Friedman and Alan Greenspan, have argued that antitrust legislation may be unnecessary; that if firms are left free to enter any market as they see fit, then the ability of any one firm to maintain a monopoly is extremely limited, if even possible. Thus, some argue that antitrust legislation merely allows the government to punish successful firms.[8]

Frank (1995) offers another reason to allow for collusive agreements; they can be an effective mechanism to prevent positional arms races. When small improvements in relative position confers a nonproportional benefit, as when a sports team hires all the best players and wins the national championship, a collusive agreement among teams to limit spending can provide a better overall outcome. Thus, the ideal policy design to achieve the procompetitive objective remains arguable. The spirit and intent of the competition laws is clearly appropriate but their application may or may not be necessary.

However, not all national laws are consistent with the moderate principles, even though all laws are established in a legal process. For example, some laws establish regulations that provide competitive advantages for some businesses over others. A protective tariff is one such example. Political support is often obtained by arguing that protection of domestic firms is necessary to ward off the unfair behavior of foreign firms. But the reality of protection is that domestic consumers of protected products will suffer losses while the benefits accrue to the protected industries. As such these policies, though legal, are nonetheless examples of involuntary transfers.

This suggests that policy prescriptions can never be as simple as saying we need more government or less government. Government plays two roles. First, government establishes laws and regulations, many of which are very important to protect citizens from unbridled involuntary transfers, the smooth functioning of a judicial system that protects property and provides for the enforcement of contracts being perhaps its most important role. Many countries do need more government if by that we mean more enforcement of laws that protect individuals from involuntary transfers. On the other hand, government is also a major facilitator of anticompetitive rules and regulations. Many of the tax and subsidy policies discriminate in favor of politically influential groups and serve to transfer money involuntarily from taxpayers, consumers, and other firms. Thus, less of this type of government is consistent with the compromise principles. Epstein (2003b, 21) points out that, "the dark side of human nature does not disappear just because fallible human beings have assumed the trappings of public office. What are needed are clear rules that define the ends to which public force may be directed."

Thus, groups who argue that government is the source of our problems because they restrict free market outcomes are certainly right. Government is empowered to act this way legally, and they certainly do so. Other groups are suspicious that multinational corporations use the political process to manipulate outcomes in their favor. These concerns are also valid. Business always has an incentive to restrict competition when that competition is strong, or to open up competition when they know they will have a competitive edge. Businesses frequently solicit the government to implement rules to achieve these goals.

Finally, government can play one other role in its capacity to facilitate voluntary transfers. Because public goods such as national defense can be difficult to finance privately, it can make sense for government to collect taxes from its citizens to provide for the national security. Most people accept this role for government and are willing to pay taxes to finance these expenditures. Thus, to a degree, the provision of public goods is another role to play for government. What is the appropriate level of expenditures is disputable, though. Some citizens will clearly prefer greater provision while others will prefer less. How to determine an acceptable level is an issue worthy of further discussion and is beyond the scope of this study. Clearly the compromise principles are consistent with some level of government expenditures to provide for public goods.

Conclusion

Most policy guides have a unique problem; a problem this book shares. That problem arises because, after offering one's policy suggestions, together with the logic or empirical support that is meant to convince one's audience, someone, somehow is just supposed to implement the plan. However, there is no single person with the power to implement any proposed plan. Even if you could convince a large group to support one's proposals, that too may be insufficient to ensure implementation. Perhaps in a dictatorship the conditions are ripe, but even then, there is a process that must be followed that determines which policies will ultimately be implemented.

For most countries today the process is a representative democracy. Democratic processes rarely take good information about policies and implement them. Instead there is considerable discussion, rhetorical debate, compromises, and adjustments. Each of these steps in the process, and many more, influence the final outcome. Thus, to really offer policy prescriptions, one should ideally provide instructions about how to begin and proceed through a political process to achieve the intended result. Examples of this are rare; which implies two things. First, it means that the policy suggestions listed here (as well as in all other policy guides) are impractical. Even if they are convincing to some, they are unlikely to be the outcome of the current political process. Second, recognition that the guidelines are impractical should inspire readers to think very hard about how such policies might be realizable in the future.

For these reasons, it is important to remember that these policy options should be considered as *goals to strive for* in the future. The intention of this work is to provide a vision of a policy end state that we might like to achieve, along with a rationale to justify that end state, because, if we do not know where were going, how can we ever end up there, except by chance.

In the next and final chapter, I suggest how the United States could begin a transition toward implementing some of these globalization policy proposals. The United States as the largest and most productive economy is one country that could withstand the adjustment costs and lead the world by example. Unfortunately, whether the United States could achieve such a policy adjustment is unlikely, unless, the current economic crisis builds up enough disillusion with the current system that a popular demand arises to strike out in a new direction.

CHAPTER 11

A Policy Plan for the United States

The key policy proposal in this study is unfettered free trade. How is the world supposed to achieve that goal? Currently, movements toward trade liberalization, either through the implementation of free trade agreements or within the WTO, involve a process of reciprocity. Each country agrees to reduce some of its trade barriers, but only if the other countries agree to lower their barriers reciprocally. If other countries refuse to reduce barriers sufficiently, then progress toward liberalization is halted. Furthermore, if another country raises its trade barriers and reneges on a previous promise, current trade agreements allow the other country to retaliate by removing some of its previous trade concessions.

Although this method of reciprocal trade concessions has had considerable success reducing barriers to trade over the past half century, recent trends suggest the process may be stuck. The failure to achieve even modest trade concessions under the Doha round of WTO talks and the difficulty in the United States to approve negotiated free trade agreements are two bits of evidence that reciprocity may no longer work. At the same time the process prevents powerful players like the United States and European Union from unilaterally reducing barriers since to do so would give up possible bargaining chips for future negotiations. Finally, the economic crisis of 2008 has led to a modest increase in protectionism and to greater suspicions that free market philosophy is a failure. So can anything be done to stem the rising tide against free international markets?

Well one alternative, although admittedly a somewhat fanciful suggestion, is for the United States to give up the strategy of reciprocity in trade negotiations and instead to unilaterally accept and implement the principles of free markets over a designated adjustment period. But why should the United States do this?

The United States is the largest, most dominant, and most dynamic economy in the world today. As such, it is best suited to withstand moderate strains and pressures that would arise in a truly competitive international environment. Because of its dynamism and innovative capacities, the United States is also best suited to demonstrate how unleashing the full forces of a free market, reigning in the undue influence of corporations to restrict competition, and providing for an adequate generalized social safety net, can generate a renewed vitality and dynamism that other countries will wish to follow. In other words, the United States can and should lead by example. Friedman (2002, 73) suggested precisely the same approach more than 50 years ago when he wrote:

> Given that we should move to free trade, how should we do so? The method we have tried to adopt is reciprocal negotiation of tariff reductions with other countries. This seems to me the wrong procedure. In the first place, it ensures a slow pace. He moves fastest who moves alone. In the second place, it fosters an erroneous view of the basic problem. It makes it appear as if tariffs help the country imposing them, but hurt other countries, as if when we reduce a tariff we give up something good and should get something in return in the form of a reduction in the tariffs imposed by other countries. In truth, the situation is quite different. Our tariffs hurt us as well as other countries.

A practical proposal could include the following elements:

a. Start now with immediate free access for all goods and services for the least developed countries.
b. Begin and complete a transition to free trade with all countries within five to ten years.
c. Begin and complete a transition to the elimination of all agricultural supports within five to ten years.
d. Dismantle trade remedy laws; or as a more modest first step, require that injury determinations incorporate consumer effects.
e. Expand the allowances for legal immigration
    i. Maintain strong restrictions for dangerous persons.
    ii. Restrict access to social services for illegal immigrants.

f. Transition to a generalized social safety net for all who suffer catastrophic losses regardless of the source of the distress.
g. Strengthen private property protections and reduce government interventions.

The easiest change to make is the removal of all trade barriers with the least developed countries. The volume of trade with these countries is very small, and the change would only affect a few agricultural, textile, and apparel industries. Therefore adjustment costs would be minimal. Complete free trade with the rest of the world would require considerably greater adjustment, which is why it makes sense to spread the adjustment over five to ten years. The same is true for the reductions in agricultural supports. Previous investments are likely to have been based on the presumption that trade barriers and agricultural supports would be maintained. Allowing a phase-in period would enable new investments to be redirected with regard to the new policy circumstances.

Elimination of the trade remedy laws is an important step in demonstrating a commitment to free trade. However, because these laws are so firmly entrenched in U.S. law and because they are sanctioned for all WTO members, it would be difficult to eliminate them entirely. As a compromise, one simple adjustment would be to require that injury determinations take into account the impact on consumers as well as producers. In this way, domestic consumers will be less likely to be shortchanged because of the involuntary transfers to import-competing businesses.[1]

Expansion of legal immigration would also solidify a U.S. commitment to free market principles. In a dynamic economy, new workers are like injections of oxygenated blood. Not only do the majority of immigrants have the motivation to succeed but also by coming into a competitive system they are able to be absorbed in ways that will stimulate additional production. It is immaterial whether high or low skilled workers are allowed to enter. At all levels they will enable new production at lower prices for more consumers. Although immigration will take some jobs away from Americans in the transition, they will also act to promote greater expansion of the size of the overall economy.

Of course, whether due to increased competition from the removal of trade barriers, or the increased immigration, the additional competition will inspire a faster churning process in the labor and capital markets, and more people will be temporarily injured in the adjustment process. For some, hard times will be persistent in which case a compassionate society can and should provide assistance. Thus, improving the generalized safety net is an important component of this policy strategy. The key feature should be to avoid policies like trade adjustment assistance, which help workers who are hurt because of only one type of competitive circumstance. Instead, assistance should go to any worker that suffers much greater than usual harm caused by competition in general. Thus, a worker who loses out due to local competition should have equal claim to services as one who loses out due to import competition or because of expanded immigration. Of course the benefits should not be too generous and should only go to citizens who are suffering the most. If the safety net is too generous, the incentive to adjust quickly to the new market circumstances will be reduced.

It is certainly true that unilateral free trade and agricultural support reductions will give an advantage to some foreign firms over domestic firms. It would be easy, as is always done, to claim the advantage is unfair and to insist that protections be maintained. Indeed this is the standard operating procedure and the reason why it is unlikely that such a policy change could be implemented. Political pressures would prevent it from happening. Nonetheless this proposal suggests a completely new mindset.

The United States can compete regardless of what unfair practices others may follow. It is important to realize that for all the competitive advantages countries such as China and Vietnam enjoy in some industries, they endure countless disadvantages as well. Among these are immature legal systems, lack of contract enforcement, considerable governmental red tape, poor security, poor corporate governance practices, and weak financial systems. When one country has advantages in some sectors, either natural or government induced, other countries will have advantages somewhere else. That is the principle of comparative advantage. Thus, if the United States dismantled its system of protection unilaterally, despite competitive gains by foreign countries in some sectors, it would realize gains in new sectors. The trick is to discover what those new sectors will be. This is something governments cannot do effectively; neither can academic researchers, think tanks, or any other group of smart people. Only through the private competitive discovery process will we learn where the newly viable sectors will be.

To accept and promote competition requires business owners and workers to be ready and willing to adjust to changing circumstances. Removing trade barriers and agricultural supports will change the costs of doing business in some industries and force them to adjust to the new conditions. Allowing greater immigration will do the same. If they cannot adjust appropriately, it is true that they will fail. Those that do fail will release their capital and workers to be reallocated to other sectors where they can be relatively productive once again. However, these business failures do not represent a failure of the system. Instead they are the strength of the system. It is through the continual business creation and destruction process that workers and companies learn resiliency, learn to be quick and nimble, and learn how to provide most effectively for the wants and needs of the people of the country and the world. It is through this process that businesses discover the most efficient means to satisfy consumer demands. It is also the way for the United States to show leadership and economic strength and to contend with the ever-growing pressures of competition from China, India, and other expanding economies abroad. Friedman (2002, 73–74) emphasized how free trade raises a nation's economic power when he noted that,

> I believe that it would be far better for us to move to free trade unilaterally, as Britain did in the nineteenth century when it repealed the corn laws. We, as they did, would experience an enormous accession of political and economic power.... Let us live up to our destiny and set the pace, not be reluctant followers.... We could say to the rest of the world: We believe in freedom and we intend to practice it. No one can force you to be free. That is your business. But we can offer you full cooperation on equal terms to all. Our market is open to you. Sell here what you can and wish to. Use the proceeds to buy what you wish. In this way cooperation among individuals can be world wide yet free.

A much weaker economic strategy is the path the United States is on now. Continual complaints about the unfair trade practices abroad and persistent demands for protections are not indicators of economic strength and global leadership. If the largest most successful economy in the world cannot compete with the competitive pressures from China or India, then who can?

Implementation of unilateral free trade also achieves one other important effect; it would redirect currently unproductive resources toward more productive activities. Considerable resources are currently used discussing and arguing about future trade policy changes with other countries. In addition, corporations and business groups maintain large legal and lobbying staffs in Washington DC to both monitor and influence international policy decisions. Once unilateral free trade is implemented, the motivation behind many of these efforts will cease. Perhaps most importantly, a commitment to promote competition and free trade would enable businesses to redirect their attention to making a better product for their customers rather than protecting and promoting their individual competitiveness by lobbying Washington. The savings to business, consumers, and taxpayers could be considerable.

Obstacles along the Way

Those interests vested in the way the system currently operates have enormous influence over proposed changes. Chances are very good that sound proposals to change the way we conduct trade policy would be viewed as a radical departure from standard practices and would have little chance of making it through the legislative process. The agents who stand to lose from a change in the system are precisely the ones who can most influence the outcomes produced by the system.

In addition, policy makers will not easily give up policy leverage they can use to please the voting public and procure votes in the next election. Lawyers and lobbyists will not easily give up their influence in the political process and the salaries that come with it. Workers will not easily be convinced that competition with foreign businesses and foreign workers and the adjustment it requires will make the economy stronger. Finally the agricultural industry will not be easily convinced that they should give up their subsidies. Thus, despite calls for change by U.S. politicians, it seems unlikely that the political process, as it is currently configured, can produce very much change.

Arguments against this proposal and in favor of the status quo require its supporters to accept an important assumption that this book has argued is simply not true. For example, supporters of interventionist trade policies would have to argue that their policies will be an improvement for the country overall; and act as if their sophisticated analysis provides a clear conclusion about the national welfare effects of their proposed policies. However, as we have argued in chapters 2 and 3, there is no way for anyone to know with confidence whether policy interventions will be good or bad in some overall sense. The same is true for the suggestion that the United States pursue free trade. There is no way to know whether free trade will be an improvement in some overall sense. Nonetheless free trade is suggested here, not based on a presumption of superior knowledge, but rather because it is consistent with the moderate principles of justice and the larger understanding that every policy choice has uncertain impacts.

Of course there is an intellectually honest way to argue in support of an interventionist trade policy or the status quo. That approach would accept the ambiguity of the national welfare effects of policies and argue that it is appropriate to give special favor to politically influential groups. Special interests could argue that protection in the form of antidumping duties or safeguard actions should be given to import-competing industries because these industries have more effectively influenced politicians to implement competition-reducing policies that work in their favor and against the interests of other citizens. Since the losing groups (e.g., consumers) were clearly not influential enough to prevent the legislation enabling these trade policies, their losses are less consequential than the benefits accruing to the winning groups. Agricultural interests could equally argue that we should just accept that subsidies transfer billions of dollars into their pockets each year at the expense of domestic taxpayers and consumers as well as the poor in less developed countries. And it is not because there is anything special about agriculture over other sectors, except that they have been more effective getting government to provide special involuntary transfers. Such an honest assessment of why to implement trade interventions is unlikely to be heard, and so it remains likely that special interests will be relegated to argue on the basis that they have superior knowledge of the effects.

Conclusion

Nevertheless all hope need not be lost. In order to achieve a new result, an important first step is to clearly define the goals and provide the justification for achieving them. This book has taken that step. In this case, the goal is not really an outcome as much as a process; the competitive process of free and voluntary exchanges and the freedom for private businesses to make their own decisions in their own interests and the interests of their customers. What outcome that process produces is completely unknowable because it will be the result of numerous independent microeconomic decisions resulting in numerous successes and failures. It will be an experimental process in which businesses are continually investigating what best serves consumer demand in the current moment, while recognizing that what is best in future moments may be completely different, thereby requiring ongoing discovery.

The goal is also a set of government policies that will inhibit involuntary transfers. This means laws protecting the security of individuals, in their persons, their homes, and their businesses. It means maintaining a judicial system to enforce contracts and render judgments about appropriate punishments for violations of laws. However it also means dismantling the current government policies that have enabled influential groups in the past to use the government regulatory system as a means to transfer money and resources from others involuntarily. This does not mean dismantling all government, only that part of government that clearly violates the proscriptions against involuntary transfers.

Finally, the goal is also a set of government policies that will encourage and promote voluntary transfers. Voluntarily doing good things for others less fortunate is the least contentious way to promote a compassionate response for those who would otherwise suffer in a competitive system. In many societies today that may involve a democratic choice to use government to provide an acceptable social safety net.

The moderate compromise is a new way of thinking about how to choose policies. It is much like looking at the world with a new set of eyeglasses. The old glasses revealed a different view of the world depending on who wore them. Some saw free trade and free markets as good for everyone. They analyzed the costs and benefits of alternative policies and argued that policies be chosen to maximize net benefits. Others saw a world dominated by profit-grabbing multinational corporations who exploited workers and threatened the natural environment. They longed for a world in which social justice prevailed, but saw little evidence of it in the real world. Everyone was convinced that the view through their set of glasses was the true and accurate view of the world; no one ever doubted what they saw.

The new glasses correct the distortions that were seen and propagated under the old view. They provide a comprehensive perspective on the world by allowing one to see how economic, political, and social considerations interact and affect each other. At the same time, the new glasses do not allow one to predict the future, or project future outcomes. Instead they more clearly show why attempts at prediction of social and economic outcomes are hopeless. This is why the compromise principles, the moderate solution, seeks to establish a simple, straightforward set of rules to guide behavior rather than attempting to achieve particular final outcomes.

Perhaps most important, these new glasses are not rose-colored. They do not offer a vision of a utopian economy. They should not convince the wearer that, with the right set of policies, all good will come to all people. Instead the glasses reveal the sometimes harsh reality of the competitive economic system. Competition provides a means for all people to achieve the very best outcome for themselves, but there are no guarantees for anyone. Because abilities, effort, and luck will naturally vary across people, different people will not achieve the same level of success and happiness. Indeed, if the moderate compromise works as intended, some people will most certainly fail within the system. Despite these misfortunes, the glasses also reveal the ways in which a society can be compassionate toward its weaker and less fortunate members. There is no reason why the harshness of competition cannot be tempered with compassion, as long as compassion does not come at the expense of competition itself.

Finally, although these new glasses offer a whole new perspective on the policies and behaviors of people and countries in a globalizing world, the clarity is not absolute. Using these glasses most effectively will take some practice. Some of the issues are so complex that the new perspective from the glasses alone may not be enough to solve the problem. Therefore, much more work remains to be done. Although the heuristic mechanism provides a simple guide to policy, as was shown in chapter 10, there are both easy cases and hard cases. Choosing appropriate policies in the more difficult cases may require much more thoughtful research. The design of this research would be somewhat different than is typical in the economics literature, though: rather than attempting to predict the welfare effects of policies or identifying potential winners and losers, research would focus instead on furthering awareness of the market mechanism, or ascertaining policy consistency with the basic principles. Research also needs to be directed toward implementation: how does one progress to a moderate compromise solution within a representative democratic system? Unless we can overcome the political obstacles, these policy proposals will remain very difficult, perhaps impossible, to implement. In the meantime, my hope is that these new glasses offer a glimpse of what a moderate compromise global policy plan with people working together toward a common goal could look like, and why that plan can truly promote economic well-being and justice for people around the world.

NOTES

Preface

1. See Friedman (2000, 2005).

1 Introduction

1. In contrast, in scientific fields, near consensus on many issues is much more common. For example, although there are some individuals who still object to the use of modern medicine, most doctors and patients (a near consensus) would accept that antibiotics are the most effective way to treat a bacterial infection or that surgical removal is the most effective treatment for a ruptured appendix.
2. The first major WTO protest took place during WTO ministerial meeting in Seattle in 1999. The protestors, representing an extremely diverse set of interests, became labeled antiglobalization because they were all objecting to an agreement designed to promote international trade and investment. However, it is perhaps more accurate to describe the groups as supporters of fairness and social justice, variously defined.
3. Alan S. Blinder, "Offshoring: The Next Industrial Revolution?" *Foreign Affairs,* March/April 2006, pp. 113–128.
4. David Wessel and Bob Davis, "Pain from Free Trade Spurs Second Thoughts," *Wall Street Journal,* March 28, 2007, http://online.wsj.com/article_email/SB117500805386350446-lMyQjAxMDE3NzI1ODAyMDg4Wj.html? (accessed March 17, 2008).
5. See Samuelson (2004).
6. The hypothetical objective observer is akin to John Rawl's decision maker in an "original position," or under a "veil of ignorance." Rawls (1971) argued that the choice of a political and economic system should be done by a decision maker who does not know what position he or she will be in once the final outcomes in the system are realized. This *veil of ignorance* prevents the decision maker from using power or influence to shift outcomes in his preferred direction because, not knowing who he will be, he would not know in which direction to shift. As such, it is a useful construct to imagine how an individual would evaluate a policy when he does not have a direct interest in the outcome, but at the same time has some interest, as he expects to be randomly placed into some position at some future time. In this way the objective observer is thought to care equally, or nondiscriminately, about the outcome for everyone. This book will imagine the perspective of an observer in this original position when making judgments or comparisons about policy options.

2 Why Economic Theory Cannot Tell Us What to Do about Policy

1. See especially Mill (1864).
2. Most economic models assume that welfare (or utility, or happiness) is derived exclusively from the consumption of goods and services. This is why analyses focus on changes in real incomes; if real income rises for an individual then that person can buy more goods and services and consequently is happier. This is what Kuenne (1993) defines as materialism. However, the more general results that will be presented here easily apply to more complex situations in which individuals receive utility from more than goods and services; e.g., from knowing that natural ecosystems are being preserved, or from the safety that one feels with job security.
3. His argument is not based on the market imperfection issue discussed in this chapter, but the points he makes are equally valid under these circumstances. See Samuelson (2004).
4. I make a subtle distinction here. Many economic models show that free trade WILL not maximize national welfare. In a simple model we can make definitive statements. However, when we translate that result to the more complex real world we can only say that countries MAY not benefit from trade.
5. Trade liberalization may increase government revenue, but only if the initial tax rate were nearly prohibitive and if the tax reduction were not too large. In some industries in some countries, tariff rates are nearly prohibitive, thus tariff revenue would actually rise before it eventually falls with further liberalization.
6. A country is "large" if its imports are sufficiently large so that a change in import volume can influence world demand and cause a change in the world price. In contrast, for small countries, trade liberalization would have no effect on prices in countries in the rest of the world. The United States, European Union, Japan, and other large economies are large countries with respect to most imports.
7. This is a *general equilibrium model* because it establishes equilibria (i.e., supply = demand) in several markets (food, clothing, labor, capital) in both countries (United States and Mexico) simultaneously. This model is much more complex than the simpler *partial equilibrium* model described above, but is also more comprehensive.
8. The one exception I know of is the standard Ricardian model of comparative advantage. It that model, with only one homogeneous factor of production—labor—all workers benefit with trade, or are at least as well off, in both countries.
9. From *The Wealth of Nations,* book 1, chapter 1.
10. The phrase "economic nirvana" was used is a similar way by Demsetz (1969).
11. Inelastic demand means that demand does not fall very much in response to a price increase.
12. For a modern rendition of this argument, see Chang (2005).
13. See Lipsey and Lancaster (1956).
14. See Irwin (1996) for an historical account of the cases made for and against free trade.
15. See Viner (1950).

3 Why Empirical Data Cannot Tell Us What to Do about Policy

1. Kehoe, Srinavasan, and Whalley (2005, 9).
2. See Robinson, Cattaneo, and El-Said (2001).

3. See Arrow (2005).
4. See, for example, Lakatos and Musgrave (1970) and Popper (2002).
5. For example, see the remarks by Vaclav Klaus, President of the Czech Republic, at the National Press Club, Washington DC May 27, 2008, http://www.realclearpolitics.com/articles/2008/05/blue_planet_in_green_shackles.html, Accessed June 2010.
6. Proxy data is an alternative data series that are presumed by the researcher to be highly correlated with the preferred data series. However, since the preferred data series is not available it is also impossible to prove that a strong correlation exists.

4 Why Fairness Cannot Tell Us What to Do about Policy

1. See Hayek (1984), chapter 5 for a useful discussion of the history and use of the term social justice in public policy discussions.
2. See Sen (1992).
3. See Barry (1995).
4. See Burke (1994) for an elaboration of the "Do No Harm" principle applied to free markets.
5. Kant introduced the categorical imperative in the "Groundwork of the Metaphysics of Morals," originally published in 1785. See Kant (2005).
6. See Smith (1971), part 2, section 1.
7. Note, foreign government export subsidies are independently considered an unfair trade practice and can be defended against using the WTO-sanctioned anti subsidy procedures. In this case, price comparisons need not be made. Instead a country need only to show that a foreign government is providing an export subsidy and that the subsidy is causing injury to the domestic import-competing firms. If both conditions are satisfied, a country is allowed to implement a countervailing duty (an import tariff) at the level of the foreign subsidy.

5 Why Democracies Will Not Choose the Best Policies

1. Downs (1957, 139).
2. The payoffs could be measured as monetary payoffs; perhaps millions of dollars accruing to each group.
3. Here we're imagining perfect information, albeit with a bit of a lag.
4. Although, bribery could involve some unproductive activity if there were transactions costs to make the bribe.
5. See Bhagwati (1982).
6. Economists use the term asymmetric information to denote the situation where one agent has knowledge about something but another does not. There is a large literature in economics that addresses problems such as these.
7. Of course this assumes the agents know the ranges and the distribution of probabilities, which by itself is a lot of information. In reality agents do not even know this. However, in all economic analyses assuming uncertainty it is necessary to assume that agents at least know the nature of the uncertainty.
8. Dorgan (2006).
9. See Nichols (1987, 661).

6 The Pursuit of Profit

1. See Naomi Klein, *No Logo* (Toronto: Knopf, 2000).
2. As there are two types of transfers, voluntary and involuntary, we might imagine there would be both an voluntary and involuntary exchange. Indeed, there are. Symbiotic relationships, which are those in which both parties benefit, are often involuntary, in which case they fit the bill for an involuntary exchange. Examples in nature include the birds that pick parasites off the backs of large animals, providing themselves food and relief to the large animal. Another example is the mutual benefits obtained between animals and the bacteria in their stomachs. However, since examples among humans seem rare, I have not added this as another category.
3. The disutility of work is really the same thing as the benefit of leisure. The worker dislikes work, presumably, because he compares it to the value of not working.
4. Note if the lender used his own money, the opportunity cost is the interest he could have earned had he deposited the money into a bank. So even in this case the lender profit is the difference between lending interest rates and deposit rates.
5. Although, technically, the nonhunting members of the household are the recipients of a gift.
6. Bastiat (1998, 6).
7. "Greed, for lack of a better word, is good. Greed is right, greed works. Greed clarifies, cuts through, and captures the essence of the evolutionary spirit. Greed, in all of its forms; greed for life, for money, for love, (for) knowledge has marked the upward surge of mankind." These words were spoken by the character Gordon Gekko (played by Michael Douglas) in the movie *Wall Street*. The movie was released in 1987, at the tail end of the heady times of the Reagan-Thatcher revolution that ushered in conservative governments in the United States and Great Britain. It was a time when the belief in the potential of free markets, unfettered by government intervention, was perhaps at an all-time high.
8. See endnote 7 for the reference to Gordon Gekko.
9. This natural state is precisely the motivations of man described by Hobbes in Leviathan. Quoting Hobbes from Kuenne (1993, 35), "Man, therefore, obsessed by pleasure and power, and essentially equal in ability with his fellows in the Hobbsian natural state, is unsocial, brutal in his treatment of others, utterly selfish in his goals, and frightened by the consequences of the like motivations of others for his life and freedom. Life in such conditions is a 'war of all against all, . . . solitary, poor, nasty, brutish, and short.' "
10. Gilbert (2007) argues that the fundamental difference between humans and other animals is the human ability to think about the future. This is possible because of its relatively large cerebral cortex. He suggests that other animals, which seem to plan for the future, like birds building nests or squirrels hiding nuts, are merely acting out of instinct. It seems plausible that the contemplation of the future enabled many important advances in human society.
11. Bastiat (1998) wrote, "... there is also another tendency that is common among people. When they can, they wish to live and prosper at the expense of others. This is no rash accusation. Nor does it come from a gloomy and uncharitable spirit. The annals of history bear witness to the truth of it: the incessant wars, mass migrations, religious persecutions, universal slavery, dishonesty in commerce, and monopolies. This fatal desire has its origin in the very nature of man—in that primitive, universal, and insuppressible instinct that impels him to satisfy his desires with the least possible pain" (4–5).
12. This simple idea can also provide an explanation to an age-old question: why is there war? The answer may be as simple as noting that some communities (nations) may determine, perhaps inspired by their envy or greed, that it would be more profitable to take from other countries than to satisfy one's desires for oneself. However, once offensive actions are taken

and plunder is successful, the aggrieved parties are sure to feel a desire for retribution, for revenge. Thus, successful aggressions can inspire future retaliations, which in turn can lead to conflicts that can stretch over centuries, as history can readily attest to.

13. Nozick (1974) discusses a principle of justice in rectification, governing the proper means of correcting for past injustices in acquisition and transfer. In other words, what happens if someone trades something he does not own?

7 Involuntary Transfers

1. See Callahan (2004) for a description of the Sears auto repair scam.
2. Moira Herbst, "The Costco Challenge," Labor Research Assn., Available online at http://www.politicalaffairs.net/article/articleview/1422/, accessed June 25, 2010.
3. Friedman (2002, 167) writes that "Marx argued that labor was exploited. Why? Because labor produced the whole of the product but got only part of it; the rest is Marx's 'surplus value.'"
4. Frank (1985) argues that workers are not paid the value of their marginal product in developed countries. Instead, low wage workers tend to be paid "too much," while higher paid workers tend to be paid "too little." Frank accounts for this discrepancy by noting that individuals have a desire for status and that one way to pay for the status conferred by higher wages is actually for high wage workers to bribe, or transfer money to the lower paid workers. This account contradicts the typical worker exploitation story since in this case it is the high paid workers who are being paid less than their VMP.
5. Assuming a 50-week, 6 days per week work schedule. Salary information from http://www.forbes.com/lists/2006/12/X0NY.html, Accessed June 25, 2010.
6. In truth the shoe consists of much more than merely the physical product. The customer is also paying for transportation, insurance, advertising, packaging, retail service, new product development, and much more.

8 Voluntary Exchange and Competition

1. See Hayek (1944; 2002).
2. See "NAFTA-related job losses have piled up since 1993," *Economic Snapshots,* Economic Policy Institute, December 16, 2003, http://www.epinet.org/content.cfm/webfeatures_snapshots_archive_12102003, accessed June 27, 2010.
3. Schumpeter (1942).
4. Of the 5.8 million U.S. businesses, 99.9 percent of them are classified as small, having fewer than 500 employees. Only 17,000 U.S. businesses have more than 500 employees.
5. See, for example, this U.S. Small Business Administration FAQ at http://www.sba.gov/advo/stats/sbfaq.pdf, accessed June 27, 2010.
6. Drawn from various news stories. See this online page for a running tally of job losses in 2008. http://www.sadanapalli.net/blog/2008/11/16/global-economy-crisis-layoff-tracker-in-the-technology-sector/, Accessed June 27, 2010.
7. See U.S. Bureau of Labor Statistics, Employment Situation Summary. The most recent version is posted online at http://www.bls.gov/news.release/empsit.nr0.htm, Accessed June 27, 2010.
8. Even these statistics do not report all of the churning taking place within an industry. Every industry loses many workers and immediately replaces them with new hires. These numbers only report the net effect in each industry.

9. See Boo, Katherine *The Churn: Creative Destruction in a Border Town*, New Yorker Magazine, March 29, 2004. Accessed online at http://www.newyorker.com/archive/2004/03/29/040329fa_fact, on June 27, 2010.
10. Friedman (2002, 118) wrote, "... it is desirable to let men follow the bent of their own interests because there is no way of predicting where they will come out."
11. Hayek (2002, 17): "In a constantly changing world, merely maintaining a given level of welfare requires constant adjustments in how the efforts of many individuals are directed; and these will only occur when the relative compensation of these activities changes. Under relatively stationary conditions, however, these adjustments—which are needed simply to maintain the income stream at its previous level—will not generate a surplus that could be used to compensate those who are disadvantaged by the price changes. Only in a rapidly growing economy can we hope to prevent an absolute decline in the material level of particular groups."
12. If MBA study, or law school, were judged to be the best route to become a highly paid CEO, then more people would enter those professions than would otherwise be optimal from a social perspective.
13. See Frank (1995) for many more examples.
14. Rothbard (1974, 90) argues that "for an economist to say that X and Y should be free to trade Good A for Good B unmolested by third parties, he must also say that X legitimately and properly owns Good A and that Y legitimately owns Good B. But this means that the free market economist must have some sort of theory of justice in property rights; he can scarcely say that X properly owns Good A without asserting some sort of theory of justice on behalf of such ownership."
15. Robert Nozick (1974) indicated that for mutually voluntary trades to be fair, individuals must have acquired the object traded legally. Thus, if someone steals an object and then proceeds to exchange it for something else with someone else, the second exchange may not be deemed as fair acquisition.
16. Richard Epstein (2003a, 36) regards this as "one of those easy cases that is absolutely vital to get correct: there must be no compensation or protection against economic losses sustained through the operation of competitive markets. It is a principle that is widely acknowledged and violated in practice."
17. See Nozick (1974).

9 Voluntary Transfers

1. See for example, http://www.wisdomquotes.com/topics/giving/, accessed June 28, 2010.
2. A complete and more recent list can be found at http://foundationcenter.org/findfunders/topfunders/top100giving.html, accessed on June 28, 2010.
3. A complete and more recent list can be found at http://foundationcenter.org/findfunders/topfunders/top50giving.html, accessed on June 28, 2010.
4. A complete recent list can be found at http://foundationcenter.org/findfunders/topfunders/top25giving.html, accessed on June 27, 2010.
5. See "Taxation Is Robbery," The Ludwig von Mises Institute, http://www.mises.org/etexts/taxrob.asp (accessed April 21, 2008).
6. See Chodorov (1962, 216–39).

10 A New Guide to Policy Choice in an Era of Globalization

1. Rodrik (1997, 73) recognizes this problem when he says, "... the world is too complicated for first-best solutions, and realistically we will have to sacrifice some efficiency."

2. As Friedman (2002, 129) wrote, "Tariffs have of course been largely imposed to 'protect' domestic industries, which means to impose handicaps on potential competitors. They always interfere with the freedom of individuals to engage in voluntary exchange."
3. It is worth noting that the effects involve more than just the domestic and foreign firm; domestic and foreign consumers and governments are also positively and negatively affected by the policy changes. This complication means that simple fairness comparisons—e.g., that their firm's actions have injured our firms, therefore it is fair to retaliate—are not as straightforward when one considers the full range of the effects.
4. According to a recent Gallop poll approximately 700 million people worldwide would prefer to live and work in another country. Of that, 210 million would prefer to move to Europe and 165 million to the United States. (The Others, *The Economist,* December 17, 2009, pp 107–110).
5. Speech to the Labour conference, September 26, 2005. Excepts reprinted online at The Globalist, Tony Blair on Globalization, http://www.theglobalist.com/storyid.aspx?StoryId=4833 accessed on June 29, 2010.
6. London (2005) makes the argument that much of America's prosperity during the 1990s was due to the advancement of competition in several key industries such as automobiles, steel (Nucor), telecommunications (AT&T breakup), finance, and retailing (Walmart).
7. Lindert (2004) conducts a careful and detailed empirical analysis of the effects of social spending on GDP growth. The conventional wisdom is that there is an equity efficiency tradeoff, that should imply that greater social spending, tending to equalize incomes, would also tend to reduce GDP growth. However, Lindert finds that higher social spending has a negligible effect on GDP growth suggesting failure of the equity-efficiency tradeoff. This study is consistent with the engineering approach to policy making: if we can measure the efficiency effects of a policy then we can design an approach that satisfies society's concerns for equity and efficiency. This approach is problematic for all the reasons discussed in chapters 2 and 3, and it is those deficiencies that inspire a quest for policy choice on the basis of sound principles.
8. See the FAQ page about antitrust at capitalism.org at http://www.capitalism.org/faq/antitrust.htm, accessed June 29, 2010.

11 A Policy Plan for the United States

1. Rodrik (1997, 83) suggests replacing the serious injury test with the following: "… demonstrate broad domestic support, *among all concerned parties,* for the proposed safeguard measure."

BIBLIOGRAPHY

Aghion, Phillipe and Rachel Griffith (2005), *Competition and Growth: Reconciling Theory and Evidence*. Cambridge, MA: MIT Press.

Arrow, Kenneth J. (2005), "Personal Reflections on Applied General Equilibrium Models," in Timothy J. Kehoe, T.N. Srinavasan, and John Whalley (eds.), *Frontiers in Applied General Equilibrium Modeling*. Cambridge: Cambridge University Press, Chapter 1.

Baker, Raymond W. (2005), *Capitalism's Achilles Heel: Dirty Money and How to Renew the Free-Market System*. New Jersey: Wiley.

Barry, Brian (1995), *Justice as Impartiality*. Oxford: Clarendon Press.

Bastiat, Frederic (1998), "The Law," translated from the French by Dean Russell, Foundation for Economic Education, Irvington-on-Hudson, NY. Online at http://fee.org/library/books/the-law-by-frederic-bastiat-free-download/

Bhagwati, Jagdish (1982), "Directly Unproductive, Profit Seeking Activities," *Journal of Political Economy*, 90, 988–1002.

Bhagwati, Jagdish (2004), *In Defense of Globalization*. New York: Oxford University Press.

Bradford, Scott C., P.L.C. Grieco, and G. Hufbauer (2006), "The Payoff to America from Globalization," *The World Economy*, 29(7), 893–916.

Burke, T. Patrick (1994), *No Harm: Ethical Principles for a Free Market*. New York: Paragon House.

Callahan, David (2004), *The Cheating Culture: Why More Americans Are Doing Wrong to Get Ahead*. New York: Harcourt, Inc.

Chang, Ha Joon (2005), "Why Developing Countries Need Tariffs: How WTO NAMA negotiations Could Deny Developing Countries' Right to a Future," South Centre, OXFAM. http://www.southcentre.org/publications/SouthPerspectiveSeries/WhyDevCountriesNeedTariffsNew.pdf

Chodorov, Frank (1962), *Out of Step: The Autobiography of an Individualist*. New York: The Devin-Adair Company, pp. 216–239.

Cohen, G.A. (1986), "Self-ownership, World-ownership and Equality," in F. Lucash (ed.), *Justice and Equality Here and Now*. Ithaca, New York: Cornell University Press.

Cowen, Tyler (2002), *Creative Destruction: How Globalization Is Changing the World's Cultures*. Princeton, NJ: Princeton University Press.

Demsetz, Harold (1969), "Information and Efficiency: Another Viewpoint," *Journal of Law and Economics*, 12, 1–22.

De Soto, Hernando (2000), *The Mystery of Capital: Why Capitalism Triumphs in the West and Fails Everywhere Else*. New York: Basic Books.

Dorgan, Byron, L. (2006), *Take This Job and Ship It: How Corporate Greed and Brain-Dead Politics Are Selling Out America*. New York: St. Martin's Press.

Downs, Anthony (1957), "An Economic Theory of Political Action in a Democracy," *Journal of Political Economy,* 65(2), 135–150.

Easterly, William (2001), *The Elusive Quest for Growth: Economists' Adventures and Misadventures in the Tropics.* Cambridge, MA: MIT Press.

Edmonds, Eric V. and Nina Pavcnik (2005), "The Effect of Trade Liberalization on Child Labor," *Journal of International Economics,* 65(2), 401–419.

Epstein, Richard A. (2003a), *Free Markets Under Siege; Cartels, Politics and Social Welfare.* 33rd Wincott Lecture, October 13, 2003, Institute of Economic Affairs.

Epstein, Richard A. (2003b), *Skepticism and Freedom: A Modern Case for Classical Liberalism.* Chicago: University of Chicago Press.

Frank, Robert H. (1985), *Choosing the Right Pond.* New York: Oxford University Press.

Frank, Robert H. (1995), *The Winner-Take-All-Society.* New York: The Free Press.

Friedman, Milton (2002), *Capitalism and Freedom.* Chicago: University of Chicago Press.

Friedman, Thomas (2000), *The Lexus and the Olive Tree: Understanding Globalization.* New York: Anchor Books.

Friedman, Thomas (2005), *The World Is Flat: A Brief History of the 21st Century.* New York: Farrar, Straus and Giroux.

George, Henry (1949), *Protection or Free Trade.* New York: Robert Schalkenbach Foundation.

Gilbert, Daniel (2007), *Stumbling on Happiness.* New York: Vintage Press.

Greenspan, Alan (2007), *The Age of Turbulence: Adventures in a New World,* New York, Penguin Press.

Greenwald, B., and J. Stiglitz (1986), "Externalities in Economies with Imperfect Information and Incomplete Markets," *Quarterly Journal of Economics,* 101, 229–264.

Grieben, Wolf-Heimo (2005), "A Schumpeterian North–South Growth Model of Trade and Wage Inequality," *Review of International Economics,* 13(1), 106–128.

Hayek, Friedrich A. (1944), *The Road to Serfdom,* Chicago, IL Chicago University Press.

Hayek, Friedrich A. (1984), *The Essence of Hayek,* Chiaki Nishiyama and Kurt Leube (eds.). Stanford, CA: Hoover Institution Press.

Hayek, Friedrich A. (1988), "The Fatal Conceit: The Errors of Socialism," in *The Collected Works of F.A. Hayek, vol. 1,* W.W. Bartley III (ed.). Chicago: University of Chicago Press.

Hayek, Friedrich A. (2002), "Competition as a Discovery Procedure," *The Quarterly Journal of Austrian Economics,* 5(3) (Fall), 9–23, trans. Marcellus S. Snow.

Irwin, Douglas A. (1996), *Against the Tide: An Intellectual History of Free Trade.* Princeton, NJ: Princeton University Press.

Kant, Immanuel (2005), *Groundwork for the metaphysics of morals,* trans. Thomas Kingsmill Abbott (1829–1913), edited with revisions by Lara Denis (1969–). Peterborough, Ontario; Orchard Park, NY: Broadview Press.

Kehoe, Timothy J. (2005), "An Evaluation of the Performance of Applied General Equilibrium Models on the Impact of NAFTA," in Timothy J. Kehoe, T.N. Srinavasan, and John Whalley (eds.), *Frontiers in Applied General Equilibrium Modeling.* Cambridge, MA: Cambridge University Press, Chapter 13.

Kehoe, Timothy J., T.N. Srinavasan, and John Whalley (eds.) (2005), *Frontiers in Applied General Equilibrium Modeling.* Cambridge, MA: Cambridge University Press.

Kuenne, Robert E. (1993), *Economic Justice in American Society.* Princeton, NJ: Princeton University Press.

Lakatos, I., & Musgrave, A. (1970), *Criticism and the Growth of Knowledge.* Cambridge: Cambridge University Press.

Lal, Deepak (2006), *Reviving the Invisible Hand: The Case for Classical Liberalism in the Twenty-First Century.* Princeton, NJ: Princeton University Press.

Leamer, Edward E. (1983), "Let's Take the Con Out of Econometrics," The *American Economic Review,* 73(1) (March), 31–43.

Lindert, Peter H. (2004), *Growing Public: Social Spending and Economic Growth since the Eighteenth Century, vol. 1.* Cambridge: Cambridge University Press.

Lipsey, R.G., and K Lancaster (1956), "The General Theory of the Second Best," *Review of Economic Studies,* 24, 11–32.

London, Paul A. (2005), *The Competition Solution: The Bipartisan Secret Behind American Prosperity.* London: AEI Press.

Mill, J.S. (1864), *Utilitarianism,* 2nd edition. : London: Longman, Green, Longman, Roberts, and Green, a digitized copy from Google Book Search, http://books.google.com/books?id=nSUCAAAAQAAJ&dq=editions:OCLC38110333&lr=&source=gbs_summary_s&cad=0.

Nichols, Mary P. (1987), "Aristotle's Defense of Rhetoric," *Journal of Politics,* 49 (3), 657–677.

Nozick, Robert (1974), *Anarchy, State and Utopia.* New York: Basic Books.

Olson, Mancur (1965), *The Logic of Collective Action.* Cambridge, MA: Harvard University Press.

Parikh, Ashok (2006), "Relationship between Trade Liberalization, Growth, and Balance of Payments in Developing Countries: An Econometric Study," *International Trade Journal,* 20(4), 429–467.

Popper, K. (2002), *The Logic of Scientific Discovery.* New York: Routledge.

Rawls, John (1971), *A Theory of Justice.* Cambridge, MA: Belknap Press of Harvard University Press.

Robinson, Sherman, Andrea Cattaneo and Moataz El-Said (2001), "Updating and Estimating a Social Accounting Matrix Using Cross Entropy Methods," *Economic Systems Research, Taylor and Francis Journals,* 13(1), 47–64.

Rodrik, Dani (1997), *Has Globalization Gone Too Far.* Washington DC: Institute for International Economics.

Rothbard, Murray (1974), *Egalitarianism as a Revolt Against Nature and Other Essays,* R.A. Childs, Jr. (ed.). Washington, DC: Libertarian Review Press.

Salamon, Lester, M. Sokolowski, and S. Wojciech (2004), *Global Civil Society, vol. 2, Dimensions of the Nonprofit Sector.* London: Kumarian.

Samuelson, Paul A. (2004), "Where Ricardo and Mill Rebut and Confirm Arguments of Mainstream Economists Supporting Globalization," *Journal of Economic Perspectives,* 18(3), 135–146.

Schumpeter, Josef (1942), *Capitalism, Socialism, and Democracy.* New York: Harper.

Sen, Amartya (1992), *Inequality Reexamined.* Cambridge MA: Harvard University Press.

Smith, Adam (1937), *Inquiry into the Nature and Causes of the Wealth of Nations.* New York: The Modern Library.

Smith Adam (1971), *A Theory of Moral Sentiments.* New York: Garland.

Suranovic, Steven M. (2000), "A Positive Analysis of Fairness with Applications to International Trade," *The World Economy,* 23 (3) (March), 283–307.

Taleb, Nassim Nicholas (2007), *The Black Swan: The Impact of the Highly Improbable.* New York: Random House.

Traca, Daniel A. (2004), "Trade Liberalization, Labour Mobility and Wages," *Journal of International Trade & Economic Development,* 13(2), 111–136.

Trefler, Daniel (2006), "The Long and Short of the Canada-U. S. Free Trade Agreement," *American Economic Review,* 94(4), 870–895.

Viner, Jacob (1950), *The Customs Union Issue.* New York: Carnegie Endowment for International Peace; London: Stevens & Sons.

INDEX